The Old Dominion
and the New Nation,
1788-1801

RICHARD R. BEEMAN

The Old Dominion
and the New Nation,
1788-1801

THE UNIVERSITY PRESS OF KENTUCKY

ISBN: 0-8131-1269-9

Library of Congress Catalog Card Number: 76-190531

Copyright © 1972 by The University Press of Kentucky

A statewide cooperative scholarly publishing agency
serving Berea College, Centre College of Kentucky,
Eastern Kentucky University, Kentucky Historical Society,
Kentucky State College, Morehead State University, Murray
State University, University of Kentucky, University of
Louisville, and Western Kentucky University.

Editorial and Sales Offices: Lexington, Kentucky 40506

For Pamela

Contents

Maps

Preface

I BEGAN THIS PROJECT hoping to trace the growth of the Republican and Federalist parties in Virginia. The finished product, however, is only in part a study of the development of the party system, for party machinery and partisan rhetoric constituted but one aspect of political life in the Old Dominion during the last decade of the eighteenth century. Coexisting with the new system of party politics was the old, oligarchic system—vividly described, but romanticized by Charles Sydnor in his small classic, *Gentlemen Freeholders*—based on wealth, influence, and social prestige. Although the techniques of party organization and mass voter participation seem hardly compatible with the closed system usually associated with oligarchic control, the two systems rarely came into conflict. The men who ruled Virginia—the wealthy planters and lawyers who dominated the county courts, the members of the legislature, and the handful of men who served in the national government—discovered ways to use the outward mechanisms of the new, partisan mode of politics while at the same time preserving traditional patterns of elite-dominated, deferential politics.

I hope therefore to tell two stories. On one level I will trace the emergence and development of Republican and Federalist party organizations in Virginia. It is here that the reader will find the details of the Virginia Antifederalists' continuing hostility to the federal Constitution, of James Madison's switch from the Federalist to the emerging Republican party, of Madison's and Jefferson's attempts to coordinate Republican opposition to Federalist foreign policy, and finally, of the Republicans' successful campaign in 1800 to replace

President John Adams with a Virginian. This is an important story that deserves to be told. Yet the second story—an account of the continuing dominance of the "old style" of politics in Virginia—is essential to understanding the first.

The opposition to the federal government, first from the Antifederalists and later from the Republican party, stemmed primarily from the desire of most members of Virginia's political elite to preserve their political institutions, and their personal power, from the threat of a new, competing agency of government. Their system of decentralized, locally controlled government had, they believed, worked equitably and efficiently for the colony and later for the state. Moreover, it had insured them a dominant role in the affairs of the Old Dominion. And they had proved that they were prepared to defend that government against "innovation." When Great Britain enacted a scheme of imperial reorganization that threatened to substitute royal for provincial authority in America, the members of Virginia's provincial elite quickly assumed political and military leadership in the struggle that followed. The Revolution brought an end to British interference in Virginia's internal affairs, but it did little to change the structure of provincial politics. If anything, the Revolution only strengthened the power of Virginia's provincial ruling class.

The prerevolutionary elite maintained almost complete control over the Virginia Convention and framed a state constitution that retained most of the features conducive to oligarchic local control. Most of the reforms brought about by the Constitution—the limitation of the governor's powers and the provisions strengthening the lower house at the expense of the upper house—resulted not from any democratic impulse, but rather were caused by the reaction against the abuses of royal government and served only to increase the power of the small group of men who constituted the provincial elite.

It is not surprising that these same men viewed proposals for a new federal Constitution in 1788 with some misgiving. Although a slim majority in Virginia voted for ratification of the federal Constitution in June 1788, a large number of those delegates believed that substantive amendments would be added to prevent the new government from threatening Virginia's interests. Accustomed to guiding their state's destiny free from outside interference, the Antifederalists and many lukewarm Federalists remained hostile to any measure that might imperil the autonomy of the Old Dominion. This suspicion, far from disappearing after ratification, was heightened by subsequent Federalist policies. In the decade following ratification, more and more Virginians regretted that they had not heeded the advice of the Antifederalists.

The political leaders of the Old Dominion were accustomed to operating within a frame of reference that was peculiarly Virginian; their response to the policies of the new government was shaped by the interests and aspirations of their own localities and not by any broad conception of the national interest. Indeed, even purely local issues tended to be settled according to the narrow and particularistic interests of individual regions and counties. As a consequence, the numerous and often bitter divisions within the elite on issues of local concern—such as those involving state banking, internal improvements, and compensation of slaveowners for executed slaves—were rarely translated into partisan gain for either national party.

I will discuss in detail those few local issues having a bearing on the debate on national questions, but I have left a thorough discussion of the other local issues to historians interested primarily in the economic and cultural structure of the state. This volume is principally concerned with the style of political life in Virginia and with the effect of that style on national party alignments. The mode of political conduct that I have discovered, while perhaps conducive to just and efficacious government in the more uncomplicated period of the seventeenth and early eighteenth centuries, proved to be increasingly self-indulgent and dysfunctional by 1800.

I have benefited from the counsel and criticism of many of my teachers and colleagues in the course of the research, writing, and revising of this work. William W. Abbot acted as a wise and patient teacher during the first stages of the study; Daniel J. Boorstin, who directed the dissertation on which this book is based, gave me the guidance and inspiration that could be expected from a man of his genius. John Hope Franklin and Lawrence W. Towner contributed not only their historical and editorial judgments but also a good measure of kindness and encouragement. Stephen Kurtz and Lee Benson read the manuscript at a later stage and offered helpful suggestions for revision. My colleague Richard S. Dunn gave me some much-needed encouragement and advice during a particularly crucial stage of the revision of the manuscript. James C. Curtis, my good friend, uncompromising critic, and mediocre tennis partner was a constant source of ideas and suggestions at virtually every stage of my work. Finally, I benefited from the painstaking editorial criticism of Robert Ferrell, chairman of the Frederick Jackson Turner Award committee.

Information in the map "Virginia Voting, 1788-1793" is taken from Norman Risjord's article "The Virginia Federalists," *Journal of Southern History* 33 (1967).

A number of institutions have been generous in their financial support for this venture. A grant from Colonial Williamsburg, Inc., financed much of the initial research on the topic. The Newberry Library provided both the funds and the facilities for a distraction-free year of writing; more important, the staff of the Newberry Library provided an intellectually stimulating atmosphere that made my year there one of the most rewarding of my life. The University of Pennsylvania awarded me a summer research fellowship which greatly facilitated many of the final revisions of the work.

My wife Pam has played an important role at every stage. A ruthless editor, she has helped me with the research, writing, typing, revising, and not unimportantly, the financing of the venture. And my two wonderful children, Kristin and Joshua, have probably hindered my progress on the book, but I love them anyway.

the federal Constitution in June 1788, a large number of those delegates believed that substantive amendments would be added to prevent the new government from threatening Virginia's interests. Accustomed to guiding their state's destiny free from outside interference, the Antifederalists and many lukewarm Federalists remained hostile to any measure that might imperil the autonomy of the Old Dominion. This suspicion, far from disappearing after ratification, was heightened by subsequent Federalist policies. In the decade following ratification, more and more Virginians regretted that they had not heeded the advice of the Antifederalists.

The political leaders of the Old Dominion were accustomed to operating within a frame of reference that was peculiarly Virginian; their response to the policies of the new government was shaped by the interests and aspirations of their own localities and not by any broad conception of the national interest. Indeed, even purely local issues tended to be settled according to the narrow and particularistic interests of individual regions and counties. As a consequence, the numerous and often bitter divisions within the elite on issues of local concern—such as those involving state banking, internal improvements, and compensation of slaveowners for executed slaves—were rarely translated into partisan gain for either national party.

I will discuss in detail those few local issues having a bearing on the debate on national questions, but I have left a thorough discussion of the other local issues to historians interested primarily in the economic and cultural structure of the state. This volume is principally concerned with the style of political life in Virginia and with the effect of that style on national party alignments. The mode of political conduct that I have discovered, while perhaps conducive to just and efficacious government in the more uncomplicated period of the seventeenth and early eighteenth centuries, proved to be increasingly self-indulgent and dysfunctional by 1800.

I have benefited from the counsel and criticism of many of my teachers and colleagues in the course of the research, writing, and revising of this work. William W. Abbot acted as a wise and patient teacher during the first stages of the study; Daniel J. Boorstin, who directed the dissertation on which this book is based, gave me the guidance and inspiration that could be expected from a man of his genius. John Hope Franklin and Lawrence W. Towner contributed not only their historical and editorial judgments but also a good measure of kindness and encouragement. Stephen Kurtz and Lee Benson read the manuscript at a later stage and offered helpful suggestions for revision. My colleague Richard S. Dunn gave me some much-needed encouragement and advice during a particularly crucial stage of the revision of the manuscript. James C. Curtis, my good friend, uncompromising critic, and mediocre tennis partner was a constant source of ideas and suggestions at virtually every stage of my work. Finally, I benefited from the painstaking editorial criticism of Robert Ferrell, chairman of the Frederick Jackson Turner Award committee.

Information in the map "Virginia Voting, 1788-1793" is taken from Norman Risjord's article "The Virginia Federalists," *Journal of Southern History* 33 (1967).

A number of institutions have been generous in their financial support for this venture. A grant from Colonial Williamsburg, Inc., financed much of the initial research on the topic. The Newberry Library provided both the funds and the facilities for a distraction-free year of writing; more important, the staff of the Newberry Library provided an intellectually stimulating atmosphere that made my year there one of the most rewarding of my life. The University of Pennsylvania awarded me a summer research fellowship which greatly facilitated many of the final revisions of the work.

My wife Pam has played an important role at every stage. A ruthless editor, she has helped me with the research, writing, typing, revising, and not unimportantly, the financing of the venture. And my two wonderful children, Kristin and Joshua, have probably hindered my progress on the book, but I love them anyway.

CHAPTER ONE

Union or No Union

THE FIRST DAY of June 1788 had been unseasonably hot in Richmond, Virginia, but it was no warmer than the debate and speculation that filled the air. The convention to consider ratification of the federal Constitution was to convene the next day; no one could be sure of the outcome. Some Federalists were so confident as to expect a majority of twenty or more, but few shared their optimism. James Madison, the most active in organizing support for the Constitution, admitted that "the business is in the most ticklish state that can be imagined. The majority will certainly be very small on whatever side it may finally lie; and I dare not encourage much expectation that it will be on the favorable side."[1]

The Constitution's opponents were equally cautious in their predictions. Patrick Henry was convinced that four-fifths of the state's inhabitants opposed the new plan of government, "yet strange as it may seem, the numbers in convention appear equal on both sides: so that the majority, which way soever it goes, will be small." Henry's Antifederalist colleague, Colonel William Grayson, agreed that the outcome was "suspended by a hair" and shared the concern of both Federalists and Antifederalists over the "seven or eight dubious characters, whose opinions are not known, and on whose decisions, the fate of this important question will ultimately depend."[2]

Historians, looking back on the final roll call vote on ratification, have had no difficulty in labeling members of the Virginia

Convention either Federalists or Antifederalists, but the delegates did not fall neatly into those two categories. The Federalists were aware of this when they began planning their
strategy for the Convention. They recognized at least three
factions in Virginia. The first, the core of Federalist strength,
was willing to ratify the Constitution with or without amendments. At the other extreme were those individuals who would
not consent to ratification unless they received a guarantee of
amendments before the new government commenced operation
—amendments which would insure that the new Constitution
would differ little from the old Articles of Confederation. The
third, and pivotal group, was convinced that amendments were
necessary, but was reluctant to reject the Constitution for fear
of jeopardizing the union.[3]

The difficulty in predicting the outcome of the Virginia
Convention was compounded by the fact that many delegates
simply did not know enough about the proposed plan of
government to have a firm opinion. Humphrey Marshall, a
delegate from the crucial district of Kentucky, could not even
locate a copy of *The Federalist* until he was on his way to the
Convention. George Nicholas, a delegate from Albemarle,
urged James Madison to distribute the essays in pamphlet
form because the "greater part of the members will go to the
meeting without information on the subject."[4]

The ordinary citizens of Virginia were even less certain,

1 George Washington to John Jay, Mt. Vernon, 8 June 1788, in *The Writings
of George Washington. . .* , ed. John C. Fitzpatrick, 37 vols. (Washington, D.C.,
1931-1944), 29: 514 (hereafter referred to as Fitzpatrick, ed., *Washington's Writings);* James Madison to Washington, Richmond, 13 June 1788, in *The Writings
of James Madison . . .* , ed. Gaillard Hunt, 9 vols. (New York, 1900-1910), 5: 179
(hereafter referred to as Hunt, ed., *Madison's Writings).*

2 Patrick Henry to John Lamb, Richmond, 9 June 1788, William Grayson to
John Lamb, Richmond, 9 June 1788, in Isaac A. Leake, *Memoir of the Life and
Times of General John Lamb* (Albany, N.Y., 1857), pp. 307, 311.

3 Madison to Washington, New York, 7 Dec. 1787, in Hunt, ed., *Madison's
Writings,* 5: 65; Henry Lee to Madison, Richmond, Dec. 1787, Papers of James
Madison, Library of Congress.

4 Hugh Blair Grigsby, *The History of the Virginia Federal Convention of 1788,*
2 vols. (Richmond, 1890), 1: 31 (hereafter referred to as Grigsby, *Virginia Convention of 1788);* George Nicholas to Madison, Charlottesville, 5 April 1788, in
Hunt, ed., *Madison's Writings,* 5: 114-15.

and considerably less informed, about the merits of the proposed Constitution. Although the Antifederalists claimed that most Virginians opposed ratification, there was in fact little basis for predicting the temper of the people on the subject. Except for those persons living in the cities of Richmond, Norfolk, Alexandria, and Petersburg, where newspapers kept them informed of the national debate over the Constitution, few Virginians were in a position to form an opinion. Nor did they seem willing to hazard an opinion at the polls. In the elections for delegates to the Ratifying Convention voter turnout rarely exceeded 25 percent of the free adult white males and often dropped as low as 10 percent.[5] If 85-95 percent of the free adult white males were eligible to vote, as recent research on the suffrage in Virginia indicates, an astonishingly large number of citizens stayed away from the polls.[6]

Those Virginians who did vote were more likely to be familiar with the wealth and prestige of their candidates than with the subtleties of the Federalist and Antifederalist arguments. In many counties a candidate's election to the Ratifying Convention, regardless of his stand on the Constitution, was a foregone conclusion. In Louisa, Warwick, Accomac, New Kent, and Chesterfield counties the delegates were not certain how they would vote, so it is obvious that their constituents did not choose them on the basis of Federalist and Antifederalist

[5] Election statistics for the Virginia Ratifying Convention are extremely rare, but a comparison of the Virginia Census of 1790, printed in Evarts B. Greene and Virginia Harrington, *American Population before the Census of 1790* (New York, 1932), pp. 154-55, with scattered returns found in the *Virginia Herald and Fredericksburg Advertiser*, 27 March 1788, the *Virginia Independent Chronicle*, 12 March 1788, the *Norfolk Journal*, 12 March 1788, the Essex County Deed Book, no. 33, and the Princess Anne County Deed Book, no. 21, Virginia State Library, gives an indication of the astonishing degree of apathy displayed by Virginia's voters.

[6] These voting percentages are the calculations of Robert E. and B. Katherine Brown, *Virginia, 1705-1786: Democracy or Aristocracy?* (East Lansing, Mich., 1964), pp. 125-46. There seems to be little reason to challenge the accuracy of the Browns' statistics, since they are based on massive research and a sophisticated evaluation of data. However, their conclusion that full political democracy existed in eighteenth-century Virginia does not necessarily follow from those statistics. The extremely high degree of voter apathy, for example, indicates that a significant number of Virginians felt that the mere right to vote was of little value.

labels.[7] And in at least four counties, the elected delegates, confident of their base of personal support, would go against the wishes of their constituents and switch sides when they arrived at the Ratifying Convention.[8] This style of personalized, nonpartisan politics, long a tradition in Virginia, would make it all the more difficult for the Federalist and Antifederalist factions to assess their strength in the Convention.

In this atmosphere of uncertainty, the delegates began their deliberations. Madison, who had already emerged as the principal spokesman for the Constitution in Virginia, would prove to be the most influential Federalist in the Ratifying Convention. Just thirty-seven years old at the time of the Convention, he had already spent thirteen years in public service, most of which had occurred not in his home state, but rather, with the continental government. In 1780, after serving briefly on the Committee of Safety for Orange County, in the Virginia Convention of 1776, and one term in the Virginia Assembly, Madison was elected a delegate to the Continental Congress. From that time until 1788 his political experience, and the range of his concerns, remained primarily continental. He had not served a long apprenticeship in either the county court or the General Assembly and, more than most of his colleagues in the Ratifying Convention, was free from attachments to local interests and more likely to give priority to national rather than local concerns.

Madison, along with Henry Lee, George Nicholas, Wilson Cary Nicholas, and John Marshall followed the Federalist strategy of defending the proposed Constitution article by article in an attempt to forestall any wholesale attack on the very conception of that document by its opponents. When the Antifederalists succeeded in arguing their case on more general terms, however, Madison and the other confirmed Federalists in the Convention enjoyed three important advantages. First,

---

[7] Jonathan Elliot, *The Debates in the Several State Conventions on the Adoption of the Federal Constitution* . . . , 4 vols. (Washington, D.C., 1836), 3: 653-62 (hereafter referred to as Elliot, *Debates*); Jackson T. Main, *The Antifederalists: Critics of the Constitution, 1781-1788* (Chapel Hill, N.C., 1961), pp. 223-33, 285-86.
[8] Main, *The Antifederalists*, pp. 223-33, 285-86.

they were able to remind the members of the Convention of the grave defects of the Articles of Confederation. Even the Antifederalists admitted that the Articles needed amending, but they were unable to devise a way in which to make the amendment process workable. New York, when it vetoed the Impost bill in 1786—a measure that would have granted to the Confederation government a limited power of taxation—proved the near impossibility of securing the unanimous vote necessary for amending the Articles.

More important, the Federalists, armed with the information that eight states had ratified the Constitution, were able to issue gloomy predictions about Virginia's fate should it stay out of the union and attempt to compete with a consolidated phalanx of the other states. Nor was this merely partisan rhetoric; most Federalists genuinely believed that Virginia would face ruin if it refused to join the union. Edmund Pendleton, a proud Virginian and a reluctant Federalist, calculated:

> 8 states have already Ratified, some with, and some without Amendments proposed; to those at least, and others who may so adopt, we shall appear with Hostile Countenances, unfavorable to a cordial reception. They will consider our Proposals [of previous amendments as a condition to ratification] as coming from Men, refusing to make a Common Stock with them of Interests, under the direction of the General Government, And therefore as dictating the admission of local Interests, Circumstances all unfavorable to Patient hearing and candid investigation. But say Gentlemen Virginia is too important in the Union, to risque her Separation by refusing her reasonable propositions. Alas Sir, with Irritated minds, reason has small force, and if those 8 states should make the Supposition of that ground's having produced our Conduct, it will add that of Insult to the other causes of Resentment, and will any Gentlemen say that Virginia, Respectable as she is, is able to *sustain* the Conflict? Does any wish to see the experiment even put in risque?[9]

9 Edmund Pendleton to Richard Henry Lee, Richmond, 14 June 1788, in *The Letters and Papers of Edmund Pendleton, 1734-1803*, ed. David John Mays, 2 vols. (Charlottesville, Va., 1967), 2: 531.

Confirmed Antifederalists such as Patrick Henry were not likely
to be persuaded by Pendleton's argument, but to many of the
undecided delegates, the consequences of refusing to join the
union seemed worse than those of joining a partially defective
one.

And finally, the Federalists capitalized on the prestige of the
Constitution's most illustrious supporter, General George Wash-
ington. Although Washington had declined to serve in the
Ratifying Convention in order to avoid the partisan quarrels
of his home state, his presence was felt. James Monroe, assessing
Washington's importance to the Federalist cause, exclaimed:
"Be assured, his influence carried this government."[10]

The Federalists, in addition to these three general advantages,
were also able to appeal to the special interests of the various
groups that stood to benefit directly from the new Constitution.
There were not enough groups in the Convention with clearly
defined interests to make this an effective tactic by itself, but
in certain cases it did prove helpful to the Federalist cause. In
particular, the western delegates, who desperately needed protection from hostile Indians, were noticeably impressed by the
Federalists' promises of a strong federal militia to patrol the
western frontiers.

The chief spokesman in the Virginia Convention for the
opponents of the Constitution was a man of quite different
background and experience than that of young nationalists
like Madison or John Marshall. Patrick Henry, at fifty-two
years of age, was revered throughout the state as the man who,
as much as Washington, had fought to free Virginians from the
tyranny of arbitrary authority.[11] Henry had served in the
colonial and state legislatures nearly every year since he entered
that body in 1765; he was chosen as the first governor of the
independent state of Virginia in 1776 and served five terms in

---

10 James Monroe to Thomas Jefferson, 17 July 1788, in *The Writings of James
Monroe . . .* , ed. Stanislaus M. Hamilton, 7 vols. (New York, 1898-1903), 1: 186
(hereafter referred to as Hamilton, ed., *Monroe's Writings*).

11 Henry's image in Virginia was, of course, not the same as that of Washington,
for Henry never was able to give all his actions the appearance of nonpartisanship
and disinterestedness that characterized the public image of Washington.

that post during the twelve years between the framing of the Virginia constitution and the Ratifying Convention of 1788. Although a delegate to the First and Second Continental Congresses in 1774 and 1775, Henry spent the greater part of his political career at home, in Virginia. When Henry exclaimed, during debate in the Ratifying Convention, "This government is not a Virginian, but an American government," he was speaking of his and other confirmed Antifederalists' fears.[12] Henry was striving to preserve everything that Virginians had fought for during the eighteenth century. They had revolted against British rule to have a Virginian government, and during the Confederation period they had continued to take pride in their local independence while defending the sovereignty of their state.

There was good cause for the Antifederalists' attachment to Virginia's decentralized, and often oligarchic, government. That government had proved exceptionally effective in the past. It had guided the Old Dominion through the Revolution and had produced an important share of the new nation's leaders. Although few of the mechanisms of that government were democratic, few Virginians were inclined to lodge any public protests against the manner of its operation. And most important, the state had prospered under that government. Men like Patrick Henry could point to the population, economic resources, and political prestige of their state and argue with some plausibility that it would be a mistake for Virginians to trade their political independence for the less-tangible benefits of a consolidated government.

Moreover, the Antifederalists had a selfish reason for desiring the continued dominance of their system of government over all other, more centralized forms. Men like Henry, William Grayson, and George Mason had devoted most of their lives to public service on the state and local level. They were quite naturally, and justifiably, proud of the way in which they had guided Virginia's destiny and were decidedly uneasy about the

---

12 Elliot, *Debates*, 3: 55.

prospect of losing their power to a competing elite in a new, federal government.[13]

Governor Edmund Randolph, who had initially opposed the Constitution in the Philadelphia Convention, would prove to be a pivotal figure during the Virginia Convention. After the Philadelphia Convention had adjourned, Randolph had reaffirmed his opposition to the Constitution in a letter to the Virginia General Assembly, later published in the *Virginia Gazette* in January 1788. In that letter he had urged Virginians not to ratify the Constitution until substantive amendments had been agreed to by the other states.[14] Although not considered to be as steadfast in his opposition as Henry, he was at least classed with those undecided delegates who would work with the Antifederalists to obtain prior amendments drastically reducing the power of the federal government over such vital areas as taxation and defense as a condition for ratification. While Washington and Madison were aware of Randolph's increasing sympathy with the Federalist cause, and indeed had been instrumental in ultimately persuading Randolph to support the Constitution, most at the Convention expected Randolph to side with the Antifederalists.[15] He would prove, however, to be the most illustrious and influential convert to the Federalist side. Some of Randolph's contemporaries ascribed his conversion to ambition for public office in the new government, but his own explanation seems more convincing. On the first day of debate in the Ratifying Convention, in answer to Henry's speech against the Constitution, Randolph voiced the motives and the misgivings of all those who, in the end, reluctantly gave their assent to the Constitution. He repeated his

13 For the most perceptive discussion of the persistence of oligarchic patterns of government in Virginia, see Charles Sydnor, *Gentlemen Freeholders: Political Practices in Washington's Virginia* (Chapel Hill, N.C., 1952), passim.

14 Edmund Randolph to the Speaker of the House of Delegates, 16 Oct. 1787, in Elliot, *Debates,* 1: 482-91.

15 Thomas Jefferson to William Short, Paris, 20 Sept. 1788, in *The Writings of Thomas Jefferson . . .* , ed. Paul Leicester Ford, 12 vols. (New York, 1904-1905), 5: 50 (hereafter referred to as Ford, ed., *Jefferson's Writings);* Madison to Randolph, 10 April 1788, George Nicholas to Madison, Charlottesville, 5 April 1788, Madison to Jefferson, 22 April 1788, in Hunt, ed., *Madison's Writings,* 5: 114, 117-21.

contention that the document was materially defective in some of its parts; in explaining his conduct at Philadelphia he avowed, "I refused to sign, and if the same were to return, again I would refuse." He then reaffirmed his determination to obtain amendments, but added: "As with me the only question has ever been between previous and subsequent amendments, so will I express my apprehensions, that the postponement of this Convention to so late a day has extinguished the probability of the former without inevitable ruin to the Union, and the Union is the anchor of our political salvation." Randolph's speech reflected the dilemma of so many reluctant Federalists. He made little attempt to defend the new plan of government as a positive good, but instead dwelt on the potential dangers facing Virginia should the state refuse to ratify the Constitution. For Randolph, the question was not whether the Constitution was a good one, but whether a union of the states under a defective Constitution was preferable to an existence outside the union.[16]

In the final speech before the vote on ratification, Randolph again emphasized the narrow range of choices open to Virginians. His tone—uncertain and apologetic—was perhaps characteristic of the manner in which Virginia entered the union. He asked future annalists to remember *"that I went to the federal Convention with the strongest affection for the Union; that I acted there in full conformity with this affection; that I refused to subscribe, because I had, as I still have, objections to the Constitution,* and wished a free inquiry into its merits; and that the accession of eight states reduced our *deliberations* to the single question of *Union or no Union."*

Immediately after Governor Randolph uttered those words, Virginia, by the slim margin of 89-79, grudgingly joined the union.[17] Young Spencer Roane, soon to become a bitter critic of the nationalist concept of union, described the occasion

---

16 Elliot, *Debates,* 3: 25-26. Some of Randolph's Antifederalist colleagues never forgave him. George Mason thereafter referred to him as the "young Arnold." Kate Mason Rowland, *The Life of George Mason,* 2 vols. (New York, 1892), 2: 308 (hereafter referred to as Rowland, *Life of Mason*).

17 Elliot, *Debates,* 3: 652-55.

somberly: "The decision has been distressing and awful to great numbers; & it is generally believed will be so received by the people. The minority is a very respectable one indeed, & made a most noble stand in defence of the liberties of the people . . . there is no rejoicing on Acct of the vote of ratification—it would not be prudent to do so; & the federalists behave with moderation and do not exult in their success."[18] Nor was there much call for exultation. The reluctant Federalists would have to wait and see if the promised benefits of union materialized. The initially uncommitted members from Kentucky and the northwest who were ultimately persuaded to vote in favor of the Constitution, would watch to see whether the new government would protect their right to navigate the Mississippi and whether the federal army would fulfill the promise to protect the frontier. Randolph and Pendleton, despite their support for the Constitution, would immediately initiate plans for calling another convention to remedy the defects of the new government.[19] They would be supported in this endeavor by a sizable number of the Federalist delegates to the Convention, most of whom would join with the Antifederalists in an attempt to effect major changes in the structure of the new government.[20]

Virginia's adherence to the union could have ended before it began had Patrick Henry been unwilling to accept his defeat peacefully. The night after the Convention adjourned, a group of dissident Antifederalists assembled to seek a way of preventing the new government from beginning its operation. They

[18] Spencer Roane to Philip Aylett, 26 June 1788, in David Mays, *Edmund Pendleton, 1721-1803: A Biography*, 2 vols. (Cambridge, Mass., 1952), 2: 272.

[19] Edmund Randolph to Madison, 18 Aug. 1788, Edmund Pendleton to Madison, 3 Sept. 1788, in Moncure D. Conway, *Omitted Chapters of History Disclosed in the Life and Papers of Edmund Randolph* (New York, 1888), pp. 117-18 (hereafter referred to as Conway, *Edmund Randolph*).

[20] The exact identity of all the undecided delegates has always been something of a mystery. That they existed is attested to by the constant references to them during the Convention. Main, *The Antifederalists*, lists ten men in addition to the uncommitted delegates from the west who were wavering on the question of ratification. I have verified Main's findings and have added a few more men to the "undecided" list by comparing those who voted "yes" on ratification with those in the convention who subsequently advocated an amendment curtailing the federal government's power over direct taxation.

asked Henry's cooperation, but the old patriot, devoted to order as well as liberty, dissuaded them. Henry had vowed that "my hand and my heart shall be at liberty to retrieve the loss of liberty, and remove the defects of the system, in a constitutional way," but he refused to thwart the will of the majority by force.[21]

The delegates to the Virginia Convention did not end their labors with the vote favoring ratification. As soon as the Constitution was adopted, many Federalists joined the Antifederalists in their drive to amend the document. George Wythe, chairman of the Federalist-controlled committee for amendments, reported his committee's recommendations to the Convention on June 27, 1788, two days after ratification.[22] In addition to a bill of rights to protect individual liberties, the committee proposed another twenty amendments designed to preserve the power of the states. The spirit of all the amendments was similar: they reflected the delegates' apprehension over what they considered the excessive power of the new government.

Two of the proposed amendments were aimed at forestalling the development of the doctrine of implied powers. The first of these was similar to what became the Tenth Amendment; it provided "that each state in the Union shall respectively retain every power" not expressly granted to the federal government. Yet unlike the Tenth Amendment, it reserved these powers not to the states and the people, but solely to each state.

The western delegates, afraid that the new government would barter their right to navigate the Mississippi River, demanded an amendment requiring approval of three-fourths of the members of both houses in Congress for ratification of treaties touching the territorial rights of any state. All the delegates were jealous of their commercial liberties and proposed that "no navigation law, or law regulating commerce,

---

[21] Rowland, *Life of Mason*, 2: 274; Elliot, *Debates*, 3: 652.

[22] Eleven Federalists and nine Antifederalists served on the committee. Grigsby, *Virginia Convention of 1788*, 1: 347.

shall be passed without the consent of two-thirds of the members present, in both houses." Control over the nation's defense, a source of much contention during debate, was to be safeguarded by an amendment requiring the consent of two-thirds of both houses for recruitment of a standing army during peacetime. Amendments restricting the federal government's control over commerce and foreign affairs passed without a division.[23]

Last, and most important, a majority of delegates sought to impose sharp restrictions on the new government's power over the purse. The committee for amendments proposed that Congress be required to requisition the states for funds before it levied taxes; Congress could levy direct taxes only if a state failed to meet its quota under the requisition. Ostensibly, the federal government would retain ultimate authority over taxation—an advance over the nonexistent taxation power of the Articles—but in fact the Virginia amendment would have crippled the power of the new government to levy taxes. Experience had proved that the requisition system was plagued by evasions, postponements, and delays. The time needed to collect taxes under the requisition system, or to prove that a state had failed to meet its quota under the system, would make it impossible for the federal government to plan its financial operations intelligently. This last amendment was the only one of the twenty proposed by the committee to meet opposition, but it passed, 85-65. Twelve Federalists voted with the Antifederalists on this crucial issue, which if adopted by the other states, would strike at the heart of the new government's authority.[24]

That an overwhelming majority in the Convention so quickly proposed to reduce drastically the powers granted by the Constitution indicated the tentative nature of Virginia's commitment to Federalism. Most of Virginia's Federalists were just as determined as their opponents to ward off the twin evils of consolidation and domination; any attempt by the new government to thwart the principles embodied in the Virginia amendments would drive supporters of the government into the arms of the Antifederalists.

---

[23] Elliot, *Debates*, 3: 662.   [24] Ibid., 3: 661.

Many Virginians were initially optimistic about securing the agreement of the other states to the proposed amendments, since it was generally conceded that Virginia's approval of the Constitution was vital to the success of the union. The residents of the Old Dominion were certain the other states would not run the risk of alienating Virginia by ignoring its demands for amendments. Their prospects seemed even brighter when the delegates to New York's ratifying convention unanimously agreed to send a circular letter to the states calling for a second convention to consider additional amendments to the Constitution.[25]

Virginia's political leaders wasted no time after they received word of New York's proposal. Even the small band of hard-core Federalists who had opposed substantive amendments were resigned to the fact that Virginia would vote in favor of a second convention to revise the Constitution. They were much more afraid that Henry and his followers would try something even more drastic. Henry had vowed "he should seize the first moment that offered for shaking off the yoke in a constitutional way" and some, like Madison, were afraid that he would use the issue of amendments as a pretext to destroy the whole system. They feared that the Antifederalists would attempt to obtain all the elective offices in the new government in order "to get a Congress appointed in the first instance that will commit suicide on its own authority."[26]

Most Antifederalists were not prepared to go that far. Their first goal was to persuade the other states to call another convention, and there was no doubt that "Mr. Henry and his friends enter with great zeal into the scheme."[27] With his large following in the counties along Virginia's southern border, Henry had succeeded in swinging the balance toward Antifederalism in the North Carolina Ratifying Convention, and the Federalists were convinced that he would lead the drive for "an early Convention composed of men who will essentially

[25] Ibid., 2: 413-14.
[26] James Madison to George Washington, Richmond, 27 June 1788, in Hunt, ed. *Madison's Writings*, 5: 234.
[27] Madison to Jefferson, 21 Sept. 1788, ibid., 5: 264.

mutilate the System, particularly in the article of taxation, without which . . . the system cannot answer the purposes for which it was intended."[28]

The critics of the plan for a second convention were too harsh with their opponents. Although some, like Henry, favored it as a means of bringing about the destruction of the new government, many others—including Randolph, Monroe, and Pendleton—supported the idea of a new convention because they genuinely believed that fundamental changes in the Constitution were essential in order to secure the benefits of union.[29]

The lower house of the state legislature, the traditional spokesman for the state and local interests of Virginia, was the obvious place to initiate the call for another convention. The members of the lower house were acutely aware of Virginia's past glories. Many of them had been in the vanguard of Virginia's opposition to Great Britain prior to the Revolution. Their fathers and grandfathers had struggled to wrest from the Crown important powers over taxation, defense, and parliamentary privilege. They had inherited a long tradition of resistance to outside authority and were determined to preserve that heritage. Moreover, they were determined to protect their own personal political power from the threat posed by the new, central government.

When the Virginia General Assembly convened in October 1788, the outnumbered Federalists realized that "a decided and malignant majority may do things of a disagreeable nature." John Beckley, clerk of the House of Delegates, reckoned the Antifederalist majority to be about fifteen, but he underestimated his opponents' strength. The Antifederalists, their ranks swelled by former Federalists who now favored a second convention, had at least a two-to-one majority.[30]

In spite of the Antifederalists' numerical preponderance, the

---

28 Ibid., 23 Aug. 1788, 5: 254.

29 Edmund Randolph to Madison, 13 Aug. 1788, Edmund Pendleton to Madison, 3 Sept. 1788, in Conway, *Edmund Randolph*, pp. 117-18.

30 Madison to Washington, New York, 5 Nov. 1788, in Hunt, ed., *Madison's Writings*, 5: 302; Edward Carrington to Madison, Richmond, 24 Oct. 1788, Madison Papers.

structure of leadership in the House of Delegates differed little from that in previous sessions. Even the position of Speaker, the most important office in the lower chamber, was not affected by the rivalry between Federalists and Antifederalists in the legislature. Thomas Mathews, a Revolutionary War general and a staunch Federalist, defeated two Antifederalists, William Grayson and Benjamin Harrison, in the contest for Speaker.[31] Mathews had served well in the post for several years; his past service and prestige within the House were enough to offset the disadvantage of his unpopular political views. This attitude toward political leadership would remain unimpaired by partisanship for over a decade. Although divisions between Federalists and Antifederalists, and later between Federalists and Republicans, came to affect the affairs of the Assembly, the members of the Virginia lower house were loathe to allow party labels to replace the more traditional means of selecting their leaders.

Mathews, entrusted with the power to appoint all committees, did not allow his desire to protect the new federal Constitution to affect his judgment. The chairmen of the six standing committees, who directed nearly all the day-to-day business of the House of Delegates, had always represented Virginia's top levels of wealth, influence, and prestige. The sudden appearance of two opposing political factions did little to alter this practice. The three Federalists and three Antifederalists appointed to these important posts were chosen not because of their role in the partisan debate over the Constitution, but because of their past experience and performance in the committee work of the lower house.[32]

Although the Federalists maintained control of many key positions in the House, their leaders were not equal to those of the Antifederalists. With Madison and Henry Lee away in the

[31] *Journal of the Virginia House of Delegates,* 25 June 1788 (hereafter referred to as *House Journal*).

[32] For an examination of the structure of leadership in the colonial House of Burgesses see Jack P. Greene, "The Foundations of Political Power in the Virginia House of Burgesses, 1720-1776," *William and Mary Quarterly,* 3d ser., 16 (1959): 485-506.

Continental Congress, and Washington and George Nicholas in temporary retirement from political life, the Federalists were at a decided disadvantage. Richard Bland Lee lamented to a fellow Federalist that the Assembly was "very weak." In Patrick Henry the Antifederalists possessed the only able orator present and "the friends to the new government, being all young and inexperienced, form but a feeble band against them."[33]

The Antifederalists wasted no time in using their majority to embarrass the Federalists. As soon as committee assignments were completed, they challenged Federalist Edward Carrington's election to the House of Delegates. Carrington had acted as chief aide and local informant of both Washington and Madison for several years and the small degree of political success that he had achieved in Virginia was due more to his ties with these national leaders than it was to his record of service in state and local government. Because of his Federalist leanings and his lack of a local political base, Carrington was a likely target for Antifederalist abuse. He had been serving in the Continental Congress until news of his election reached him in New York in June 1788, when he promptly resigned his post in Congress and returned to serve in Virginia. The Committee of Privileges and Elections examined the case and recommended that Carrington take his seat in the lower house, but the Antifederalists overruled the Committee's recommendation and unseated him, claiming that he had violated an act prohibiting officials from serving in both the state and the continental governments.[34] Although the vote on Carrington's dismissal was not recorded, there is little doubt that partisan feelings entered into the final decision; Henry had specifically mentioned Carrington's Federalist outlook during previous debate and Carrington was convinced that the Antifederalists' bitterness toward him was a decisive factor in the outcome.[35]

Carrington's unseating was merely the opening salvo. On October 29, Henry announced that he would oppose any meas-

---

[33] Richard Bland Lee to Madison, 29 Oct. 1788, Richard Bland Lee Papers, Library of Congress.

[34] *House Journal*, 23, 24 Oct. 1788.

[35] Edward Carrington to Madison, Richmond, 24 Oct. 1788, Madison Papers.

ure to put the new government into operation unless accompanied by proposals for amending the Constitution. The same day he presented his plan for a second convention. According to Henry's opponents, the language of the proposal constituted "a direct and indecent censure on all those who had befriended the new government, holding them forth as the betrayers of the dearest rights of the people." Unfortunately, there were few Federalists present who had been active enough in the Ratifying Convention to answer Henry's allegations. Francis Corbin was the only vocal supporter of the Constitution present in the House of Delegates and he seemed "not to have the confidence of those who are friends to the fair trial of the new government."[36]

Corbin was a poor match for the venerable Henry. Corbin's father had been an influential figure in the royal government of Virginia, and when the Revolution came he had fled to England with his sons. Francis Corbin was the only member of the family not to side with the Loyalists, but he nevertheless remained in England during the entire period of the Revolution and came back to Virginia only after his schooling, and the war, had ended.[37] Corbin's close attachment to England was hardly advantageous to his political ambitions in anglophobic Virginia. When Corbin attacked Henry for going against the wishes of the people by asking for another convention, the old patriot was quick to compare Corbin's past services to Virginia with his own, reminding his listeners that he had not been "basking in the beams of royal favour at St. James" during the Revolution. Though most of the legislators had taken sides on the issue of a second convention, any comparison of the principal spokesmen of the two parties in the General Assembly must have worked in favor of the Antifederalists.[38]

Henry's resolution calling for another convention asked:

[36] Charles Lee to George Washington, Richmond, 29 Oct. 1788, in U.S., Department of State, *Documentary History of the Constitution of the United States,* 5 vols. (Washington, D.C., 1894-1905), 5: 101-3 (hereafter referred to as *Documentary History*).

[37] Grigsby, *Virginia Convention of 1788,* 1: 143-44.

[38] William Wirt, *Sketches of the Life and Character of Patrick Henry* (Philadelphia, 1817), pp. 305-7.

"that for quieting the minds of the good citizens of this Commonwealth, and securing their dearest rights and liberties, and preventing those disorders which must arise under a government not founded on the confidence of the people, application be made to the Congress of the United States, as soon as they shall assemble under the said Constitution, to call a Convention for proposing amendments to the same, according to the mode therein directed." The Federalists tried to soften the proposal by offering a substitute resolution, agreeing on the need for amendments, but asking that Congress be given the first opportunity to act on them. The Antifederalists would have none of it. The Federalist proposal was overwhelmingly defeated, 39-85, and Henry's resolution passed.[39]

The next step in the Antifederalists' strategy was to elect representatives to the First Congress who would be hostile to the federal government. Although some Federalists suspected that this was part of a plan to make the new government dissolve voluntarily on its first assemblage, the purpose was to insure that Virginia's congressional delegation would do everything in its power to obtain adoption of all amendments proposed in the Ratifying Convention.[40] The election by the legislature of Virginia's two United States senators offered the first opportunity to carry out this scheme. The Antifederalists backed Madison as a candidate for the Continental Congress to diminish his influence over the senatorial elections; with Madison out of the state, they were more confident they could attract enough support to elect both their candidates, William Grayson and Richard Henry Lee. While Madison's consequent absence did not prevent his name from being placed in nomination, he failed in his bid for election. On November 8, 1788, the General Assembly balloted for two United States senators and despite Edward Carrington's enthusiastic lobbying for Madison, the results were: Lee—98, Grayson—86, Madison—77.[41] Thus,

39 *House Journal*, 30 Oct. 1788.

40 Theodorick Bland to Richard Henry Lee, Richmond, 28 Oct. 1788, Lee Family Papers, Alderman Library, University of Virginia; Patrick Henry to Caleb Wallace, Richmond, 15 Nov. 1788, Patrick Henry Papers, Library of Congress.

Virginia's two representatives to the United States Senate were men determined to curtail drastically the powers granted to the new government.[42]

The Antifederalists sought to consolidate their political supremacy the next week. On November 13 the legislature laid out districts for the election of congressional representatives; the results suggest that Patrick Henry and not Elbridge Gerry should have been given credit for the practice of gerrymandering. The Antifederalists again used their majority in the Assembly to strike at Virginia's foremost nationalist, James Madison. Madison's district was drawn to include his own county of Orange, but then was extended far into the southwest to embrace the Antifederalist counties dominated by Henry and the Cabell family. Madison would have an uphill fight to gain election, and his experience would be a lesson to Virginia Federalists with political ambitions.[43]

Henry and the Antifederalists next drafted a bill to prevent any person from holding important posts in both state and federal governments. Even the Federalists agreed that this was a necessary piece of legislation, since it was important to guard against conflict of interest among government officials, but the Antifederalists carried it a step further and used the act to attack the new government. According to Carrington, the Antifederalist version of the bill was "intended for the purposes of bringing odium upon the Federal Government and embarrassing it."[44] It stated that no one holding any lucrative position in any branch of the federal government would be allowed to hold office in the state government. It even disqualified soldiers in the United States militia from serving in the state govern-

---

41 George Lee Turberville to Madison, 27 Oct. 1788, Edward Carrington to Madison, 9 Nov. 1788, in *Documentary History*, 5: 110.

42 Richard Henry Lee and William Grayson to the Speaker of the House of Delegates, New York, 28 Sept. 1789, in *The Letters of Richard Henry Lee*, ed. James C. Ballagh, 2 vols. (New York, 1914), 2: 507-9 (hereafter referred to as Ballagh, ed., *Richard Henry Lee*).

43 *House Journal*, 13 Nov. 1788; Irving Brant, *James Madison*, 5 vols. (New York, 1941-1961), 3: 238-39.

44 Carrington to Madison, Richmond, 18 Nov. 1788, in *Documentary History*, 5: 119.

ment—although members of the Virginia militia could serve in federal posts. The bill passed, 71-52, with Antifederalists almost unanimous in support of the measure.[45] One purpose of the act was to discourage men from taking employment in the nation's capital for fear that they might lose their power in the state government. But this was sadly out of touch with reality. Instead of forcing Virginia's political leaders to continue working for the state government, the effect of the bill proved the opposite. As Carrington predicted, "the United States, being debarred from conferring their powers upon state officers, will induce the most able of these into service." The result of course would be a diminution in the number of talented and prestigious people holding office and serving in the state government.[46]

The Virginia legislature on November 14, 1788, delivered its final warning to the new national government. In an address to Congress, which was to convene in March 1789, the legislature reaffirmed its opposition to the Constitution in its present form. The legislators claimed that a desire for union had brought about Virginia's ratification, but that serious defects remained which far outweighed any benefits that union might bring. Despite their assent to the Constitution, the members of the Ratifying Convention had given "the most unequivocal proofs that they dreaded its operation in its present form." The address hinted that the new government could not hope to endure unless the apprehensions of the people of Virginia were relieved by amendments. The members of the Assembly—no doubt recalling the vacillation of the Confederation Congress —placed little faith in "the slow forms of Congressional discussion and recommendation" and questioned whether "indeed, they [Congress] should ever agree to any changes." On the same day the legislature proposed a circular letter to the other

45 William Walter Hening, *The Statutes at Large, Being a Collection of the Laws of Virginia from the First Session of the Legislature in the Year 1619,* 12 vols. (Richmond, 1823): 12: 694-95 (hereafter referred to as Hening, *Statutes at Large*); *House Journal*, 8 Dec. 1788.

46 Carrington to Madison, Richmond, 9 Nov. 1788, in *Documentary History*, 5: 111-12.

states asking their concurrence in the call for another convention.[47]

Once again the outnumbered Federalists tried to tone down the Antifederalist address. They proposed a substitute resolution which "earnestly called upon the Congress of the United States to take the said amendments under their immediate consideration," but this mere show of approval for the Virginia amendments did not satisfy their opponents; the Federalist version of the address was defeated, 50-72, and the original passed *viva voce*.[48]

The debate over a second convention provides an interesting commentary on Virginia's attitude toward union. That a decisive majority of Virginia's elected representatives agreed to call a second convention with the purpose of undoing much of the work of the first is indicative of a strong aversion to the nationalists' concept of union. Even more extraordinary is that almost no one, including most Federalists, quarreled with the ostensible aim of the Antifederalists—adoption of the amendments proposed by the Virginia Ratifying Convention. It was not a mere majority, but a near unanimity of Virginians who favored a set of amendments that would deprive the new government of many of its essential powers. Most Virginia Federalists, although they feared the disruptive effects of another convention, shared the Antifederalists' distaste for consolidated government.

The major division in Virginia in the fall of 1788 was not between confirmed Federalists and Antifederalists. Rather, it was between a band of determined Antifederalists that wanted to limit or even destroy the powers of the federal government and another group that approved of union, but nevertheless desired that Congress adopt amendments to render parts of the new system less obnoxious. The only stern criticism of these two groups came from a small group of nationalists within the Federalist faction, who were incensed that the legislature should show "the most malignant (and if one may be allowed

---

47 *House Journal,* 14 Nov. 1788.
48 Ibid.

the expression, the most unwarrantable) disposition toward the new government."[49] In particular, they resented Henry's dominance over the legislature; according to Tobias Lear, "he ruled a majority of the Assembly, and his edicts were registered by that body with less opposition than those of the Grand Monarque have met with from his parliaments. . . . And after he had settled everything . . . to his satisfaction, he mounted his horse and rode home, leaving the little business of the state to be done by anybody who chose to give themselves the trouble of attending to it."[50]

Lear and his nationalist colleagues were peevish in their criticism. The Antifederalists had not initiated the assault on the new government because they enjoyed the role of obstructionists. They feared an erosion of their liberties and prerogatives unless Virginia's amendments were adopted, and they did not believe Congress could be trusted to act in good faith on Virginia's proposals. Patrick Henry was so disturbed by the Constitution in its unamended form that he claimed he was prepared to move to North Carolina, which had refused to ratify the Constitution, and where, presumably, his liberties would go untrammeled.[51] Even a staunch nationalist like Chief Justice John Marshall, looking back on the fight over the Constitution, was able to see justification for the Antifederalists' apprehensions. One of the central tenets of Antifederalist thought, according to Marshall, was that "liberty could only be endangered by encroachments upon the states; and that it was the great duty of patriotism to restrain the powers of the general government within the narrowest possible limits."[52] This was not an unreasonable view in eighteenth-century

[49] Washington to David Stuart, Mt. Vernon, 2 Dec. 1788, in Fitzpatrick, ed., *Washington's Writings*, 30: 146.

[50] Tobias Lear to the Governor of New Hampshire, Mt. Vernon, 31 Jan. 1789, in George Bancroft, *History of the Formation of the Constitution of the United States of America*, 2 vols. (New York, 1885), 2: 488-89.

[51] Theodorick Bland to Richard Henry Lee, Richmond, 28 Oct. 1788, Lee Family Papers; Patrick Henry to Caleb Wallace, Richmond, 15 Nov. 1788, Henry Papers.

[52] John Marshall, *The Life of George Washington* . . . , 2d ed., 2 vols. (Philadelphia, 1843), 2: 205-6 (hereafter referred to as Marshall, *Washington*).

America. The central government of Great Britain had posed a threat to American liberties by its denial of colonial authority over such measures as taxation and legislative prerogative. It was natural that Henry, the champion of Virginia's right to govern her own affairs within the imperial system, would insist on that right for the Old Dominion within the new nation. He had fought centralized power throughout the course of his political career. His campaign to curtail the power of the federal government was but one more round in that fight.

The Antifederalists would be rebuffed in their attempt at another constitutional convention and would have to rely on Congress for amendments. But their efforts were not all in vain. They had registered strong opposition to the whole notion of centralized power, and their influence was being felt by even the most determined of the Old Dominion's nationalists.

The changing political fortunes of Madison best illustrate the pressure exerted by the Antifederalists. Madison was one of the few Virginians who in 1788 could be classified as an enthusiastic nationalist. He had spent most of his career in national service and unlike most political leaders in Virginia was not accustomed to subordinating national to local interests. But it was becoming apparent that the rising tide of Antifederalist sentiment in Virginia was making it necessary to do just that.

Madison's defeat, in November 1788, for a seat in the United States Senate would cause him to begin to move away from his nationalist stance and to become more solicitous of local interests.[53] Although he had originally been an unwilling candidate for the Senate, the manner of his defeat proved a shaking experience for the young Federalist. Henry had attacked him abusively during the debates on the candidates, pronouncing him "unworthy of the confidence of the people in the station of senator," and claiming that his election "would terminate

[53] The most persuasive account of Madison's switch from a national to a state-oriented position is E. James Ferguson, *The Power of the Purse: A History of American Public Finance, 1776-1790* (Chapel Hill, N.C., 1961), pp. 297-305.

in producing rivulets of blood throughout the land."[54] Vituperation might have been expected, especially from an implacable foe like Henry, but Madison was more dismayed by indications that he would also fail in his bid for a seat in the House of Representatives. His chances were dimmed by the gerrymandering of his congressional district. It was imperative that he do something to bolster his sagging popularity. His supporters pleaded with him to come home from New York and, more important, to soften his opposition to constitutional amendments. Accustomed to operating independently of local interests, Madison was averse to doing either. He did not want to stoop to "an electioneering appearance" and was not convinced of the necessity of amendments.[55] In October 1788, before the Antifederalists had blocked his election to the Senate, he wrote Jefferson explaining his position. He was willing to support a bill of rights, but only with the greatest reluctance. "I have never thought the omission [of a bill of rights] a material defect," he informed Jefferson, "nor been anxious to supply it even by subsequent amendments, for any other purpose than that it is anxiously desired by others." Under no circumstances would he support amendments to restore to the states power given to the national government.[56]

James Monroe, Madison's opponent in the congressional race, hoped that he could use the amendment issue to advantage. During November and December of 1788 he traveled through Orange, Amherst, Spotsylvania, Culpeper, Louisa, Albemarle, Goochland, and Fluvanna—the counties comprising the congressional district—informing the people that Madison opposed all amendments. The strategy seemed to work: by the end of December 1788 it appeared that the lesser-known Monroe might defeat Madison.[57] To counteract Monroe's efforts Richard

54 Henry Lee to Madison, 19 Nov. 1788, Madison Papers.

55 Madison to Edmund Randolph, Philadelphia, 23 Nov. 1788, in Hunt, ed., *Madison's Writings*, 5: 305; Carrington to Madison, Richmond, 15 Nov. 1788, in *Documentary History*, 5: 110.

56 Madison to Jefferson, New York, 17 Oct. 1788, in Hunt, ed., *Madison's Writings*, 5: 269-71.

57 Madison to Henry Lee, Philadelphia, 30 Nov. 1788, ibid., 5: 308-9; Carring-

Bland Lee began circulating pamphlets in favor of Madison.
Lee attacked the partisan spirit of Henry's criticism of Madison
and assured the voters that Madison was not as unfriendly to
amendments as Monroe claimed.[58]

It was still imperative that Madison make those assurances in
person. In January 1789 he finally yielded to the wishes of his
supporters. He came to Virginia to campaign personally and
at the same time began to shift his position on amendments.
In a letter to Baptist minister George Eve, a communication
certain to gain wide circulation, Madison openly advocated
limited amendments. He defended his decision to oppose
amendments as a condition to ratification, but admitted that
"circumstances are now changed." He vowed that, since the
Constitution had been ratified by the necessary number of states,
"it is my sincere opinion that the Constitution ought to be
revised." He then endorsed not only a bill of rights but also an
amendment increasing the number of representatives in the
lower house—this last step to eliminate complaints that adequate
representation would be impossible in a government extending
over such a large, populous territory.[59] Circumstances *had*
changed. Only a few months earlier he had repudiated the
notion of increasing the ratio of congressional representation
on the grounds that it would create confusion and dilute talent
in the House of Representatives.[60] Madison concluded his
letter to Eve by conceding that there "are sundry other alterations which are either eligible in themselves, or being at least
safe, are recommended by the respect due to such as wish for
them."[61] This last statement, suitably vague, could allow
Madison's supporters to intimate to the voters that he favored

---

ton to Madison, Richmond, 15 Nov. 1788, Alexander White to Madison, Richmond, 4 Dec. 1788, Hardin Burnley to Madison, 16 Dec. 1788, in *Documentary
History*, 5: 117-18, 128-29, 133-34.

58 Richard Bland Lee to Madison, Richmond, 12 Dec. 1788, Richard Bland Lee
Papers.

59 Madison to George Eve, 2 Jan. 1789, in Hunt, ed., *Madison's Writings*, 5:
319-21.

60 Benjamin F. Wright, ed., *The Federalist*, "Number 58" (Cambridge, Mass.,
1961), p. 392.

61 Madison to Eve, 2 Jan. 1789, in Hunt, ed., *Madison's Writings*, 5: 319-21.

a wide range of amendments without having to state specifically what those amendments were.

That Madison appealed to a Baptist minister for support was significant. The Baptists, the principal evangelical sect in Virginia, had for decades played an active role in the state's political affairs. In their desire to increase liberty for dissenters the Baptists had become the only religious group in Virginia to show an interest in political organization. They distrusted the state government because it had consistently subordinated their interests to those of the Episcopal Church and had tended to side with the Antifederalists on the Constitution out of fear that their religious liberties would fare even worse at the hands of a more powerful, highly centralized government. By soliciting the aid of the Baptists to secure his political survival, Madison had entered into an alliance with a group whose political principles were often in direct opposition to his own. An alliance containing such disparate elements would not have been possible in many states, but in Virginia, where personal influence and prestige were often more important than an individual's ideology, Madison was able to obtain Baptist aid without opening himself to the charge of having betrayed his political principles.[62]

The appeal to the Baptists proved successful. In the congressional election, held in February 1789, Madison defeated Monroe 1,308 to 972.[63] But he had been forced to make important concessions in order to achieve his victory. He had not previously been willing to agree to amendments simply out of "respect due to such as wish for them," but with his political career on the line, he modified his views.

Madison's shift was part of a trend that affected nearly all Virginia's representatives in the nation's capital. Within the next few years most of Virginia's Federalist congressmen would moderate their positions in an attempt to court powerful

[62] Wesley M. Gewehr, *The Great Awakening in Virginia, 1740-1790* (Durham, N.C., 1930), pp. 189-94. The alliance, though politically expedient, was not always a comfortable one. The extreme statements of some of the more radical Baptists often hindered, rather than helped, the cause of the antiadministration party.

[63] *Virginia Herald and Fredericksburg Advertiser*, 12 Feb. 1789.

political groups within Virginia committed to preserving their tradition of local, decentralized government. This drift of Virginia's Federalist congressmen toward the Antifederalist camp did not signify a complete capitulation to the political principles of extreme Antifederalists such as Patrick Henry or Richard Henry Lee—men like Madison would retain many of their nationalistic principles while at the same time borrowing Antifederalist rhetoric—but it was a clear sign that a large segment of the powerholders in the Old Dominion were determined to prevent any further growth in the nationalizing tendencies of the new government.

CHAPTER TWO

The Continuity of Political Life

THE RELUCTANCE of so many of Virginia's state-oriented politicians to yield power to a new federal government is hardly surprising. For those same men had successfully resisted any changes in their own state government which threatened to diminish their political power. Even the Revolution, although it succeeded in eliminating royal authority, left the structure of provincial politics intact. The Virginia constitution of 1776 merely legitimized the destruction of royal power and strengthened the grasp of the provincial oligarchy on the politics of the state. That constitution, although hardly advancing the already-slow process of democratization in Virginia, was nevertheless wholly in keeping with the ideals for which Virginia's political leaders fought the Revolution. For those leaders had rebelled against Great Britain to preserve local institutions of government, and therefore their own political power, from the threat of outside interference.

The efficacy and stability of Virginia's political system was founded on a strong tradition of vigorous and responsible local government. During the colonial period local units of government, and the county courts in particular, had gradually assumed control over the internal polity of Virginia's many counties. Royal governors and the House of Burgesses seemed far-removed from the daily concerns of small farmers and large planters alike; for most people, distant from the seat of power, the county court *was* the government.

The average number of judges in each county was twenty-two, but only four were needed to conduct the business of the county court.[1] The court was to meet each month, on a day fixed by law, to consider nearly every type of business; it often acted in a legislative and executive capacity as well as in its judicial role. In addition to being the court of first instance for all civil and criminal cases, the county court by mid-eighteenth century had assumed responsibility for collecting taxes, licensing all public utilities, and supervising all charities. The social value of the county court was perhaps even more important than its official role. It was here that the residents of a widely dispersed agrarian society could gather to transact business, renew acquaintances, and exchange gossip.[2]

Theoretically the governor had the power to appoint the members of the county court, who in turn appointed the lesser county officials, but through a long series of struggles with the royal governors, the justices assumed practical control over local appointments. When a vacancy occurred, the justices would recommend a replacement to the governor, who would generally approve it without question. The governor was not legally bound to accept the court's nomination, but since the court was usually composed of the leading men of the county, whose cooperation was invaluable for a harmonious term in office, he usually acquiesced in their decision. The justices also gradually established the precedent of a lifetime appointment, and when one of them died his successor often was a son or a close relative.[3]

The system had supposedly worked well in the past. The county court officials of colonial days had constituted a "Who's Who" of Virginia society; nearly all Virginia's revolutionary

1 Sydnor, *Gentlemen Freeholders*, pp. 78-93. The structure and function of the county courts has been accurately described by Sydnor; it is therefore necessary only to summarize briefly his findings here.

2 Albert O. Porter, *County Government in Virginia: A Legislative History, 1607-1904* (New York, 1947), pp. 9-226.

3 Sydnor, *Gentlemen Freeholders*, pp. 78-93.

heroes had served an apprenticeship as justices of the peace. Working for little or no pay, they had taken time from their business as planters or lawyers to look after the interests of their constituents in what most historians have characterized as a responsible and paternalistic fashion. With this heritage of effective local government it is not surprising that most Virginians had misgivings about the effects of national government. The vision of federal tax officials and tobacco inspectors, sent from distant states with different interests, was not comforting. To most Virginians, even the state government seemed too distant to understand their needs. Only the county government could be trusted to act in accordance with the people's wishes. No matter that officials were not popularly elected; their physical proximity to the voters insured that they would act responsively.

Yet by the 1780s this system of oligarchic, if benevolent, county rule was beginning to show signs of weakness. The county aristocracies were losing their effectiveness. The reasons for the decline are not altogether clear; an intensive study of local government in Virginia during the nineteenth century—the period in which the weaknesses of county government become most apparent—would provide at least some explanations. A few of the causes, however, can be detected in the late eighteenth century. First, the demands made upon local government were steadily increasing as the economy and social structure of the Old Dominion became more complex. The same structures of government were in many ways unequipped to cope with both the increasing and changing demands placed upon them. Moreover, the character of the people who controlled those structures of government was subtly changing. The county aristocracies were being weakened, not so much from pressure from the lower classes, as from the continual intermarriage between the many branches of prominent families and the newer, influential families. As the number of people with a claim to aristocracy grew, the answer to the question of who should rule the county was no longer as clear as it had been.[4] The appointive system, which had previously selected the educated, well born, and capable, now began to be used for corrupt purposes.

It was no novelty that political leaders were using their influence to obtain government employment for friends. This was a time-honored practice dating back into the colonial period.[5] More serious was the outright buying and selling of offices. In the past, when the social hierarchy in the counties was more stable and the choice for an office more apparent, this was not so common, but as those persons with a claim to social prominence increased, so too did applications for public office. In a system with some popular control over the selection of public officials, increased competition for public office would have led to an increased reliance on the people for support and would have tended to promote democratization of the political system. But in Virginia, with a system congenial to oligarchic control, this increased competition for office merely enlarged the possibilities of corruption. Instead of turning to the people to convince them of their qualifications for public office, the county oligarchs only intensified their efforts to use their personal influence and wealth to obtain appointive offices. Clerkships were openly purchased by those wealthy enough to invest in a position which they hoped would launch their political careers. There was also a constant maneuvering for appointments as officers in the state militia. Theoretically, a county court recommended the appointment of officers to the governor on the basis of seniority, but in practice both the court and the governor overlooked this tradition when it was politically or financially expedient. Virginians did not appear particularly concerned about the buying and selling of offices. A bill to prohibit the practice was defeated in 1789, although a milder version finally was passed in 1792. Despite this statutory prohibition, the custom continued, particularly in the western part of the state, where enforcement was more difficult

---

4 For example, there were members of the Lee, Mason, and Carrington families on each side of the question in the Virginia Ratifying Convention.

5 Drury Stith to Henry Tazewell, Brunswick, 5 Feb. 1789, Spencer Roane to Tazewell, Essex, 6 Feb. 1789, Tazewell Family Papers, Virginia State Library (VSL).

and where the tradition of responsible local government was less strong among the newer ruling elite.[6]

The county courts were faced with problems more serious than occasional cases of corruption: by the end of the eighteenth century the courts were in many instances not functioning. A common complaint by those who petitioned the General Assembly was that the system of justice in the counties was slow and inequitable. Most of the petitions pointed to the same fault: with a multiplicity of justices, working without pay and feeling no special responsibility to be present at the monthly meeting of the court, it was not uncommon for no one of them to appear at the scheduled session of the court. Without a quorum, the business of the court was at a standstill. This neglect of duty led to delays as long as five years in the settlement of even the smallest claims. Not a few residents were becoming impatient with the system. "It has become questionable," complained the petitioners from Albemarle County, "whether the condition of our aboriginal neighbours, who live without law or magistrates, be not preferable to that of the great mass of nations . . . whose laws burden them."[7]

But the county court was immune to change. For everyone who signed the petition of Albemarle County, there were many more like Benjamin Watkins Leigh, who as late as 1819 declared that the county courts were "so important that their institutions may well be considered as a part of the constitution, both of the colonial and present government. No material change was introduced by the revolution in their jurisdiction, or general powers and duties of any kind. . . . It would perhaps be impossible for any man to estimate the character and utility

6 *House Journal*, 14 Dec. 1789, 6 Oct. 1792; Samuel Shepherd, *The Statutes at Large of Virginia, 1792-1806, Being a Continuation of Hening's Statutes at Large*, 3 vols. (Richmond, 1835-1836), 1: 6-7; James McDowell to John Preston, Smithfield, 21 Oct. 1792, Francis Preston to John Preston, 24 Oct. 1792, Preston Papers, Virginia Historical Society (VHS); Henry Lee to John Preston, Richmond, 17 Feb. 1792, Executive Letterbooks, VSL; Thomas Smith to James Monroe, 28 May 1800, Correspondence to the Executive, VSL.

7 Petition of the Citizens of Loudon County, 19 Oct. 1792, Petition of Fairfax County, 6 Oct. 1792, Petition of Albemarle County, 24 Dec. 1798, all in Petitions to the Virginia General Assembly, VSL.

of this system, without actual experience of its operation."[8] Although one generation removed from the group of men who dominated the political affairs of Virginia in the 1790s, Leigh was a product of the same tradition. The county courts represented the cornerstone of effective government for both Leigh and his predecessors. This pride in Virginia's local institutions was the single most important factor working against any increase in the power of the continental government or any alteration of the structure of the state government.

The members of the lower house of the legislature, during both the colonial and post-revolutionary period, were at the pinnacle of political power within their respective county hierarchies. They had generally served an apprenticeship in county government and had advanced to a position where they served as spokesmen for their respective counties in the affairs of the state. They were understandably averse to any changes which threatened to weaken their positions. Many of the members of the House of Delegates, the post-revolutionary counterpart of the colonial House of Burgesses, would view the new federal government as precisely such a threat.[9]

The first stage in the legislative process, the election of delegates to serve in the lower house, has long been a source of historical debate. The most recent research on suffrage in the Old Dominion suggests that as many as 85 to 95 percent of Virginia's free adult white males were permitted to cast votes in local elections. In many cases citizens without the necessary fifty-acre freehold were allowed to vote despite laws to the contrary. This latitude given to nonfreeholders is best illustrated by a survey of contested election petitions presented

---

8 Benjamin W. Leigh, comp., *The Revised Code of the Laws of Virginia* (Richmond, 1819), 1: 244n, quoted in Sydnor, *Gentlemen Freeholders,* p. 86.

9 The lower house of the legislature tended to dominate the upper house. The state senate could only approve, amend, or reject legislation initiated by the lower house. On only a few occasions did it differ with the lower house on important matters. The history of the continuing fight for autonomy by the colonial counterpart of the House of Delegates, the House of Burgesses, is recounted in Jack P. Greene, *The Quest for Power: The Lower Houses of Assembly in the Southern Royal Colonies, 1689-1776* (Chapel Hill, N.C., 1963).

to the House of Delegates. In these contested elections as many as 40 percent of the total votes were cast by citizens without the necessary freehold. When a formal complaint was filed, the illegal votes were voided, but one can assume that nonfreeholders voted in elections that were not disputed and that it was only when the outcome was in doubt that their right to vote was challenged.[10]

There are questions relating to suffrage in Virginia, however, which are impossible to answer by analysis that is merely quantitative. How were elections conducted? How did the candidates view the electorate? On what criteria did the voter base his choice? What percentage of those who could vote thought it worthwhile to do so? The answers reveal much more about the nature of Virginia's political process than the simple fact that a high percentage of the people were allowed to cast a vote.

In the 1780s and 1790s, as in the past, the county sheriff controlled nearly every step of the election process. If he thought most freeholders had voted, he could close the polls after a few hours; if a heavy voter turnout or bad weather slowed the process, he might extend voting into the next day. In some cases, as in Harrison County in 1790, the sheriff could keep the polls open for as many as eleven days. The

10 Brown and Brown, *Virginia, 1705-1786,* are the most prominent of those historians arguing that the right of suffrage in Virginia was widespread. Their findings relative to the extent of the suffrage have not been successfully challenged. Their conclusions with respect to the presence or absence of "democracy" resulting from that widespread suffrage, however, have been widely questioned. The present study was not conceived either as an attempt to support or to refute the Browns' findings, but there is abundant evidence to prove that the relationship between the right to vote and the existence of democratic attitudes is a dubious one. For examples of elections where nonfreeholders voted, see House Journal, 29 Oct., 27 Nov. 1790, 15 Jan. 1800; Petition of Thomas Stith to the Convention of 1788, Election Records no. 1, Election Committee to Chairman of the Committee of Privileges and Elections, 18 Nov. 1788, Election Records no. 362, Petition of Delegates for Jefferson County, 1790, Deposition of William Robinson, Sheriff of Harrison County, April 1790. Petition of M. Roberts to the Committee of Privileges and Elections, 20 Oct. 1790, Poll List, Greensville County, 26 April 1792, Petition of John Clopton to the Committee of Privileges and Elections, 21 Oct. 1792, Charles Griffin to William Foushee, 14 April 1798, Election Records no. 363, VSL.

sheriff could also challenge any prospective voter for not possessing the necessary freehold.[11] This kind of power, when exercised responsibly, did much to insure a fair and orderly election process.

There were no institutional checks guaranteeing that the sheriff would use his power impartially. The House of Delegates served as the court of appeal in cases where the sheriff was charged with abusing his power, but it rarely ruled against him. Complaints continued to flow into the House of Delegates. Hardly a year went by when sheriffs were not accused of deliberately keeping the polls open to aid one candidate at the expense of another or that they were not charged with excluding the votes of some nonfreeholders but not the votes of others.[12]

The voting was occasionally accomplished by a showing of hands, but more often it was *viva voce,* which allowed candidates or interested spectators to calculate the results of the election while it was in progress. This method had its drawbacks, however. It lent itself to a subtle coercion, since a tenant of one of the candidates would be reluctant to cast his vote against his landlord, who was usually present at the polls watching the votes being cast. Since most candidates were wealthy planters, with many tenants, this could materially affect the outcome of an election. The defects of this method were described in 1789 by a disgruntled, defeated candidate for the Assembly: "The candidate stands upon an eminence close to the Avenue thro which people pass to give in their votes, viva voce, or by outcry. There the Candidates stand ready to beg, pray, and solicit the peoples votes in opposition to their competitors and the poor wretched people are much difficulted by the prayers and threats of those Competitors, exactly similar

11 Hening, *Statutes at Large,* 12: 120-29; Sydnor, *Gentlemen Freeholders,* pp. 18-21; Albert McKinley, *Suffrage in the Thirteen English Colonies in America* (Philadelphia, 1905), p. 35.

12 See, for example, Deposition of William Robinson, Sheriff of Harrison County, April 1790, Poll Book, Ohio County, 24-26 April 1798, Petition to the Committee of Privileges and Elections, Berkeley County, April 1798, Petition to the Committee of Privileges and Elections, Ohio County, 1 May 1799, VSL.

to the Election of the corrupt and infamous House of Commons in England."[13]

Political campaigns were sometimes hotly contested for weeks in advance and other times they merely formalized a victory that was a foregone conclusion, but nearly all the campaigns had one common denominator: a candidate was elected not because he took a stand on the issues of the day, but because he was popular and had influence in the county.

Nearly all candidates disdained appeals to the people. Madison was reluctant even to appear in his home state during his campaign for a seat in the First Congress—despite the fact that his absence might spell defeat.[14] John Marshall not only refused to campaign, he was not even aware of his candidacy in the 1795 election for the House of Delegates. He had gone to the polls to vote in a hotly contested election between two gentlemen who had been longstanding rivals.

> I attended at the polls to give my vote early and return to the court which was then in session at the other end of town. As soon as the election commenced a gentleman came forward and demanded that a poll should be taken for me. I was a good deal surprised at this entirely unsuspected proposition and declared my decided dissent. I said that if any of my fellow citizens wished it I would become a candidate at the succeeding election but that I could not consent to serve that year because my wishes and my honour were engaged for one of the candidates. I voted for my friend and left the polls for the court which was open and waiting for me. The gentleman said that he had a right to demand a poll for whom he pleased, and persisted in his demand that one should be opened for me— I might if elected refuse to obey the voice of the constituents if I chose to do so. He then gave his vote for me. As this was entirely unexpected—not even known by my brother, who though of the same political opinions with myself was the active and leading partisan of the candidate against whom I

---

13 David Thomas to Griffith Evans, 3 March 1789, in *Proceedings of the Massachusetts Historical Society*, 46 (1913): 370-71.

14 Madison to Randolph, Philadelphia, 23 Nov. 1788, in Hunt, ed., *Madison's Writings*, 5: 305.

had voted, the election was almost suspended for ten or twelve minutes, and a consultation took place among the freeholders. They then came in and in the evening information was brought me that I was elected. I regretted this for this sake of my friend. In other regards I was well satisfied at being again in the assembly.[15]

A vigorous campaign based on issues was obviously not necessary if a man like Marshall did not even have to acknowledge himself a candidate. The fate of the two original candidates is even more interesting. In this particular election, they held opposing positions on the most important political issue of the day—ratification of the Jay Treaty. That a man like Marshall, because of his popularity and prestige, could divert attention from such an important issue testifies to the role of personality in the political process. If this could occur in the city of Richmond, the most politically sophisticated area in Virginia, it could happen anywhere in the state. The conduct of Marshall's brother is yet another indication of the unimportance of political issues in Virginia's elections. Although sharing the same Federalist sentiments as John Marshall, he was the leading advocate of the Republican candidate.[16] The entire episode serves to show that political labels based on national issues were often meaningless in a state where local problems and prominent personalities were the decisive factors in the political process. Marshall's victory in Richmond in 1795 did not signify a triumph of the nationalistic principles of the Federalist party. Rather, it represented a personal vote of confidence in the character and ability of John Marshall.

Marshall was so popular, in fact, that he did not have to rely on a common Virginia practice—the liberal distribution of food and drink to potential supporters—to gain election. Some have maintained that this widespread practice of "treating" is proof of the candidates' dependence upon the will of the electorate and is therefore indicative of the democratic nature of Virginia's

15 *An Autobiographical Sketch by John Marshall,* ed. John Stokes Adams (Ann Arbor, Mich., 1937), pp. 15-16.
16 Ibid., pp. 14-15.

political process. It certainly seemed so to the Frenchman Ferdinand Bayard, traveling in Virginia in 1791. He claimed that election days in Virginia were days of reveling, of brawls, where "the candidates offer drunkenness openly to anyone who is willing to give them his vote. The taverns are occupied by the parties, the citizens flock to the standards of the candidates; and the voting place is often surrounded by men with clubs, who drive back and intimidate the citizens of the other party."[17] But treating was hardly the product of a democratic society. Its use presupposed that the candidates were wealthy enough to afford the practice. When it did influence the outcome of an election, then it inevitably worked in favor of those who could afford to be lavish in their entertainment. Its very existence also suggests a certain contempt for the voter, who needed to be bribed to vote for the best candidate.[18]

Some Virginians, like Edmund Pendleton and his fellow petitioners from Caroline County, were disgusted with this style of campaigning. They asked the House of Delegates "whether the best mode of enabling electors to judge of a candidate's qualifications, is to deprive them of their senses?" They condemned the device of treating because it gave an inordinate advantage to the wealthy, thus perpetuating oligarchic rule. But this practice had roots deep in English and colonial tradition and was therefore difficult to stop. "I am sorry to observe that such is the disposition of my countrymen," Thomas Evans of Accomac County exclaimed in exasperation, "that nothing will induce them to attend elections of however great importance without being treated."[19]

The apathy that Evans lamented persisted throughout the

17 Ferdinand M. Bayard, *Travels of a Frenchman in Maryland and Virginia, with a Description of Philadelphia and Baltimore in 1791*, ed. Ben. C. McCary (Williamsburg, 1950), p. 65.

18 For a contemporary description of the practice of treating, and of Virginia election practices in general, see Jay B. Hubbel and Douglass Adair, "Robert Munford's The Candidates," *William and Mary Quarterly*, 3d ser., 5 (1948):3-43. In addition to a perceptive textual analysis, the article also contains an interesting biographical sketch of Munford.

19 Petition of Caroline County to the Virginia General Assembly, 18 Dec. 1797, Virginia Miscellany, LC; Thomas Evans to John Cropper, 6 Dec. 1796, John Cropper Papers, VHS.

1790s in spite of statutes that punished nonvoting freeholders with a fine of one-quarter their yearly tax assessment. Although the tension between Federalists and Antifederalists in the legislature increased, voter participation remained low, averaging less than 20 percent of the free adult white male population.[20] In some counties the response of the citizens was so feeble that there seemed to be little point in holding the election at all. In the 1790 election for the House of Delegates in Essex County the two victorious candidates, each running unopposed, garnered a total of seven votes each. In Brunswick and Cumberland counties the contests for presidential elector in 1789 managed to interest only 15 percent of the voters. Even in the hotly contested election between Madison and Monroe in 1789, none of the eight counties had a voter turnout exceeding 35 percent and some had as low as 10 percent.[21]

This low turnout is explained by two factors: first, political

20 Hening, *Statutes at Large,* 12: 122. For a sampling of voter participation in Virginia during the period 1788-1792, see Poll List for presidential elector, 7 Jan. 1789, Poll List for representatives to the House of Delegates, April 1789, Poll List for congressional election, April 1789, Poll List for election of representatives to the House of Delegates, 26 April 1790, Poll List for election of representatives to the state senate, 26 April 1790, Poll List for congressional election, 26 July 1790, Poll List for special congressional election, 6 Sept. 1790, Poll List for election of representatives to the House of Delegates, 25 April 1791, Poll List for congressional election, 5 Nov. 1792, Brunswick County Election Records, VSL; Poll List for election of representatives to the Ratifying Convention, 17 March 1788, Poll List for election of representatives to the House of Delegates, 21 April 1788, Poll List for presidential elector, 10 Jan. 1789, Poll List for congressional election, 2 Feb. 1789, Poll List for election of representatives to the House of Delegates, 19 April 1790, Poll List for congressional election, 6 Sept. 1790, Poll List for election of representatives to the House of Delegates, 18 April 1791, Poll List for election of representatives to the House of Delegates, 16 April 1792, Poll List for presidential elector, 5 Nov. 1792, Essex County Deed Book, no. 33, VSL; Poll List for presidential elector, 7 Jan. 1789, Poll List for congressional election, 2 Feb. 1789, Poll List for election of representatives to the House of Delegates, 26 April 1791, Poll List for presidential elector, 25 Sept. 1792, Westmoreland County Records and Inventories, vols. 6, 7, VSL; Poll List for presidential elector, Jan. 1789, Poll List for congressional election, 2 Feb. 1789, Cumberland County Deed Book, no. 6, VSL; Poll List for congressional election, Lancaster County, Feb. 1789, Election Records no. 28, VSL.

21 Poll List for election of representatives to the House of Delegates, 19 April 1790, Essex County Deed Book, no. 33; Poll List for presidential elector, 7 Jan. 1789, Brunswick County Election Records; Poll List for presidential elector, Jan. 1789, Cumberland County Deed Book, no. 6, VSL; *Virginia Herald and Fredericksburg Advertiser,* 12 Feb. 1789.

issues were not nearly so important to the average farmer as were the more immediate demands of scraping out an existence; and second, for every election with surplus quantities of liquor and excitement, there were several which were carried out in a perfunctory and thoroughly predictable fashion. In most counties there were men who expected to be elected almost automatically. In Amherst County, Antifederalist William Cabell would be elected unanimously; in the Eastern Shore county of Accomac, Federalist Thomas Evans looked forward to similar support.[22] It is hardly likely that this unanimity of opinion came about because the residents of a county were united in common political beliefs. Rather, the prestige of the Cabells and the Evanses of Virginia commanded the support of the citizens regardless of any differences in political philosophy between them and their constituents.

In the case of men of stature, like Edmund Randolph, formal elections were not even necessary. In the middle of the important legislative session of 1788, Randolph, then governor of Virginia, decided that his presence in the House of Delegates could help reduce Patrick Henry's influence over the Assembly. He wrote to Madison, "On Friday I shall be a member. I could not get in sooner, as a vacancy could not be sooner created than today." Randolph merely persuaded the current member from his district of Williamsburg to resign and was immediately selected to take his place.[23] If this had happened in a society which was not bound by gentlemanly traditions of aristocratic control, the opposition would at least have made an issue of it. In Virginia, where respect was high for Randolph both as a gentleman and a statesman, few citizens, if any, raised an eyebrow.

Some historians would argue, however, that Randolph's case was not at all typical. In particular, Robert E. Brown and Katherine Brown, on the basis of their examination of Virginia

22 Hunt, ed., *Madison's Writings*, 5: 318n; Election Records, no. 259, VSL.

23 Randolph to Madison, Richmond, 10 Nov. 1788, in Conway, *Edmund Randolph*, p. 121; Earl G. Swem and John W. Williams, *A Register of the General Assembly of Virginia, 1776-1918, and of the Constitutional Conventions* (Richmond, 1918), p. 29.

in the eighteenth century, have concluded that the electoral
process of the Old Dominion was decidedly democratic. The
statistical evidence that they have presented to prove their case
is impressive, but one cannot help but feel that they are
describing a society that eighteenth-century Virginians would
not have recognized. Virginians were simply not concerned
over the question of whether their society was democratic or
aristocratic. Equity and efficiency, not democracy or aristocracy,
were the attributes of the political system that were most highly
valued by Virginians. And most of Virginia's voters, despite
the rather limited range of choices presented them by the
county oligarchs, were probably generally satisfied with the
form of representation they received from the state government.
Although most representatives to the legislature were far
wealthier and more socially prominent than their constituents,
the representatives' interests tended to be consistent with those
of the rest of Virginia's overwhelmingly agrarian-oriented population. The interests of different counties were often dissimilar, with conflicts between counties or regions carried over
into the legislature; but these differences were seldom apparent
in the politics of the individual counties. Apathy, far more
than divisiveness or discontent, was the characteristic political
attitude. Most Virginians were reasonably satisfied with the
men who served them and did not give much thought to the
mechanism by which their representatives were selected.

The casual manner in which delegates were elected was in
keeping with the informal way in which they conducted business when they reached the capital city of Richmond. Dr.
Johann Schoepf, traveling through Richmond in 1784, described
the scene with amazement:

> It is said of the Assembly: It sits; but this is not a just ex-
> pression, for these members show themselves in every possible
> position rather than that of sitting still, with dignity and atten-
> tion. An assembly of men whose object is the serious and im-
> portant one of making laws should at least observe a simple
> *decorum*, but independence prevails here. During the visits
> I made I saw this estimable assembly quiet not 5 minutes

together; some are leaving, others coming in, most of them talking of insignificant or irrelevant matters, and to judge from the indifference and heedlessness of most of their faces it must be a trifling business to make laws. . . . In the ante-room there is a tumult quite as constant; here they amuse themselves zealously with talk of horse-races, runaway negroes, yesterday's play, politics, or it may be, with trafficking.[24]

Schoepf's description was in some ways unfair, since most of the business of the General Assembly was not accomplished on the floor, but in committee. Nevertheless, his description was in one important respect an accurate one: surely one of the major functions of the annual meeting of the General Assembly was to bring together men of experience throughout the state to conduct business, renew acquaintances, and meet the newer, rising group of Virginia gentry. The only change in this easygoing atmosphere came in 1787, when the delegates were finally required by law to be prompt in their attendance at the opening of the session. St. George Tucker marveled at the change: a "fine of ten pounds upon each individual had had an operation which the consideration of saving thousands to the community could not effect."[25]

Representation in the House of Delegates was weighted slightly in favor of the eastern and particularly the wealthy Northern Neck sections of Virginia, but the disparity was not nearly so great as critics of the system claimed. The eastern coastal region, extending from the most southerly portion of the James River northward to the Rappahannock and from the Chesapeake Bay to the fall line, had a free white adult male population of 36,758 and a total of seventy-one delegates. The Piedmont, running roughly from the fall line to the Blue Ridge Mountains, had a free white adult male population of 41,815 and fifty-two delegates. The 31,520 free white adult males in the transmontane west, that portion of Virginia west of the Blue

24 Johann David Schoepf, *Travels in the Confederation,* ed. Alfred J. Morrison. 2 vols. (Philadelphia, 1911), 1: 55.

25 St. George Tucker to Francis Tucker, Richmond, 17 Oct. 1787, Tucker-Coleman Papers, College of William and Mary.

Ridge Mountains, were represented by thirty-six delegates. Thus the eastern region of the state, with 33 percent of the free white adult male population, possessed 45 percent of the delegates to the lower house; the Piedmont, with 39 percent of that population, sent only 32 percent of the delegates to the legislature; and the transmontane west, with 28 percent of the free white adult male population, comprised only 23 percent of the total delegation to the House of Delegates.

The most serious problem in the west, however, was not the inequity in its representation, but the new problems that were created in correcting that disproportion. Because delegates were apportioned two to a county, the only way in which to equalize representation was to divide the larger, western counties. This was done frequently, sixteen new counties being added in the years 1788-1800 alone. But each division created new problems. Certain groups in the underrepresented areas clamored for more representation, but others opposed any division on the grounds that it would double the expense of local government. And their argument was not without merit. The creation of a new county required new justices of the peace, sheriffs, and other lesser officials. The usual result was higher tax assessments and a chorus of complaints from residents of the new counties.[26]

The major complaints from the west were aimed not at the failure of the eastern delegates to provide additional representatives, but rather, at the expense involved in obtaining those representatives.[27] The citizens of Greenbrier County, protesting the division of their county, actually refused to pay the increase

[26] A chronological listing of the divisions of Virginia's counties can be found in a number of sources, including J. R. B. Daniel, ed., *A Hornbook of Virginia History* (Richmond, 1965), pp. 12-30. The data on representation was based on the *United States Census, 1790*. Free white adult males rather than total population was chosen as the basis for comparison because it is the category that more closely (although not exactly) corresponds with the number of eligible voters in Virginia. It is also perhaps important to note that the western sections were even more underrepresented in the Senate. The transmontane west, with 28 percent of the free adult white male population, comprised only about 17 percent of the membership of the upper house in 1790.

[27] Petition of Amelia County, 16 Nov. 1789, Petition of Mecklenburg County, 2 Nov. 1793, Petition of Ohio County, 26 Dec. 1798, Petition of Greenbrier County, 12 May 1797, Legislative Petitions, VSL.

in their new tax assessment. The legislature relented and the next year enacted a special measure reducing their assessment. Although the desire for additional representation in the west was undoubtedly great, it is clear that a great many of Virginia's citizens were unwilling to pay the price of that representation.[28]

The counties in northwest Virginia, because of their large land area and sparse population, suffered most from this awkward and expensive method of increasing representation. Not surprisingly, these same counties were to constitute a stronghold of Federalist sentiment in Virginia by the turn of the century. Their attachment to the federal government stemmed not from any devotion to the ideology of Federalism, but from a dissatisfaction with the way in which the Republican-dominated state government had handled their problems in the past.

The structure of the new House of Delegates differed little from that of the colonial House of Burgesses. The bulk of its business was carried on by the five standing committees. Nearly all the 170-odd delegates served on at least one of these committees. The Committee of Propositions and Grievances was the largest and most important. It received reports and complaints from citizens in the counties asking for amendment, enactment, or repeal of a law. It was from this committee that most public and private bills emerged. The Committee of Claims, the second most powerful, considered and passed judg-

28 Petition of Greenbrier County, 12 Nov. 1791, 7 Dec. 1797, 4 Dec. 1799, Legislative Petitions, VSL; Shepherd, *Statutes at Large,* 2: 245. Van Beck Hall, "A Quantitative Approach to the Social, Economic and Political Structure of Virginia, 1790-1810" (unpublished paper presented at the annual meeting of the Southern Historical Association, October 1969), has quite properly stressed that underrepresentation in the legislature was a major western grievance. He further demonstrates that the western delegates in the legislature invariably voted overwhelmingly in favor of the division of western counties. These votes generally took place, however, only after a preponderance of petitions from the counties affected indicated that the residents of those counties approved of a division. Once an individual county agreed to bear the financial burden that a division of the county entailed, the other western counties had absolutely nothing to lose by voting in favor of such a division. But it is also clear that a great many proposals to divide counties were never brought to a vote in the legislature because of the flood of petitions from the county involved which protested division.

ment on all claims filed by counties and individuals against the state. As had been the case since the Revolution, most of its work consisted of old war claims.[29] The Committee of Courts of Justice had the most difficult task. The House, because it so dominated affairs of state, exercised executive and judicial functions in addition to its regular legislative business. The Committee of Courts of Justice decided whether a claim or petition should be considered by the House or sent to another state agency. If it fell under the jurisdiction of the House they sent it to the appropriate standing committee for further scrutiny.[30] The Committee of Privileges and Elections, so important in the colonial House of Burgesses, lost much of its usefulness when the threat of imperial authority to parliamentary privilege was eliminated. In the post-revolutionary period its function was to certify elections and to rule on election disputes.[31] The Committee of Religion, always the least important of the standing committees, was weakened by the disestablishment of the Episcopal Church. Its duty was to see that no House business was conducted during the morning prayer. The committee also had jurisdiction over suits for divorce—another indication of the imbalance of power between the judicial and legislative branches.[32]

Except for the Speaker, who was in charge of committee appointments, the chairmen of the five standing committees were the most powerful members of the House. They not only controlled the House proceedings from their own committees but also served on the greatest number of special committees as well. These committees, ranging from the committee charged with the responsibility of drafting the tax bill to the committee to prepare a bill "for the killing of wolves," usually drafted the specific pieces of legislation which the standing committees had recommended.[33]

The House leaders were an impressive group of wealthy,

29 *House Journal*, 15, 24 Nov. 1794, 18 Nov. 1796.
30 Thomas Evans to John Cropper, 30 Nov. 1794, John Cropper Papers.
31 *House Journal*, 9 Nov. 1796.
32 Ibid., 19 Nov. 1794, 18 Nov. 1796.
33 Ibid.

well-born, and well-respected men. Thirty-three men dominated the business of the House of Delegates between the years of 1788 and 1800.[34] This number would have been even smaller had there not been a flow of prominent Virginians from the state legislature to the various branches of the new national government. This exodus opened up committee chairmanships that had been held by the same men for years. When prominent figures such as John Taylor, James Madison, or William Branch Giles returned from the politics of the nation's capital, they immediately stepped back into the chairmanships of their respective committees.[35]

The men who controlled the affairs of the House had impressive family ties. Eighteen of the thirty-three leaders came from the highest strata of Virginia society. In this group were three Lees, two Harrisons, two Cabells, two Taylors, Francis Corbin, John Page, Wilson Cary Nicholas, Carter Braxton, Wilson Miles Cary, William Overton Callis, Edmund Randolph, French Strother, and Patrick Henry. Another seven, John Wise, Zachariah Johnston, Larkin Smith, Thomas Madison, William Branch Giles, William Tate, and John Marshall had improved their own lesser-gentry background by marrying into more prominent Virginia families. Only eight of the thirty-three, Nathaniel Wilkinson, Robert Andrews, Joseph Eggleston, Thomas Mathews, Thomas Evans, William Foushee, John Guerrant, and Miles King, were without immediate ties to the first families of Virginia.[36] Although influential family con-

---

[34] See Appendix 1.

[35] *House Journal*, 3 Dec. 1789, 9 Nov. 1796.

[36] It is much easier to prove that men did have prominent family connections than it is to prove that they did not, since the absence of information attesting to distinctive heritages is not irrefutable proof that they did not exist. Information for those listed in Appendix 1 was gleaned from *William and Mary Quarterly*, 1st ser., 9: 39; Beveridge, *Life of Marshall*, 1: 9-11, 148-200; *Virginia Magazine of History and Biography* 12: 434; Barton H. Wise, *The Life of Henry A. Wise* (New York, 1899), pp. 8-12; Hugh H. McIlhany, *Some Prominent Virginia Families* (Staunton, Va., 1903), 100-107; Dice Robins Anderson, *William Branch Giles: A Biography* (Menasha, Wis., 1915), pp. 1-36. I have not felt it necessary to give references for those men, such as the Lees, Cabells, and Harrisons, whose family names were enough immediately to identify them as members of the aristocracy. A search of Lyon G. Tyler, *Cyclopedia of Virginia Biography* (New York, 1915); *Tyler's Quarterly Historical and Genealogical Magazine* (all volumes);

nections were important to a man's political career, they were
not a guarantee of political success. Intermarriage between the
many branches of the prominent families (and the newer,
increasingly prominent families) had become so widespread
by the 1790s that the number of those included in the circle
of Virginians with an impressive genealogy had become legion.
A politician from a prominent family seeking to capitalize on
his family connections might find that he had competition not
only from other prominent families but also from members
of his own family. Thus, there were also many delegates
possessing impressive family lineages who were excluded from
positions of leadership.[37]

The House leaders were generally men of substantial wealth.
Ten were among the one hundred richest men in Virginia,
with land holdings ranging among them from 4,000 to 22,000
acres.[38] The remainder were men of comfortable means.
Twelve were farmers and planters on a more modest scale.
Three of these owned between 2,000 and 4,000 acres and seven
between 1,000 and 2,000 acres. Only two could be classed as
small farmers, holding less than 500 acres. The other nine were
professional men, whose wealth is more difficult to ascertain
because it was not usually tied up in taxable property. Their
security holdings and slaveholdings however indicate that they
too were men of affluence. There were six lawyers, two phy-
sicians, and one minister among this last group. The only
leader whose wealth is not known, Thomas Mathews, was
probably a merchant.[39]

Although nineteen of the thirty-three House leaders lived
in the eastern coastal region, the role of the west in the House
was steadily increasing. In the 1790s the Piedmont area was

William and Mary Quarterly, 1st and 2d ser. (all volumes); *Virginia Magazine of
History and Biography* (all volumes); and myriad county histories and genealogies
failed to turn up evidence on the eight men without apparent influential family
ties.

[37] Swem and Williams, *Register of the General Assembly,* pp. 30-31.

[38] Property holdings for the one hundred wealthiest men in Virginia are listed
in Jackson T. Main, "The One Hundred," *William and Mary Quarterly,* 3d ser.,
10 (1954): 368-83.

[39] See Appendix 1.

the home of eleven prominent leaders; the remainder of western Virginia had three men in positions of leadership.[40] The increasing power of the western region in the House was not the product of any gradual democratization; it merely meant that the same families who had dominated the affairs of the state in the past had themselves begun to move westward.

A composite picture of leadership in the lower house shows an impressive continuity with the past. The prominent names in the House of Delegates differed little from those in the colonial House of Burgesses, and wealth continued to be an important ingredient in political power. Nearly all leaders had college educations, a distinctive mark of the upper class in agrarian Virginia. Although the west was contributing more prominent legislators than it had in the past, this only indicated that the state was becoming more homogeneous, with the Piedmont and even the transmontane west adopting the settled and oligarchic characteristics of the coastal region. Perhaps the most significant thing about the House leaders was their experience. They had served their county and state for many years, and their fathers and grandfathers had often served before them. They were acutely conscious of their role as the statesmen of Virginia and this sense of duty impelled them to assume the bulk of the committee work of the House. More important, it made them jealous of any encroachment on their power, whether from the state or from the new national government.[41]

By the 1780s, at least, some of Virginia's more perceptive citizens were beginning to question certain features of their mode of government; there were signs that it was becoming antiquated and was now inadequate to the needs of an increasingly complex society. Thomas Jefferson, who had for a long time expressed dissatisfaction with many of the provisions of the Virginia constitution, subjected it to a detailed, systematic criticism in 1782 when he wrote his *Notes on Virginia*. He

40 Ibid.
41 Jack P. Greene, "Foundations of Political Power in the Virginia House of Burgesses," pp. 485-506.

saw three principal defects. First, he objected to the property qualification for voters and asked that all "who pay and fight" for the support of government be given the franchise. Second, he disliked the method of representation in the lower house; instead of the outmoded and often unfair system of allowing each county two representatives, he thought that representation should be apportioned by population. Finally, he deplored the lack of an adequate separation of powers between the three branches of government, and in particular, he decried the grant of excessive power to the lower house.[42]

By 1788 Jefferson had gained the support of other progressive-minded Virginians. Madison, Edmund Randolph, and Archibald Stuart joined the fight to convince local leaders of the need for constitutional reform. Stuart had acted as lobbyist for Jefferson and Madison in the Virginia General Assembly. He had prepared a new draft of a constitution in 1785 in case the legislature should agree to call a convention to consider revision. Unfortunately, hostility to state constitutional reform was so great that he never had an opportunity to use it. Stuart had even suggested that the Virginia Federalists in the Ratifying Convention of 1788 should try to gain two objects at once: adoption of the new federal Constitution and major amendments to Virginia's old constitution. He was dissuaded by Madison, who feared that the opponents of either object would band together to defeat both.[43]

Most of Virginia's ruling elite viewed revision both as a threat to their own positions and as unnecessary tinkering with institutions that had served Virginia well, but many of the citizens of the state, particularly the disfranchised, were not satisfied with the operation of the existing constitution. "A Mechanic" complained to the editors of the *Columbian Mirror and Alexandria Advertiser* that it was grossly unfair to prevent

42 Thomas Jefferson, *Notes on Virginia,* in Ford, ed., *Jefferson's Writings,* 3: 222-35.

43 "Proposed Draft of Virginia Constitution, 1785," Stuart Family Papers, VHS; James Madison to Archibald Stuart, New York, 30 Oct. 1787, Stuart Family Papers; Jefferson to Stuart, Philadelphia, 23 Dec. 1791, in Ford, ed., *Jefferson's Writings,* 5: 408-11.

a skilled artisan who worked hard, paid taxes, and served in the
militia from participating in the political process simply because
he lacked the necessary freehold. He could find no other reason
for this inequity "but that the dregs of Monarchy and British
influence were not quite purged off at the formation of the
laws."[44] "Analyticus," writing shortly after the presidential campaign of 1796, laid the blame much closer to home. He thought
it strange that the very people who had complained the loudest
over the aristocratic elements in the federal government were
the same men who had strongly opposed attempts to eliminate
undemocratic features of the state constitution. He then gave
his readers a lesson in practical political theory:

> An aristocracy is a government where all the power is possessed
> by a few titled individuals—an obligarchy is a government
> where a few individuals are possessed with the same power,
> but without titles; and such was the government of Virginia
> before the establishment of the Federal constitution—where a
> few influential individuals, (if not families) had, in a consider-
> able degree, the direction of the affairs of the whole state. This,
> it is true, was not established by any law, but circumstances
> and the habits of the people, gave it a sufficient sanction; yet
> I have often thought it extraordinary to hear those very gentle-
> men loudest in the cry against aristocracy. But it is a trick,
> common enough with those who are most guilty, to be always
> first in accusing their neighbors. There is no other way in
> accounting for the violent opposition of persons of this cast,
> to the general government, than by bringing into view the
> chagrin they have experienced, by the federal constitution hav-
> ing in a great measure, stripped them of those oligarchical
> powers which they enjoyed in their own state, without giving
> them an equivalent for it in the government of the union.[45]

"Analyticus," although writing for partisan ends, had hit
upon the major contradiction between the rhetoric and the
reality of the Antifederalists' opposition to the new government.
The Antifederalists, and later the Republicans, constantly con-

[44] *Columbian Mirror and Alexandria Advertiser,* 27 Sept. 1796.
[45] Ibid., 15 Dec. 1796.

demned the central government as an engine of aristocracy, while at the same time they rebuffed all attempts to alter or weaken their own oligarchical control over the state and county government of Virginia. Although they would ally themselves with men like Jefferson in their struggle against the centralizing tendencies of the new government, their reasons for opposing that government were not entirely consonant with those of the planter-statesman from Monticello. Jefferson combined his belief in the efficacy of local government with at least a mild commitment to egalitarianism; his followers in Virginia shared his attachment to local government, but they too often used that system of government as an instrument to thwart the advancement of those egalitarian ideals. As a result, few Virginians were willing to apply to their own government the same critical standards that they insisted in applying to the federal government. For every citizen like "Analyticus," there were many holding the views of "A Real Farmer," who asked, "from what human production may we not expect defects; is it not therefore safer to remain as we are rather than risk a reform which probably may be more defective?"[46] This disinclination to experiment for fear that things might be made worse, or for fear that their own power and prestige might be threatened, was a common thread through the Antifederalists' arguments against adoption both of the federal Constitution and of major amendments to the state's plan of government.

Despite this widespread aversion to innovation, Edmund Randolph, in December 1789, attempted to persuade the Virginia House of Delegates to consider a plan of revision for the state constitution.[47] Randolph prefaced his remarks with a tribute to the framers of the Constitution of 1776, but added "that having always lived in a dependency on the English monarchy, they were destitute" of any practical knowledge in the

[46] Ibid., 15 Sept. 1796.
[47] Although the resolution criticizing the Virginia Constitution has been mentioned by Albert J. Beveridge, *The Life of John Marshall*, 4 vols. (New York, 1916-1919), 2: 56n, its authorship has been hitherto unknown. I have found evidence that Randolph was the author in John Dawson to James Madison, Richmond, 17 Dec. 1789, Madison Papers; and Arthur Campbell to Zachariah Johnston, Richmond, 21 Nov. 1791, Zachariah Johnston Papers, VSL.

techniques of constitution-making.[48] His first criticism was
aimed at the "unbounded extent of the legislative power." The
framers, he said, had overreacted to the abuses of the royal
governors. By vesting the legislature with nearly unlimited
power they had created a new source of tyranny, and the result
was that the "constitution has been invaded by some law or
another of almost every session." By passing bills of attainder,
ex post facto laws, and general assessments for the support of
religion the legislature had ignored principles contained in the
Virginia Declaration of Rights. The first two were now for-
bidden by the federal Constitution and the last by action of
the legislature itself, but the Assembly still possessed power to
suspend *habeas corpus* regardless of any clear indication of
public danger.[49]

Randolph also objected to the Assembly's control over appointments. The legislators elected the governor, members
of the Council of State, militia generals, United States senators,
state judges, and a host of lesser state officials. In addition, the
governor and his council appointed justices of the peace, sheriffs,
county clerks, and militia officers below the rank of general.
Since the governor and council were dependent upon the legislature for election each year, they were careful not to appoint
anyone of whom the legislature might disapprove. Because of
its hold on the executive branch, the legislature had practical
control over nearly every state and local office in the Old
Dominion. The overseers of the poor, who were elected in
their individual counties, were the only public officials who
escaped this influence of the Assembly. Nor was the legislature
always vigilant in maintaining a high standard in its appointments. Randolph observed that in spite of an office-seeker's
"merit out of doors [he] will be too weak to combat the solicita-
tion of a brother in office. . . . The obstacles then are multiplied
against talents and virtue, which are sufficiently countenanced
by the feeble discernment of a large assembly, considered as
the source of all appointments."[50]

48 *House Journal,* 8 Dec. 1789.
49 Ibid.   50 Ibid.

Randolph would have agreed with the eminent jurist St. George Tucker in his assessment of the executive branch. Tucker, in an appendix to his 1803 edition of *Blackstone's Commentaries,* noted that the "executive department in Virginia is *chosen, paid, directed,* and *removed* by the legislature. It possesses not a single feature of independence."[51] And the post-revolutionary governors did not complain of their dependent status; most of them had served as leaders in the lower house and were in harmony with its policies. In times of crisis, the governor had even been known to resign his post to take a seat in the House of Delegates, where his influence on legislation might be greater.[52]

The judiciary was even less independent of legislative influence than was the governor. Virginia's constitution never fully defined the jurisdiction of the various state courts—the result being that no one was sure who had the authority to hear a given case. Nor did it define the extent of the judiciary's power. It was still an open question whether any of the state courts could void an act of the legislature. Randolph believed that the result of this lack of definition in the courts' authority would be "that every command of the Legislature is to be executed without hesitation, or the Judiciary and Legislature will be in eternal strife." Since the legislators controlled the appointments, salaries, and removals of state judges, there could be no doubt as to which side would win such a contest.[53]

The lower house was also plagued by defects within its internal structure. Randolph was particularly displeased with the system of electing new delegates each year, for he believed that it resulted in a multiplicity of laws, in a disregard of past policy, and in a continual loss of valuable experience among the membership of the legislature. He was similarly distressed with the method of legislative apportionment which stipulated that

---

[51] Ibid.; St. George Tucker, *Blackstone's Commentaries; with Notes of Reference, to the Constitution and Laws of the Federal Government of the United States . . .* (Philadelphia, 1803), bk. 1, pt. 1, Appendix, p. 119.

[52] Sydnor, *Gentlemen Freeholders,* pp. 95-96; Edmund Randolph to James Madison, Richmond, 10 Nov. 1788, in Conway, *Edmund Randolph,* p. 121.

[53] *House Journal,* 8 Dec. 1788.

each county be given only two representatives in the House of Delegates, regardless of population. Randolph was not so much concerned with the inequity, as he was with the inefficiency, of this system. The House had been willing to subdivide counties when their population warranted additional representation, but the effect of this was to make itself too large to deal efficiently with the problems of the state. The House had grown from 126 members in 1776 to 173 members in 1789, and new counties were being added every year.[54]

Randolph concluded his critique by asking that "our own Constitution be compared with that of the United States, and retrenched where it is repugnant." This plea could hardly have appealed to those who were hostile to the new federal Constitution, and the delegates' reaction to his suggestion made it obvious that it did not. A counterresolution was offered, bluntly stating that Randolph's proposals contained "principles repugnant to Republican Government, and dangerous to the freedom of this country, and therefore ought not to meet with the approbation of this House, or to be recommended to the consideration of the people." With that hostile response, the resolution to amend the state constitution was laid on the table, never to be revived.[55]

Efforts to amend the state constitution engendered as much heat as did the fight to call a convention to amend the federal Constitution. The friends of state constitutional revision were disconsolate and not a little displeased with the heavy-handed manner in which Randolph presented his critique of the state government. Most of Virginia's political leaders took offense at the bluntness of his attack on the state government. Such was their attachment to their traditional forms of local, decentralized government that Randolph's proposal served only to strengthen their determination to preserve the state constitution from amendment and to set back the cause of constitutional revision a few more years.[56]

---

54 Ibid.; Swem and Williams, *Register of the General Assembly*, p. 31.
55 Ibid.
56 John Dawson to James Madison, Richmond, 17 Dec. 1789, Madison Papers.

It is all too easy to blame Virginia's leaders for being obstructive and self-interested in matters relating to state constitutional reform. Most of them, however, were genuinely outraged at Randolph's attack on the state government. That government had, after all, been a significant factor in the growth of a strong and independent-minded ruling class during the colonial period and had provided the state with a measure of stability during the hectic years of the Revolution. The members of the Virginia legislature, who constituted the social, political, and economic elite of their society, viewed themselves as just and responsible rulers and therefore saw no need for innovation in the structure of their state government. And their opposition to such innovation sprung from the same source of political belief as did their efforts to amend, and weaken, the new federal Constitution. Both were products of the desire to preserve and protect the institutions which they believed had worked so well for Virginians for over a century.

CHAPTER THREE

Antifederalist Fears
Confirmed

IT WAS NOT UNTIL the First Congress of the United States had
convened that Virginians faced the full consequences of their
decision to join the union. All the charges and countercharges
over the nature of the general government had been, up to
that date, pure conjecture. But when the new government
actually commenced operation, the Antifederalists faced the
unhappy prospect of seeing all their dire predictions come true.

The months following adjournment of the state legislature
in November 1788 had not been particularly encouraging for
the Antifederalists. The attempt to call a second convention
had proved abortive. Virginia and New York alone advocated
such a drastic measure; the other states either failed to respond
or declined on the grounds that a convention at such an early
date would be inexpedient and potentially disruptive for the
union.[1] Virginia's Antifederalists grudgingly came to realize
that they would have to depend on Congress to frame the necessary amendments. Worse, the congressional elections had not
gone well for the Antifederalists; of the ten representatives
elected from Virginia, only three had opposed ratification of
the Constitution.[2] Yet this was not as disastrous for the Antifederalists as it first appeared, since many of Virginia's Federalist
congressmen were also committed to major alterations in the
Constitution. In fact, the Federalist representatives from Virginia sided more often with the Antifederalist opponents than

with their Federalist colleagues from the North. As soon as Congress began its deliberations it became clear that the Federalists in Virginia, when faced with the choice of remaining loyal to Federalist orthodoxy or acting in accordance with their own, locally oriented interests, would usually choose the latter.[3]

The Antifederalists were most heartened by Madison's continuing transformation from a confirmed nationalist to a staunch defender of Virginia's interests. He not only had ceased to oppose amendments but also had actually initiated the call for them in the First Congress. Hoping to win over his Antifederalist opponents by leading the fight for amendments, he was at the same time attempting to keep the proceedings under his own control so as to prevent the Antifederalists from enacting measures drastically curtailing the power of the central government. This strategy had been suggested to him by his Virginia ally, Henry "Lighthorse Harry" Lee, who had warned against offering the opposition any improper concessions, but who at the same time had urged that the House of Representatives "disarm them by complying with the rational views of the advocates for amendments spontaneously."[4] In pursuing this course Madison walked a fine line. He risked alienating those staunch Federalists who were opposed to any alteration of the Constitution, while at the same time failing to satisfy those who wanted amendments of a more radical nature. Considering the feeling on both sides, Madison did not fare badly.

Congress drafted twelve amendments, including the ten

---

[1] George Clinton to Governor Beverly Randolph, New York, 5 May 1789, Thomas Mifflin to Randolph, 6 March 1789, John Hancock to Randolph, 21 Feb. 1789, Communications to the Executive, VSL; Randolph to the Speaker of the House of Delegates, Oct. 1789, Executive Letterbooks.

[2] The seven Federalists were Andrew Moore, Alexander White, Richard Bland Lee, John Page, Samuel Griffin, John Browne, and James Madison. The three Antifederalist congressmen were Josiah Parker, Isaac Coles, and Theodorick Bland. James Madison to Thomas Jefferson, New York, 27 March 1789, in Hunt, ed., *Madison's Writings*, 5: 334.

[3] See the speeches by Virginia's congressmen in U.S., *Annals of Congress*, 1st Cong., 1st sess., 1789, 1: 424-49, 660-65, 704-76.

[4] Henry Lee to George Washington, Stratford, 1 July 1789, The Papers of George Washington, LC.

eventually adopted by the states; the two amendments excluded from the Bill of Rights—one to augment the number of representatives in the House and the other to prevent senators and representatives from increasing their compensation while in office—were ultimately rejected by the states.[5] The amendments were the result of many compromises; they did much to allay the fears of those who were concerned with the protection of individual liberties, but were less successful in appeasing those Antifederalists who desired a radical transfer of power away from the central government to the states. Few people in Congress were satisfied, but Madison had at least met some of his constituents' demands without substantially weakening the Constitution.

Perhaps the most helpful factor in reconciling Virginians to the set of limited amendments, as well as to the Constitution itself, was that George Washington of Mount Vernon, Virginia, occupied the chair of the chief magistrate. The Constitution probably would never have been carried in Virginia had it not been a generally accepted fact that Washington would be the first president, and his influence continued to muffle criticism when the government commenced operation.[6]

Yet despite Washington's prestige and Madison's amendments, many Virginians remained unreconciled to the Constitution in its present form. Senators William Grayson and Richard Henry Lee had tried in vain to obtain amendments of a more substantial nature; their failure to do so served only to increase their disenchantment with the federal government. Lee wrote to Patrick Henry in despair: "We might as well have attempted to move Mount Atlas upon our shoulders. In fact, the idea of subsequent amendments was little better than putting oneself to death first, in expectation that the doctor, who wishes our destruction, would afterward restore us to life."[7]

---

[5] For a discussion of the framing of the Bill of Rights see Robert Allen Rutland, *The Birth of the Bill of Rights, 1776-1791* (Chapel Hill, N.C., 1955), pp. 190 218.

[6] James Monroe to Jefferson, 17 July 1788, in Hamilton, ed., *Monroe's Writings*, 1: 186.

Henry agreed. He was convinced that the congressional amendments would "tend to injure rather than serve the cause of
liberty." They would have the effect of lulling the suspicions
of those initially hostile to the government without removing
the cause for those suspicions. Henry was willing to trade the
whole pack of amendments for just one limiting Congress's
authority over direct taxation.[8]

The Antifederalists pointed to other portents of danger in
the new government. The debate in Congress over the proper
form of address for public officials seemed symptomatic of the
government's monarchical tendencies. Vice President John
Adams, the leading advocate of a formal title for the chief
executive, seemed to personify the faults of the new government. His political theory, his New England bias, and his
cantankerous nature were abhorrent to most Virginians. Even
the Virginia Federalists were perturbed by the attempt to
bestow titles on the president.[9] This effort was in the end
unsuccessful, but the episode did little to ease the minds of
those initially hostile to the government.

The apparent victory of the North in the contest for the
permanent site of the nation's capital provided another cause
for suspicion. Here was an issue upon which Virginia's Federalists and Antifederalists could unite; their common regional
interests took precedence over any ideological differences. Consequently, Virginia's representatives in Congress and, indeed,
all southern representatives desired that the capital site be
fixed on the Potomac River. Toward the close of the first
session however, congressmen from Pennsylvania and New
England devised a plan to locate the capital in Pennsylvania,
on the Susquehanna River. The House adopted this plan, but
the Senate amended it slightly by moving the site closer to

7 Richard Henry Lee to Patrick Henry, New York, 14 Sept. 1789, in Ballagh, ed.,
Richard Henry Lee, 2: 501-4.

8 Patrick Henry to Richard Henry Lee, Prince Edward County, 28 Aug. 1789,
Henry Papers; David Stuart to George Washington, Abingdon, 12 Sept. 1789, in
Documentary History, 5: 205.

9 John Page to St. George Tucker, New York, 7 Feb. 1790, Tucker-Coleman
Papers.

Philadelphia. The spirit of the amended version was the same;
the capital would be located in the North, far from the interests
of Virginia. The hasty adjournment of Congress, however, and
possibly the grumblings of Southern congressmen postponed
final action on the bill until the next session.[10] The representatives from Virginia were nevertheless faced with the unpleasant fact that the Northern members of Congress, by in-
sisting on a Northern site for the capital, had proved themselves
willing to use their majority to further their interests at the
expense of those of the South. And Virginians were not pleased
with the prospect. Madison, increasingly mindful of Southern
interests, warned the Northern representatives in Congress that
Virginia never would have ratified the Constitution if the
members of the Ratifying Convention had been aware that their
wishes would be disregarded with such impunity.[11]

Despite their fears of "Northern domination," Virginians
could, by the time the General Assembly convened in October
1789, take some comfort in the fact that Congress had not
actually passed any legislation adversely affecting their interests.
A set of moderate amendments had been adopted, the idea of
titled officers had been rejected, and the North's bid for the
permanent seat of government had been at least temporarily
delayed. The other two major pieces of congressional legislation
—an act initiating an impost and one establishing a judiciary
system—had met with a generally friendly reception in Virginia.[12] The fears of Virginians were further assuaged by the
changing attitudes of their Federalist representatives. Madison

10 For a good brief treatment of this issue, and indeed of all the early operations of the federal government, see Richard Hildreth, *History of the United
States,* 6 vols. (New York, 1854-1855), 4: 127-29.

11 The issue of the location of the permanent capital was merely one of the
first of many where the interests of the North and South conflicted, and where
Southerners came to realize that their sectional interests were substantially
different from those of the North. It is a mistake, however, to read into these
differences the more basic conflicts that would ultimately lead to civil war.
There was, it seems, a qualitative difference between the issues of the 1790s,
which were all capable of compromise, and the more deep-seated differences of
the antebellum period. *Annals of Congress,* 1: 857.

12 Mann Page to Richard Henry Lee, Mann's Field, 23 July 1789, Lee Family
Papers; Henry Lee to Madison, Alexandria, 10 June 1789, Madison Papers.

was now considered the patron of amendments and Virginia's other Federalist congressmen had followed his lead. In their first year in Congress they had proved that, while they continued to support the idea of a national government and remained unwilling to join the Antifederalists in their sweeping attacks on the new government, they also were not prepared to vote in opposition to Virginia's interests merely for the sake of maintaining harmony with Northern Federalists.[13] This combination of moderation on the part of Congress as a whole and of Virginia's Federalists in particular made circumstances more favorable for the federal government in Virginia than at any time since the Ratifying Convention. As the Virginia Assembly began its fall session, it appeared that the federal government might finally receive the approbation of the Old Dominion's state officials.

Some of the foes of the federal government were not prepared to allow it to escape censure. Senators Lee and Grayson made one more attempt to alert the state legislature to the dangers of the government. On September 28, 1789, they wrote a formal letter to the Speaker of the House of Delegates apologizing for their inability to procure more radical amendments. They refused to take their defeat lightly, declaring: "It is impossible for us not to see the necessary tendency to consolidated empire in the natural operation of the constitution, if no further amended than as now proposed; and it is equally impossible for us not to be apprehensive for Civil Liberty, when we know of no instance in the records of history, that shew a people ruled in freedom, when subject to one undivided government, and inhabiting a territory so extensive as that of the United States." They were persuaded that unless the states renewed their efforts to revise the Constitution, the present system would bring "the annihilation of the state governments."[14]

13 Edward Carrington to Madison, Richmond, 9 Sept. 1789, Madison Papers; see esp., *Annals of Congress* 1: 836-900.

14 Richard Henry Lee and William Grayson to the Honorable Speaker of the House of Representatives in Virginia, New York, 28 Sept. 1789, in *Documentary History*, 5: 217-18.

The call for renewed opposition went forth. It contained the familiar refrains; it cried out against consolidation and bemoaned the destruction of state sovereignty by a Northern majority. This time, however, the Virginia legislature did not respond favorably to the challenge. The congressional amendments, submitted to the General Assembly for ratification during the first week of November, were discussed intermittently during the next month. Patrick Henry "was disposed to do more antifoederal business," but all his efforts were in vain.[15] He tried to round up support for an address thanking Lee and Grayson for their efforts to obtain more radical amendments in Congress, but the two Virginia senators seemed to have temporarily lost the confidence of most of the members of the state legislature. Even some Antifederalists considered their letter to the Speaker of the House to be intemperate, and consequently, Henry's proposed address failed to come to a vote.[16]

Henry also attempted to postpone for a full year consideration of the congressional amendments on the grounds that the legislators had been elected prior to the drafting of them and thus were not competent to know the sense of their constituents on the question. This was a tactical maneuver, since neither Henry nor anyone else in the House of Delegates previously had shown any concern for the constituent power. Only in a few cases had the citizens of a county ever instructed their delegates how to vote. Henry and his colleagues, when elected to the lower house, had always considered themselves free agents. It was their duty to protect the interests of their county, but the best way to do this, they believed, was to vote and act independently of the influence of their less-informed constituents. Faced with the proposal to postpone action on the amendments for a year, the delegates decided to act independently of Henry's influence as well; the motion for postponement was killed before it could be brought to the floor for a vote.[17]

Once Henry's tactical ploys were exhausted, debate on the

---

15 Edward Carrington to Madison, Richmond, 20 Dec. 1789, Madison Papers.
16 Ibid.   17 Ibid.

amendments began in earnest. The first ten amendments received near-unanimous approval from Federalists and Antifederalists alike, but the eleventh and twelfth amendments, those reserving power to the people and the states, ran into difficulty. Randolph, who continued to support the new government while at the same time remaining steadfast in his advocacy of major amendments to the Constitution, led the opposition. The eleventh amendment was worded: "The enumeration in the Constitution, of certain rights, shall not be construed to deny or disparage others *retained* by the people."[18] Randolph objected to the vagueness of the amendment; in his opinion the first ten amendments did not include all those rights necessary for the preservation of the liberties of the people, and the eleventh amendment set down no criterion by which it could be determined whether a right was retained or not. He believed that an amendment explicitly limiting Congress's powers would be more effective than a vaguely worded one protecting unspecified rights of the people. His opposition to the twelfth amendment, which reserved power to the states, was based on the same grounds.[19]

Randolph's opposition to the eleventh and twelfth amendments threatened the passage of the other ten. Not everyone was able to comprehend the logic behind his objections, but there were some Antifederalists in the legislature, unhappy because the congressional amendments were too weak, who were perfectly willing to use his opposition as an excuse to reject the whole package of amendments. In addition, there were many delegates, including some reluctant Federalists, who believed that the eleventh and twelfth amendments were vital to the proper limitation of the new government's authority. They approved of all the amendments, but thought it unwise to adopt the first ten if the last two were stricken. Randolph succeeded in persuading the Committee of the Whole to reject the eleventh and twelfth amendments, but, after a few days of behind-the-scenes wrangling a coalition of Federalists and

18 Ibid.; Hardin Burnley to Madison, Richmond, 28 Nov. 1789, Madison Papers.
19 Edward Carrington to Madison, Richmond, 20 Dec. 1789, Madison Papers.

moderate Antifederalists, weary of bickering over amendments and anxious to ensure the peaceful operation of the new government, succeeded in obtaining the necessary majority to overrule the committee's recommendation. On November 30, 1789, the House of Delegates adopted all twelve amendments.[20]

The amendments next went to the state senate for approval, and in a relatively infrequent display of independence, the senate confronted the lower house with unyielding opposition. Antifederalist Stevens Thomson Mason persuaded his colleagues to reject the third (freedom of speech, press, and religion), the eighth (trial by jury), and the eleventh and twelfth amendments on the grounds that they were too weak. According to Hardin Burnley, Madison's neighbor in Orange County, the senate was not really dissatisfied with the twelve amendments, but was "apprehensive that the adoption of them at this time will be an obstacle to the chief object of their pursuit, the amendment on the subject of direct taxation."[21] In short, the Antifederalist strategy was to reject the most popular amendments, such as that guaranteeing religious liberty, and throw the whole subject back at Congress, where the project for an amendment regarding direct taxation might be revived.[22]

The House of Delegates refused to accede to the senate's rejection of the third, eighth, eleventh, and twelfth amendments and the senate in turn refused to be bullied into adopting all twelve. By the middle of December it was apparent that a stalemate could not be averted and supporters of amendments in the House decided to postpone any consideration of amendments until the composition of both houses was more favorable. With this tactical retreat, the controversy temporarily subsided. Although Virginia was the first state to consider the congressional amendments, it was the last to adopt them. Two years later, in December 1791, after it had become clear that other states were willing to ratify the congressional amendments

20 Hardin Burnley to Madison, Richmond, 5 Dec. 1789, Madison Papers.
21 Ibid.
22 Irving Brant, *James Madison*, 3: 286-87.

in spite of the opposition to them in Virginia, the upper and lower houses of Assembly finally came to an agreement and added their assent.[23]

The Antifederalists in the House of Delegates, despite their support of the congressional amendments, did not abandon their attempts to obtain additional amendments of a more substantial nature. On December 5, 1789, they proposed a harshly worded resolution demanding that Congress adopt the amendments proposed by the Virginia Convention, but the Federalists, by the tie-breaking vote of Speaker Thomas Mathews, managed to defeat the measure.[24] Patrick Henry, dismayed by his inability to dominate the House as he had done in the past, had left the city for his home in Prince Edward County when the vote was taken. Even the Federalist members admitted that the result might have been different had he been present to exert his influence on the delegates who were undecided.[25] As it was, a milder resolution urging Congress to reconsider the Virginia amendments passed without division.[26]

The Virginia senate's refusal to ratify the congressional amendments and the resolution asking Congress to amend the Constitution more drastically were signs that the general government had not met with full acceptance by all Virginians. On the other hand, supporters of the government had cause for some optimism: most Virginians had at least recognized the new government as a fact of life. The obstinacy of the state senate, far from rallying support for those who wished to bring about the downfall of the government, only served to discredit them in the eyes of those who opposed the government in its present form, but who nevertheless hoped that the amendments would remedy its defects. The Baptists were especially angry. Although they had initially opposed the Constitution, the Federalists had begun to court their support. The senate's rejection

23 *House Journal,* 13, 14 Dec. 1789; *Senate Journal,* 14 Dec. 1789; Hening, *Statutes at Large,* 12: 327-29.
24 *House Journal,* 5 Dec. 1789.
25 Edward Carrington to Madison, Richmond, 20 Dec. 1789, Madison Papers.
26 *House Journal,* 5 Dec. 1789.

of the amendment concerning religious freedom—a provision deemed vital by the dissenting sects—helped cement the alliance between the Baptists and increasingly moderate Federalists such as Madison.[27]

The Federalists must have been particularly encouraged by the defeat of the Antifederalist resolution on amendments. To be sure, it was defeated by only one vote and a milder substitute was passed overwhelmingly, but for the first time since the Ratifying Convention, a sizable number of Virginia's elected representatives had expressed limited confidence in the general government and had not gone to great lengths to denounce it. Even Patrick Henry, though he had by no means given up his fight for amendments, began to change the tone of his arguments. Where he had once refused even to recognize the new government, he now counseled his supporters to get into the government and make the best of a bad situation.[28] This limited support on the part of some and reluctant acquiescence on the part of others was actually the zenith of Federalist sentiment in Virginia.

Support for Federalist programs was at best temporary, however. Arthur Lee did not think the mood would last. He predicted that "the expectations raised of the benefits of the new Constitution are most unreasonable and therefore cannot be satisfied. Its additional weight upon the people, has not been considered, yet may be felt, and tho' its benefits should be more than proportionate, yet we know how much a small burthen outweighs a great benefit; and therefore how probable it is that dissatisfaction with the new government should exceed the present extravagant expectations from it."[29] Although it was an overstatement to say that the people's expectations of the government were extravagant, Lee was on the mark with his prediction that "a small burthen outweighs a

27 B. Ball to Madison, Fredericksburg, 8 Dec. 1789, Reverend John Leland to Madison, 1789, Madison Papers; Madison to the President of the United States, Orange, 20 Nov. 1789, in *Documentary History*, 5: 215.

28 Fisher Ames to George Minot, New York, 13 Jan. 1790, in Seth Ames, ed., *The Works of Fisher Ames*, 2 vols. (Boston, 1854), 1: 72.

29 Arthur Lee to Charles Lee, 8 May 1789, Ludwell-Lee Papers, VHS.

great benefit." Virginians would soon forget the advantages of union and remember only the hardships.

From the day Congress assembled in 1790 until the end of the decade, the policies of the new government became increasingly offensive to the residents of the Old Dominion. From that time on an increasing number of Virginia Federalists were driven toward the Antifederalist camp by their aversion to the actions of the Northern majority in Congress. As it became apparent that Federalist policy conflicted with the interests and traditions of their home state, Virginia's Federalists abandoned their faction and joined with the Antifederalists in fighting that policy. The alliance between the two groups was not always comfortable. Most of the Federalists who defected from their faction retained their faith in the basic structure of the new government and in the necessity of union; they only objected to the particular policies the government was pursuing. The Antifederalists, on the other hand, were eager to make radical changes in the structure of the federal government. But it was a coalition formed out of the necessity of defending Virginia's interests. As the Northern majority in Congress embraced each of Alexander Hamilton's programs, other disenchanted Federalists recognized the importance of the alliance. In this fashion, the Republican party took shape in Virginia.

When Alexander Hamilton, on January 14, 1790, delivered his First Report on the Public Credit, the dangers of union assumed a tangible form. It was on the question of finance that the Confederation had foundered and it was imperative that the new government straighten out the nation's tangled debt structure. Hamilton's task was to rescue the United States' declining credit at home and abroad without further dislocating the American economy. Nearly everyone agreed that it was necessary to pay the principal and interest on the foreign debt in full—Hamilton did not even bother to discuss this matter in his report—but the question of the domestic debt was not susceptible to such a simple solution.[30]

30 The most sophisticated account of public finance during the Confederation

Hamilton proposed that continental certificates of indebtedness, of which there were many types differing widely in value, be redeemed from their owners at face value plus 4 percent accumulated interest, all payable in specie or western lands. The 4 percent interest rate was less than the full 6 percent that some of the security holders expected, but Hamilton was confident he would not lose their support and hoped that the 2 percent reduction might win over some of those hostile to redemption at the full interest rate. Hamilton also proposed that the federal government assume the debts of the individual states on the ground that the states' obligations had been contracted in a common cause, the American Revolution, and that the payment of them by a single government unit would provide a more efficient and equitable means of liquidating them.[31]

The government's obligation to fund the national debt was generally recognized; the major question on funding concerned the amount and method of payment. Assumption of state debts was another matter. The federal government had no legal obligation to pay the states' debts; the reasons for assumption were more political than financial. The purpose was not to strengthen the nation's credit structure, but to make the states more dependent upon the federal government, thereby tightening the bonds of union.[32] Hamilton's report was criticized on two grounds therefore; his opponents disliked the method of funding the national debt and they denounced the whole concept behind assumption of state debts.

The vast majority of Virginia's political leaders thoroughly detested both the funding and assumption proposals. Most agreed that funding was well within the limits of the Constitution, but few thought that continental securities should be redeemed at nearly full value, and more important, almost no one believed that those who purchased securities at depreciated prices should receive the same compensation as original

and early national periods is Ferguson, *Power of the Purse*. Ferguson has done such a masterful job of untangling the complicated details of this period that I have relied heavily on his work.

31 Ibid., pp. 293-97, 306-7.
32 Ibid.

holders. They opposed assumption even more vehemently; they thought it both a violation of the Constitution and inequitable in operation, since they believed that their state had liquidated most of its debt.[33]

Although most Virginians would have agreed that contracts ought not to be impaired and that the national debt should be funded, they objected to Hamilton's plan because they believed it was based on the British monocratic system and because it would reward those who were least deserving of payment—the Northern speculators. There was enough substance to these objections to make anti-administration rhetoric effective. There were widespread rumors, some with a grain of truth, that men like Robert Morris and William Duer were dispatching ships laden with money to buy up depreciated loan certificates.[34] This seemed in keeping with all that Virginians had heard about the economy of the commercial North. While the Southern states acquired wealth from productive labor—tilling of the soil—the Northern states accumulated profits through artificial means, in this case by using depreciated paper currency to buy continental securities.

The original security holders in Virginia, so the story went, had invested the just profits of their labor in federal securities to help the common cause, only to be duped into selling them during years of inflation by unscrupulous Northern speculators. Now these same Northern speculators were clamoring for payment at a value many times more than their initial investment, while industrious Virginians, who had invested honest profits or had fought in the continental army for the public welfare, were to receive nothing. This, at least, was the way in which the scheme was viewed by its opponents. The business of funding seemed to symbolize a fundamental difference between North and South: the agrarian system of the South was based on the notion that a man's profits should equal his total invest-

[33] James Madison to Edmund Pendleton, New York, 4 March 1790, in Hunt, ed., *Madison's Writings*, 6: 5-7; Edmund Randolph to Madison, Williamsburg, 10 March 1790, John Dawson to Madison, 13 April 1790, Madison Papers.

[34] Whitney K. Bates, "Northern Speculators and Southern State Debts: 1790," *William and Mary Quarterly*, 3d ser., 19 (1962): 30-31.

ment of money and labor, while that of the North was based on artificial devices, some of them bordering on usury.[35]

The kinship between the older English and the newer American funding systems made the evils of Hamilton's proposals seem even more invidious. The Federalist administration, dominated by men subservient to the interests of Great Britain, was using the corrupt financial policy of that nation as a model for its own operations. The new government was creating a monopoly of the monied interests which differed little from that which Americans had fought to overthrow in the Revolution. John Taylor of Caroline, a bitter foe of the plan, claimed that Hamilton's financial plan "was invented in England to prop a revolution by corruption; extensively used to sacrifice the nation to German interests; and it has been continued to feed avarice and silently to revolutionize the revolution. It was introduced, into America, after that nation had been defended, to enrich a few individuals, and also to revolutionize that revolution. . . . It taxes them, enriches a credit or paper faction; changes property; forms a party; and transforms the principles as in England."[36]

This denunciation of the monied interests represented more than a defense of Virginia's own economic interests; it was a defense of a whole way of life. In a state where agrarianism was lauded as the highest virtue, the creation of a new class of security speculators and "paper factions" was deemed a positive menace.

Congressman James Madison was aware of the reaction to Hamilton's funding scheme in his home state. Accordingly, he announced a departure from the orthodox Federalist position by proposing that original creditors who still held securities

35 Jefferson to Washington, 14 Aug. 1787, in Julian Boyd, ed., *The Papers of Thomas Jefferson*, 17 vols. (Princeton, N.J., 1950-1969), 12: 38 (hereafter referred to as Boyd, ed., *Jefferson Papers*); *Virginia Independent Chronicle*, 18 Oct. 1786; William Grayson to Patrick Henry, New York, 29 Sept. 1789; Richard Henry Lee to Patrick Henry, New York, 10 June 1790, in William Wirt Henry, *Patrick Henry: Life, Correspondence and Speeches*, 4 vols. (New York, 1891), 3: 405-7, 420-22.

36 John Taylor, *An Inquiry into the Principles and Policy of the Government of the United States* (Fredericksburg, 1814), pp. 253-54.

be paid the principal plus the full 6 percent interest, but that those who had purchased depreciated securities receive only the highest market value (about 50 percent of face value) of those securities. The balance of the payment, Madison proposed, should go to those who originally owned the securities. This scheme had great appeal, for it appeared under the banner of equity, but it was probably illegal, since it would have impaired the government's contract with the owners of the depreciated securities and if adopted would have raised the public debt even higher.[37]

It is likely, as E. James Ferguson has suggested, that Madison's proposal was yet another step in his transformation from a nationalist to a state-oriented politician. Madison had opposed making a distinction between original and recent security holders in 1783 and had remained silent on the issue during the Constitutional Convention, but as the anguished cries of Virginians began to reach him in New York, he began to change his position. His plan was designed to appeal to only a limited number of states, most notably Virginia, and would have cost more than Hamilton's original proposal.

If Madison had been genuinely concerned with scaling down the public debt, and not merely with increasing Virginia's share of the booty, he would have cooperated with the other opponents of funding, who were urging that the interest rate be lowered to 3 percent and that redemption be paid only by the sale of western lands. His adherence to Virginia's interests, and his refusal to cooperate with opponents of the measure from other states caused Pennsylvania's Senator William Maclay to grumble that "the obstinacy of this man has ruined the opposition."[38] Madison's proposal was defeated 13-36; nine of the thirteen votes in favor of the scheme came from the new coalition of Virginia Federalists and Antifederalists. Hamilton's system for funding the national debt was eventually adopted,

37 *Annals of Congress,* 2: 1191-95; again, for a lucid summary of Madison's proposal, see Ferguson, *Power of the Purse,* pp. 297-301.

38 Ferguson, *Power of the Purse,* pp. 297-301; William Maclay, *The Journal of William Maclay: United States Senator from Pennsylvania, 1789-1791,* ed. Edward S. Maclay (New York, 1927), p. 197.

but Madison had made his point; by denouncing the funding plan as the brainchild of a few greedy merchants and speculators, he had enhanced his reputation as a defender of the liberties and interests of the citizens of his home state.[39]

Most Virginians considered funding of the national debt to be merely inequitable, but they viewed assumption of state debts as an open violation of the Constitution. Virginia's Federalists joined the Antifederalists in complaining that the assumption proposal was unconstitutional. Nowhere, they claimed, did the Constitution give the federal government power to enter into the domestic finance of the states. Theodorick Bland, a leader of the Antifederal forces in the Ratifying Convention, predicted "that our state government will have little else to do than to eat, drink, and be merry" if the assumption bill were passed. He had warned the delegates to the Convention that consolidation would be the natural result of such a large grant of power, and he now felt the grim satisfaction of seeing his predictions come true.[40]

Edmund Randolph, wavering between the two political camps, was beginning to see that there was some foundation to the Antifederalists' fears. He estimated that "the people of Virginia are . . . almost unanimous against the assumption of the state debts," and he admitted that the danger of consolidation was no longer the slogan of a few hysterical Antifederalists.[41] Even such supporters of the Constitution as Henry Lee, Richard Bland Lee, and Archibald Stuart felt assumption to be an open defiance of the Constitution.[42] Loudest in their complaints were those who believed that the assumption proposal would be prejudicial to Virginia's economic interests. They had reason to grumble: approximately 87 percent of the state's remaining debt was no longer in the hands of the original creditors and

[39] *Annals of Congress*, 2: 1298.

[40] Theodorick Bland to St. George Tucker, New York, 6 March 1790, Tucker-Coleman Papers.

[41] Edmund Randolph to Madison, Williamsburg, 20 May 1790, Madison Papers.

[42] Henry Lee to Madison, Richmond, 18 March 1790, Madison Papers; Richard Bland Lee to Theodorick Lee, New York, 14 March 1790, Archibald Stuart to Richard Bland Lee, Abingdon, 23 May 1790, Richard Bland Lee Papers.

over 30 percent was owned by people living outside the state.[43]
More important, Virginians believed, mistakenly, that they had
discharged the greater part of their war debt and would therefore be taxed under the assumption plan to pay for the heavy
indebtedness of states like Massachusetts and South Carolina.[44]

At the time Hamilton proposed assumption there was a
scheme in operation for adjusting inequalities in the contributions of the states to the war. By this plan, adopted by the
Confederation Congress in 1785, a commission would examine
claims by the states against the continental government. Presumably, the findings of this commission would serve as the
basis for the settlement of accounts under Hamilton's assumption proposal. The Southern states, however, had been slow
in establishing their claims with the commission and, as a
result, would be materially injured by an immediate settlement
of accounts under the assumption act. Thus, it was not only
assumption that Virginia opposed, but particularly assumption
before her accounts could be brought up to date and accepted
by the commission in charge of validating the debts owed to
the states.[45]

In Richmond, Governor Beverly Randolph was doing all
he could to improve Virginia's position in the final settlement.
He instructed agents throughout the state to use all possible
speed in locating old vouchers. Unfortunately, the business
was moving much too slowly. Many holders of certificates were
afraid to turn their vouchers over to state officials, fearing
that they would not be paid after they relinquished them.
Moreover, Virginia's accounts were in hopeless disarray. Governor Randolph, just before Hamilton issued his report, admitted
to the secretary of the treasury that he was unable to give a
reasonable estimate of Virginia's debt.[46] The legislature resorted

43 Bates, "Northern Speculators and Southern Debts," pp. 32-33.
44 Ferguson, *Power of the Purse*, pp. 308-9.
45 Ibid., pp. 308-11.
46 Beverly Randolph to William Davies, 13 Nov., 30 Dec. 1789, 20 March 1790,
Randolph to Richard Banks, 12 Aug. 1789, Randolph to P. Williams, 20 March
1790, Randolph to the Secretary of the Treasury, Oct. 1789, all in Executive
Letterbooks.

to issuing duplicate certificates to people who claimed their originals had been lost, but this resulted in dual claims being presented at the Treasury Office, and the laws permitting the issuance of duplicates often had to be repealed.[47]

Virginians in Congress, temporarily forgetting their constitutional objections, tried to find ways to make the assumption bill work to the advantage of their state. Madison was able to add a provision to the bill extending the time allowed for submitting vouchers to the General Board for the Settlement of Accounts, but he was less successful in other areas.[48] In particular, he was unable to fulfill Governor Randolph's request that additional Southern members be appointed to the General Board in order to insure a more friendly reception for Virginia's claims.[49]

Madison's effort to improve Virginia's position in the settlement of state debts took the form of an amendment to the assumption proposal, presented in March 1790, seeking to compensate the states for both their existing debts and those they had redeemed. The proposal was hardly in keeping with Madison's constitutional objections to assumption, since it would have resulted in a federal involvement in the states' affairs even wider than Hamilton had envisioned. The scheme was at length defeated, for it would have placed a prohibitive cost on the entire plan. When Hamilton's original plan came to a vote in June 1790, it too was defeated, 29-31, thus setting the stage for one of the most famous compromises in American history.[50] Virginia's congressional representatives, realizing they did not have enough votes to secure the Potomac River as the site of the nation's capital, let it be known that they might be willing to change their minds on assumption in exchange for Northern support for a Southern location for the capital. Jefferson and Madison persuaded Congressman Richard Bland

[47] Beverly Randolph to the Speaker of the House of Delegates, 22 Dec. 1790, Executive Letterbooks; Hening, *Statutes at Large*, 13: 219.

[48] Ferguson, *Power of the Purse*, pp. 314-15.

[49] Beverly Randolph to Madison, Richmond, 17 July 1790, 10 Aug. 1790, Madison Papers.

[50] Ferguson, *Power of the Purse*, pp. 315-18.

Lee that "the poison of the [assumption] measure would be very much diminished" by the advantages of having the capital located on the Potomac. On June 28 Lee and his Virginia colleague Alexander White, a representative of northwest Virginia, the only consistent source of Federalist support during the 1790s, reversed their former positions and voted in favor of assumption, providing the necessary margin for passage.[51] Lee and White, by voting for assumption, spared Madison the necessity of voting in favor of the compromise which he had co-authored. Madison, by casting his vote against assumption, was able to stay in the graces of the Antifederalists in his home state.

In the end, assumption of state debts was not nearly so prejudicial to Virginia's interests as it was first feared. The Old Dominion's share of the $21,500,000 debt owed to the states was fixed at $3,500,000, a sum which even Virginia's two Antifederalist senators felt reasonable. In addition, the General Board began to take a much more liberal attitude toward some of Virginia's shakier claims. By 1794, when the states' claims were settled, Virginia, instead of being taxed to pay for the debts of the other states, emerged as the federal government's single largest creditor.[52]

Although Madison and his Virginia colleagues in Congress seemed content with the bargain they had made, most of the local leaders within Virginia were irate over the passage of the assumption bill. Several years would pass before they discovered that their state had fared well in the settlement of accounts; for the present, they could see no way in which Virginia would benefit from the act and were not at all sure that the Northern congressmen could be trusted to keep their promise regarding the site of the capital. James Monroe reported to Jefferson that assumption "would create great disgust if adopted under any

[51] Richard Bland Lee to Theodorick Lee, New York, 9 April, 26 June 1790, Richard Bland Lee Papers; Jefferson, "Memorandum on Assumption," [1792?]. in Boyd, ed., *Jefferson Papers*, 17: 205-7.

[52] Ferguson, *Power of the Purse*, p. 324; Richard Henry Lee and William Grayson to the Governor of Virginia, New York, 25 July 1790, in Ballagh, ed., *Richard Henry Lee*, 2: 534.

shape whatever, and I doubt whether the immediate removal to the Potomak would reconcile [the people to it]."[53] Federalist Henry Lee was even more dismayed. He thought the measure abhorrent to Republican government. Writing to Madison, he predicted: "This government, which we both admired so much, will I fear prove ruinous in its operation to our native state." Lee had become so disillusioned with the new government that he hoped Patrick Henry, whom he had opposed bitterly the year before, would take a seat in Congress to help fight for Virginia's interests.[54]

Hamilton's financial program was not the only cause of anger. Congress had managed to antagonize Virginians on a number of other, unrelated matters. For the second consecutive year, the United States Senate rejected a petition from the Virginia General Assembly asking that the public be allowed to witness the Senate's proceedings.[55] In rejecting the request, the Federalist-dominated Senate seemed oblivious to the concerns of Virginia. After Richard Henry Lee and William Grayson had spent two full days pleading with their Senate colleagues to open their doors to the public, only one other senator, William Maclay of Pennsylvania, was willing to join the Virginia senators.[56] More serious, Congress also spent some time deliberating on petitions from the Quakers asking for the abolition of slavery. Someone had spread the rumor that Congress was prepared to pass an act for emancipation, hoping to panic Virginians into selling their slaves at a low price. Congress, in the spring of 1790, eased the fears of Virginia's slaveholders by passing a resolution denying its authority to interfere in matters relating to emancipation, but the incident provided Virginians with yet another glimpse of the dangers that lurked in union.[57]

As news of the activities of Congress reached Virginia, discon-

53 James Monroe to Jefferson, Richmond, 13 July 1790, in Boyd, ed., *Jefferson Papers*, 16: 597.
54 Henry Lee to Madison, Richmond, 13 March 1790, Madison Papers.
55 *Annals of Congress*, 1: 967-68.
56 David Stuart to Washington, Abingdon, 2 June 1790, in Worthington C. Ford, ed., *The Writings of George Washington*, 14 vols. (New York, 1889-1893), 11: 482-84 (hereafter referred to as Ford, ed., *Washington's Writings*).
57 Ibid.; *Annals of Congress*, 2: 1472-74.

tent appeared in unexpected quarters. Federalist Henry Lee was led to declare: "Henry is already considered a prophet, his predictions are daily verified—His declarations with respect to the division of interests which would exist under the constitution and predominate on all the doings of the government already have been undeniably proved. But we are committed and we cannot be relieved, I fear, only by disunion." Lee ventured that even disunion might be preferable to an existence dominated by "an insolent northern majority."[58] Even David Stuart, President Washington's close friend, relative, and confidant, could not contain his displeasure:

> I have now gone through the catalogue of public discontents, and it really pains me much, and I believe every friend to the government, to think that there should be so much cause for them; and that a spirit so subversive of the true principles of the constitution, productive of jealousies alone, and fraught with such high ideas of their power, should have manifested itself at so early a period of the government. If Mr. Henry has sufficient boldness to aim the blow at its existence, which he has threatened, I think he can never meet with a more favorable opportunity. . . . It will be the fault of those who are the promoters of such disgustful measures, if he ever does, or indeed anyone else.[59]

Lee and Stuart were two of Virginia's staunchest Federalists. Despite their dissatisfaction with government policy, they remained Federalists. But like most other Virginians who stayed in the Federalist camp, they refused to endorse many of the specific policies of the new government. They retained their faith in the wisdom of union under the new Constitution, but were unwilling to sacrifice Virginia's interests simply to achieve harmony with Northern Federalists. The differences between the Virginia Federalists and their counterparts to the North were so great, in fact, that it is misleading to speak of a unified Federalist party in eighteenth-century America.

[58] Henry Lee to Madison, Berry-Hill, 3 April 1790, Madison Papers.
[59] David Stuart to Washington, Abingdon, 2 June 1790, in Ford, ed., *Washington's Writings*, 11: 482-84.

The mood of the Virginia General Assembly toward the proposals of the 1790 Congress was decidedly hostile. Governor Beverly Randolph had warned Madison that the assumption act would "produce some warm animadversions from the legislature," but he underestimated the strength and depth of the opposition.[60] He had not envisioned that a new political faction —a coalition of Antifederalists and disenchanted Federalists— would arise from the debates in the legislature over federal policy. It was the members of the General Assembly, far more protective of local interests than their counterparts in the United States House of Representatives, who would exert pressure on Virginia's national leaders and bring about the movement known and mislabeled as Jeffersonian democracy.

Patrick Henry, on November 3, 1790, introduced a resolution in the House of Delegates declaring the assumption act "repugnant to the Constitution, as it goes to the exercise of power not expressly granted to the General Government."[61] The Federalists in the Assembly, knowing they lacked the numbers to obtain a resolution applauding assumption, or even postponing a condemnation of it, attempted to tone down Henry's proposal. They suggested that the House draw up a remonstrance to Congress stating that assumption "will, in its operation, be highly injurious to those states which have by persevering and strenuous exertions redeemed a considerable portion of the debts incurred by them . . . and will particularly produce great injury to this state." They concluded by warning Congress that assumption was so unjust, that unless it was immediately repealed, it "will very much alienate the affections of the good citizens of this commonwealth from the government of the United States; will lessen their confidence in its wisdom and justice, and finally, tend to produce measures extremely unfavorable to the interest of the union."[62]

The Federalist resolution was hardly an apologia for assumption. It condemned the act on every ground except that of

60 Beverly Randolph to Madison, Richmond, 26 May 1790, Madison Papers.
61 *House Journal*, 3 Nov. 1790.
62 Ibid.

constitutionality. Some supported it only to forestall Henry's resolution, but that it was necessary to resort to such a harshly worded substitute is indicative of Virginia's intense dislike of assumption. Denunciatory as it was, the Federalist version was defeated, 47-88, and the resolution proclaiming the assumption act unconstitutional passed, 75-52. On December 21, 1790, the Virginia senate added its approval and the resolution became official state policy.[63]

Embittered Virginians were not content with a brief resolution proclaiming the unconstitutionality of assumption. On November 22, 1790, a special committee of the lower house proposed an address to Congress; three weeks later a large majority in both houses of the state legislature voted to adopt it.[64] The rhetoric of the *Address of the General Assembly of the Commonwealth of Virginia to the United States in Congress Assembled* would be echoed through the decade. Republican leaders in the nation's capital, when they began to organize their forces in Congress, leaned heavily upon this address and on others like it for their own attacks on the government.[65] The Virginia Address was the opening round in a barrage of criticism that would culminate in the defeat of the Federalist administration.

The memorialists from the Virginia legislature first condemned the close resemblance between the Hamiltonian and English systems of finance; they decried the effects of the latter, whose "unbound influence, pervading every branch of government, threatens the destruction of everything that pertains to English liberty."[66] This was prerevolutionary rhetoric, dusted off and applied to the new national government. It was to be so frequently employed that it would become impossible for any Federalist to escape the charge of being under English influence.

The second part of the *Address* accused the Federalist adminis-

---

[63] Ibid.; *Senate Journal*, 21 Dec. 1790.

[64] *House Journal*, 22 Nov., 16 Dec. 1790.

[65] See the similarities between the *Address* and the later letter of Thomas Jefferson to George Washington, Mt. Vernon, 29 July 1792, in Ford, ed., *Washington's Writings*, 12: 147-51.

[66] Hening, *Statutes at Large*, 13: 237.

tration of attempting to "perpetuate a large monied interest" which "must in the course of human events, produce one or other of two evils, the prostitution of agriculture at the feet of commerce or a change in the present form of the federal government fatal to the existence of human liberty."[67] This was not only an outcry against the monied interest but also another reminder of the delegates' revolutionary heritage. By lifting a phrase from the Declaration of Independence, Virginia's agrarian republicans explicitly linked the evils of imperial rule with those under the new federal government.

The third section of the *Address* recapitulated the specific grievances against the assumption act. The act would operate against the interests of those states which, like Virginia, had already paid the major share of their debts; it would also impose an intolerable burden of taxation on the Old Dominion. Moreover, the legislators could find no clause in the Constitution which could possibly enable Congress to take such action; they had ratified the Constitution under the express condition "that every power not granted was retained" by the states, and state debts were surely a case where the individual states, not the federal government, were vested with authority.[68]

The *Address,* as adopted, would serve as a practical guidebook for anyone wishing to attack the federal government in the future. Anglophobia, fear of Northern monied interests, and a doctrine of strict construction—these were all present in the *Virginia Address* and would become staple commodities for the opponents of the Federalist administration during the next decade.

One phrase was expunged in the final version of the *Address,* however. A majority in the House had agreed to it, but at the last minute the Senate deleted it. It declared assumption unconstitutional and added: "it is manifest then, that the consent of the State legislatures ought to be obtained before the said act can assume a constitutional form."[69] The legislators were no

67 Ibid.   68 Ibid.
69 "Senate Amendments to Address Concerning Assumption," 21 Dec. 1790, Rough Bills of the Legislature, VSL. There is no evidence to explain why the

longer giving a simple opinion on the constitutionality of a specific act. They were taking a step toward a general constitutional principle upholding the right of the states to exercise authority in cases where the policies of the state and national governments conflicted. They had mounted a brief, but meaningful assault on the notion of divided sovereignty and had temporarily resolved the issue in favor of the states. Although the *Address of 1790* did not pronounce the assumption law null and void, it did hint at a way in which the constitutionality of an act could be determined and prepared the way for the doctrine of nullification expressed eight years later in the Kentucky Resolutions.

Looking back from a vantage point where the implications of the Virginia and Kentucky Resolutions, Calhoun's nullification doctrine, and secession can be viewed, it is easy to speak of the evils of the doctrine propounded by the Virginia legislature. To condemn the members of the lower house for a radical attempt to undermine the union is to ignore the fact that, in 1790, there were few precedents to establish the final locus of sovereignty; most of the existing precedents were derived from the experience of the states under the Articles of Confederation and these were consonant with the position taken by the lower house. The *Virginia Address,* while antithetical to the doctrine of political sovereignty which emerged after 1790, was in complete harmony with the principles upon which Virginia had fought the Revolution and with the spirit with which it had agreed to ratify the Constitution.

Although Virginians may have had some cause to voice constitutional objections to the assumption proposal, much of the harsh language of the *Virginia Address* was not warranted.

Senate deleted this important passage from the *Address,* and—even more surprising—why the House acceded to the Senate's action. Since technically the *Address* was not an official piece of legislation, but rather, merely a resolution giving the "sense" of the House on the subject, the members of the House of Delegates could have insisted on their version of the *Address* and then published it under their auspices alone. It is possible that the members of the House, when faced with Senate opposition, were made to realize that they had gone too far, but it is perhaps more likely that, failing to recognize the full ramifications of what they had said, the legislators dropped it out of convenience.

To be sure, the Northern monied interest was aided by establishment of the public credit, but the interests of agrarian Virginia had not been sacrificed. Instead of being burdened by assumption, Virginia proved to be the greatest beneficiary. But in 1790 many Virginians were still convinced that English influence and Northern greed were combining to destroy them. The *Virginia Address* was an expression of those fears and a warning to Congress that Virginians would never submit to the trend of the government.

An analysis of voting behavior in the House of Delegates on the major national issues of 1788-1790 dramatically illustrates the antipathy of the members of Virginia's ruling elite to the general government. The two voting blocs that emerge are notable for their substantial number of members, for the impressive agreement among members within each bloc, and for their consistent and sharp opposition to each other on all national issues. Of the fifty-four men who served all three sessions in the House of Delegates during the years 1788-1790, thirty-two were Antifederalists and ten were Federalists. Thus, forty-two of the fifty-four sample delegates are readily identifiable as supporters of one or the other of the two factions. Over three-fourths of the men in the Antifederalist bloc were in agreement all the time, the rest, at least 80 percent. Eight of the ten members of the Federalist bloc agreed on all issues, and the other two, on at least 80 percent of the national issues brought before the House of Delegates.[70] Although the Anti-

70 See Appendix 2. The divisions listed in the appendix are based on a computer analysis of the voting behavior, on national issues, of the fifty-four men who served in the House of Delegates every year between 1788 and 1790. A rate of 80 percent agreement was set as the minimum requirement for inclusion within either voting bloc. Since the General Assembly was elected annually and its turnover was high, it was impossible to make an accurate evaluation of the individual voting behavior of all the members of the Assembly. There is no indication, however, that the voting behavior of the three-term delegates was atypical. While the data listed in the appendix shows the similarities in occupation and property holdings among the members of the Federalist and Antifederalist voting blocs, I have not been able to find enough information on other variables (e.g., ethnic group, religion, age) to provide a complete explanation for the voting behavior of Virginia's political leaders.

federalists would have outnumbered the Federalists in any case, the small band of Federalists might have been larger had it not been for the controversy-filled session of 1790. In fact, many of the twelve delegates who are not included in either bloc were former Federalists who deserted their faction on the issues of funding and assumption.

The alignments in the House of Delegates were not drastically dissimilar from the divisions between the supporters and opponents of the policies of the new government in the United States House of Representatives. Although Madison calculated that the Virginia delegation to the First Congress consisted of seven Federalists and three Antifederalists, it is clear that Virginia's Federalist representatives could no longer be considered friends of Federalist policy by the end of the second session of Congress. The final vote on assumption in the House, which was perhaps the most severe early test of a representative's commitment to Federalist policy, found eight Virginians opposed to Hamilton's proposal and only two in favor.[71]

It is imperative that one use considerable caution in drawing inferences from this data. There is no reason to doubt that the voting behavior of the fifty-four delegates in the sample is an accurate reflection of the political attitudes of the members of Virginia's political elite, but it does not follow that the partisan divisions among the delegates are representative of the divisions of opinion among the great mass of Virginia's citizens. The electoral process in Virginia was more often guided by personality and prestige than issues and ideology. The political attitudes of the delegates included in the sample group are therefore not necessarily a reflection of the views of their constituents. Rather, the delegates tended to align themselves with either the Federalist or Antifederalist factions only after they were elected and had taken their seats in the lower house.[72]

71 Madison to Jefferson, New York, 27 March 1789, in Hunt, ed., *Madison's Writings,* 5: 334; Jefferson, "Memorandum on Assumption" [1792?], in Boyd, ed., *Jefferson Papers,* 17: 205-7.

72 The high rate of annual turnover in the lower house which necessitated the use of the sample of "three term" delegates should not be interpreted to mean that the members of the lower house were being closely watched by their con-

The delegates, because of their prestige and power within their own regions, were able to exert significant political pressure on Virginia's representatives in Congress—the changing political philosophy of Madison is testimony to that fact—but that same prestige and power allowed them to make their political decisions relatively free from the demands of their constituents.

If the composition of this sample group is at least a key to the division of opinion on national issues among Virginia's political leaders, then two distinct camps did exist among the ruling elite, each bound by common beliefs as to the direction their society should move. This division within the elite was apparent as early as 1788, when the Antifederalists attempted to call a second convention to amend the new Constitution, and as Jackson T. Main and Norman Risjord have shown, probably predated the Ratifying Convention, arising from differences during the Confederation period.[73] The solidarity of the two groups is particularly impressive when one realizes that there is no record of an attempt to organize them into political parties. The high rate of agreement within each faction during the period 1788-1790 was the product of a near-unanimity of sentiment which made organization or party discipline superfluous. There was undoubtedly the same amount of backstage maneuvering in the Virginia legislature as there was in any body accustomed to operating within the framework of factional politics, but at this early stage, there were no overt attempts to organize either the legislators or the people into two permanent parties.

It would be helpful if we could arrive at some neat pattern of economic or regional interests that determined an individual delegate's voting behavior. No such pattern emerges. The

---

stituents and were therefore rapidly replaced. The high turnover, rather than being a sign of democratic stirrings among the electorate, was in fact only an indication that the leading members of the county oligarchies could enter and leave the legislature when they pleased. Although annual turnover in the legislature was high, the total years of service of most legislators was extraordinarily long.

73 Jackson T. Main, "Sections and Politics in Virginia, 1781-1787," *William and Mary Quarterly*, 3d ser., 12 (1955): 96-112; and Norman Risjord, "The Virginia Federalists," *Journal of Southern History* 33 (1967): 486-517.

economic interests of the members of the Federalist and Anti-federalist voting blocs were strikingly similar. Three of the Antifederalists were lawyers, one a merchant, and twenty-six were planters. Of the Federalists, seven were planters, one a lawyer, and one a merchant and planter of substantial means.[74] Six Antifederalists were men of distinct affluence, twenty possessed at least enough property to be labeled "planters" rather than "farmers," and only three could in any sense be typified as farmers of moderate means. Of the Federalists, three could count themselves among the extremely wealthy, four were moderately wealthy planters, and two were merely farmers. That the economic holdings and interests of the members of both groups were so similar is hardly surprising; the members of each faction were drawn from the same group of predominately wealthy and well-born citizens that had always ruled the affairs of Virginia.[75]

Norman Risjord, who has examined voting behavior in the Virginia lower house by studying the votes of each county

[74] It is of course difficult to be precise about occupation in an overwhelmingly agrarian society like Virginia. In particular, those men who are listed as "lawyers" or "merchants" in Appendix 2 were also often affluent planters as well. Conversely, some of those listed as "planters" were often lawyers and merchants. In all cases I have attempted to discover the delegate's primary occupation and label him accordingly. No record of occupation could be found for two of the Antifederalists and one of the Federalists.

[75] See Appendix 2. There was no record of property holdings for three of the Antifederalists and one Federalist. I have divided landholders into four categories: 0-50 acres—subsistence; 51-399 acres—farmers of moderate means; 400-1,500 acres—planters of moderate wealth; 1,500 acres or more—affluent planters.

Although categories of wealth vary from county to county in Virginia it is possible to calculate averages and medians for representative areas in Virginia. According to the tax lists for 1795, the average landholding in Surry County, in the southern Tidewater, was 290.8 acres, the median, 150 acres. In Lancaster, in the northern Tidewater, the average holding was 213.8 acres, the median, 131. The average holding in Pittsylvania County, in the southern Piedmont, was 273.6, the median, 198. The tax lists for Washington County, in the extreme southwest, show an average holding of 321.6 acres, a median of 205.5. In Shenandoah County, in the northwest, the average was 277.5, the median, 200. The dramatic difference between the average and median landholding in each of the counties suggests that the gap between the affluent and the middle-class farmer was a significant one, with the vast majority of Virginia's landowners possessing estates of one or two hundred acres and a tiny minority of planters owning estates of over 1,500 acres. I will deal with patterns of landholding in Virginia, and the implications of those patterns, in a forthcoming article.

unit rather than the votes of the individual legislators themselves, has provided us with our most accurate picture of the
geographic divisions in the legislature on national issues during
this period.[76] Two significant conclusions can be derived from
a comparison of Risjord's findings and my own. First, there
is a clear continuity in the geographic divisions arising from
the Federalist-Antifederalist split in the Virginia Ratifying
Convention and those occurring during the early years of the
operation of the new government (see maps on pages 244-46).
Second, Federalist strength declined drastically from its 1788
level in nearly every area in the state and dropped particularly
sharply in the Tidewater.[77] It is also apparent, however, that
although individual counties often voted the same way from
year to year, relatively few blocs of counties in the same geographic region voted together consistently enough to warrant
any broad-scale generalizations about patterns of regional voting
in Virginia. The one exception was the extreme west, encompassing the Shenandoah Valley and the land west of the Blue
Ridge Mountains, which continued to be solidly Federalist
throughout the decade. The reasons for this were connected
more to purely local issues relating to problems of defense
and state constitutional revision than they were to any fundamental divisions between the extreme west and the rest of

[76] Risjord, "The Virginia Federalists," pp. 486-517, esp. p. 492, for an explanation of methodology. Risjord's method of analyzing votes by county unit.
because it accounts for the voting behavior of all, rather than merely some of
Virginia's counties, is preferable to my sample of individual legislators if one
is interested primarily in charting the geographic divisions within the state.
This approach does, however, tend to limit seriously the number of possible
variables under consideration. By using a geographical unit, the county, one is
prevented from making any meaningful generalizations about the personal attitudes and interests of the delegates. Thus, while it is clear that Risjord's geographic analysis and my sample of individual voting behavior each have limita-
tions, the two methods, when used in conjunction with one another, constitute a
relatively accurate guide to the political divisions over national issues occurring
in the lower house.

[77] Ibid.; Risjord used the period 1788-1793 for his analysis of roll call votes.
Although longer than the 1788-1790 period that I have used, it does not render
our data incomparable. The nature of the divisions in the lower house was
firmly fixed by 1790, when former Federalists began to desert their faction over
the issues of funding and assumption. Moreover, there were relatively few roll
call votes on national issues in the lower house between 1791-1793.

the state on any of the important national issues of the period.[78]

The other possible geographic division suggested by historians, that between the Northern Neck and Southside counties, does not add substantially to our understanding of the nature of the Federalist-Antifederalist split in the legislature. According to Jackson Main, the Northern Neck counties were characterized by a wealthy aristocracy controlling a large share of the state's wealth and property, a high percentage of tenant farmers, and a favorable position along the coastlines of the navigable rivers and bays. Although predominately agrarian, the Northern Neck counties were oriented toward the commercial economy of the North. The Southside counties had a larger middle class population, fewer tenant farmers, and were primarily interested in subsistence, as opposed to commercial farming. In a study of the 1780s Main found that the Northern Neck counties were overwhelmingly Federalist in sentiment, the Southside, Antifederalist.[79]

The divisions suggested by Main begin to blur during the period 1788-1790, however. Again using Risjord's analysis of voting by county in the Virginia lower house, it is clear that the Southside Virginia counties were overwhelmingly Antifederalist. The importance of this should not be overestimated, however, since the vast majority of representatives from the Northern Neck were Antifederalists as well. The only area of appreciable Federalist strength, the northwest, was not considered by Main to be identifiable as belonging definitely to either the Northern Neck or the Southside bloc.[80]

---

78 Ibid.; Risjord, while he recognizes the importance of purely local issues as causes of the divisions between the northwest and the remainder of the state, also argues that the Federalist and Antifederalist counties tended to have different economic interests. In some ways the economic structure of some Federalist and Antifederalist counties was different, but these differences had no relation to questions of national policy.

79 Main, "Sections and Politics in Virginia," pp. 96-112.

80 The Northern Neck-Southside alignments are derived simply by comparing ibid. and Risjord, "The Virginia Federalists," p. 494. It is impossible, however, to make an exact correlation between the Federalist-Antifederalist and the Northern Neck-Southside divisions because Main was unable to identify many of Virginia's counties as belonging to either the Northern Neck or the Southside blocs.

The shortcomings of a geographic interpretation based upon a commercial-agrarian division are perhaps best illustrated by the political behavior of the town of Richmond. It has become almost axiomatic that Richmond, as the political and commercial center of Virginia, was a Federalist stronghold, yet this holds true only during those years when illustrious Richmonders such as John Marshall ran for office. Marshall's colleague from Richmond in the House of Delegates was Miles Selden, a man who sided with the Antifederalists on every issue during the 1788-1790 period. Nathaniel Wilkinson, the other delegate who served from Richmond during these years, did not vote on enough national issues to be definitely classified as a member of either faction, but on the few occasions when he did vote he sided with the Antifederalists. This pattern of representation would remain, even in the politically sophisticated town of Richmond, for the remainder of the decade. During those years when Marshall decided not to serve in the House of Delegates, his seat would most often be filled by a member of the opposing faction. It would seem that Richmond was a Federalist-dominated town not because it had a commercial orientation but because prestigious Federalists such as Marshall, who could have been elected to office in any area of the state, happened to reside there.[81]

The most striking feature about the geographic distribution of the two political factions is that Antifederalists were in the majority in nearly every section of the state. It seems likely that Federalists like Marshall won election in spite of their support for the federal government. That there were so few Federalist leaders in Virginia is not surprising. Most members of the ruling elite in Virginia, after seeing the new government in operation for less than two years, were convinced that it constituted a threat to the interests of their state in general and to their political power in particular. Marshall might have supported Federalist policies because he saw in them a way for America to achieve national greatness, Edward Carrington

---

[81] Selden is included in the Antifederalist bloc listed in Appendix 2. Wilkinson's voting records may be checked in *House Journal*, 30 Oct., 18 Nov. 1788.

might have supported them because his political fortunes, meager as they might have been, were tied to those of prominent leaders in the nation's capital, but for most of Virginia's political leaders, the first two years of the operation of the new government had confirmed the worst of Patrick Henry's fears.

CHAPTER FOUR

Federal Policy and
Domestic Affairs

A COALITION OF Antifederalists and disenchanted Federalists, which, by 1791, would assume the name of the "republican interest," had dominated the Virginia legislature in 1790 and had passed overwhelmingly the *Address to Congress,* a memorial critical of the federal government. In so doing, the members of Virginia's ruling elite had expressed decisively their fears of consolidated government. Despite this heavy preponderance of leaders opposing the policies of the new government, there remained in the legislature a small band of Federalists, who though personally uncertain of the wisdom of government policy, nevertheless voted consistently against their republican opponents in the General Assembly. This polarization of political sentiment was not a completely new phenomenon in Virginia politics; two distinct political factions had developed in the legislature as early as the mid-1780s. But never before had the number of issues causing those divisions been so great nor the membership in those factions so broadly based. What had the new government done in the past three years to warrant this polarization of opinion and to cause such a large proportion of Virginia's leaders to turn against it? The issue is a particularly puzzling one, for in spite of widespread dissatisfaction with Alexander Hamilton's financial schemes, the first years of union worked few changes in the internal structure of the Old Dominion.[1]

The voting behavior of the state legislators on issues of purely local concern offers the best indication of the continuity within Virginia's internal political structure. The same planter-gentry who had dominated the government of Virginia for over a century continued to hold power after ratification of the federal Constitution. The divisions over national policy did not change the way in which they viewed their local problems. Although most of Virginia's political leaders joined the vanguard of the movement labeled Jeffersonian democracy, they were not transformed into democrats. They continued to vote in the same fashion as before ratification, and indeed, as before the Revolution. Narrow, regional interests, not ideology or egalitarian principles, shaped their attitudes toward the important issues of the day.

An analysis of the voting behavior on local issues of the fifty-four men serving all three terms in the House of Delegates during the years 1788-1790 does not yield the same clear-cut divisions as does the analysis of national issues. Two opposing voting blocs emerge, but they are substantially different from those arising over the divisions of opinion on national issues.[2] The two blocs, Group A and Group B, were smaller than the Federalist-Antifederalist factions. They had fourteen and fifteen members respectively; almost half the delegates did not fall into either group. To the extent that these blocs represent a division in Virginia's internal political structure, and the small size of each group suggests that they did not represent a major one, the most important general source of disagreement lay in the different interests of the eastern and western delegates. Group A contained thirteen delegates from the Tidewater,

[1] Union under the federal Constitution did of course necessitate some procedural changes in the administrative relations between the state and the central governments, but these had little effect on the people of the state as a whole. For a discussion of some of the administrative adjustments made necessary by the Constitution see Richard R. Beeman, "The Old Dominion and the New Nation, 1788-1801" (Ph.D. diss., University of Chicago, 1968), pp. 144-46.

[2] See Appendix 3. Because issues of purely local concern were both more numerous and encompassed a wider variety of questions than did those of national concern, it has been necessary to lower the minimum rate of agreement required for inclusion within a bloc from 80 to 70 percent.

one from the Piedmont, and none from the transmontane west. Of the fifteen delegates in Group B, nine lived in the Piedmont, three in the transmontane west, and only three in the Tidewater.[3]

There is no correlation between the members of the Federalist-Antifederalist voting blocs and those of blocs A and B. Group A contained twelve Antifederalists and two Federalists; Group B, eleven Antifederalists and four unaligned delegates; there were very few Federalists in either bloc and the Antifederalists were evenly split between the two.[4] It is conceivable that the Federalist members of the legislature, as proponents of a system of government which thought in terms of national rather than local interests, were less likely to be tied to any one set of local or regional interests and thus were not supporters of either voting bloc. It seems more likely that there were few Federalists in either of the two groups because there were very few Federalists in the Virginia House of Delegates.

The small size of the two local voting blocs is yet another indication of the lack of national partisan influence on local affairs, but it should not be interpreted to mean that political divisions on local issues in Virginia were slight. Indeed, as recent research on local politics in Virginia indicates, there were often, despite the deferential, nonissue oriented pattern of voting in the individual counties, bitter and divisive clashes of interests among the representatives from the various counties and regions in the state legislature.[5] The members of Virginia's political elite, although elected on the basis of prestige and personality within their respective counties, proved more than willing to fight for the special interests of their own con-

3 Ibid. The relatively small size of the sample group makes any generalization about the exact nature of the divisions on local issues tentative. In "A Quantitative Approach to the Social, Economic and Political Structure of Virginia, 1790-1810" (unpublished paper presented at the annual meeting of the Southern Historical Association, October 1969), Van Beck Hall suggests that there were discernible voting patterns on individual or related sets of local issues. It is also clear from Hall's findings that the complexity and diversity of the total number of local issues confronted by Virginians renders the formation of large voting blocs based on any single factor—e.g., class or geography—extremely unlikely.

4 See Appendix 3.

5 See Hall, "A Quantitative Approach to Virginia, 1790-1810."

stituencies. For the most part these divisions within the elite occurred outside the framework of the two national political parties that were beginning to emerge in Virginia and, in fact, were usually so localized as to prevent the emergence of sizable factions that voted cohesively on a whole slate of local issues. But the divisions, however localized, were frequently present nonetheless. Although a systematic discussion of purely local politics lies outside the scope of this study, a cursory survey of attitudes toward two of the persistent sources of conflict on the state level—the issues of separation of church and state and the status of Negro slaves—will at least suggest the particularistic nature of local politics in the Old Dominion. And it is, of course, precisely this particularistic view of politics that provides the general explanation for the hostility of so many of Virginia's citizens and political leaders to the consolidating tendencies of the federal government.

In December 1785, after nearly ten years of piecemeal action, the Virginia legislature passed the bill for Religious Freedom, disestablishing the Episcopal Church. The quest for complete separation of church and state did not end with passage of the bill, however. Following that action the dissenting sects, particularly the Baptists, engaged in constant but unsuccessful agitation to divest the Episcopal parishes of the glebe lands originally given them by the Crown. The impetus behind their efforts came in part from the desire to carry the principle of separation of church and state to its conclusion, but a more practical consideration was also involved. The Episcopal Church was not using its lands for the purpose for which they were designed—the care of the poor; the job needed to be handled by a more efficient agency.[6] When an individual parish proved incapable of discharging its duties to the poor, the Assembly was able to force the sale of its lands, but attempts to institute a statewide sale of the church's glebe lands had failed.[7]

[6] Robert Usry, "The Overseers of the Poor in Accomac, Pittsylvania, and Rockingham Counties, 1787-1802" (M.A. thesis, College of William and Mary, 1960), passim.

[7] Ibid., pp. 1-7; Shepherd, *Statutes at Large*, 1: 311.

The issue of the glebe lands was brought before the Assembly once again in 1789. On November 27 the House of Delegates agreed to hear a joint petition from the seven major Baptist associations of Virginia. The petition asked that the legislature order the sale of all the lands of the Episcopal Church, the proceeds to be used for a state-administered program of education and care for the poor. The Baptists' opponents argued that the lands were a private donation from the king of England to the Episcopal Church of Virginia and that independence did not alter their status; the lands remained the private property of the individual parishes. As private property, they could not be disposed of by legislative act. If anyone had the right to tamper with private property, and opponents of the Baptist petitioners doubted that anyone did, it was the courts, not the legislature.[8]

As in the past, supporters of the Episcopal Church brushed aside the issue. When the Baptists tried to bring the issue to a vote on December 9, the majority in the General Assembly succeeded in postponing further discussion until the next session.[9] On November 19, 1790, the Baptist petitioners finally succeeded in bringing the matter to a vote, but it was hardly worth the effort. A resolution calling for a statewide sale of the lands of the Episcopal Church was decisively defeated, 52-89.[10]

The division on the question of the glebe lands reflected the special interests of the delegates. Of the fifty-two men in favor of the sale of the glebes, fifty were from the west, where the dissenting sects were strongest. Of those opposing, fifty-nine were from the Episcopalian-dominated east, thirty from the west. The western delegates favoring sale of the lands were almost exclusively from areas where the impact of Protestant revivals had been greatest. The far western counties, dominated by the dissenting sects, were unified in support of the measure. They were joined by Piedmont counties such as Orange and Loudon. In Loudon County the powerful Ketoctan Baptist

8 *House Journal,* 27 Nov. 1789.
9 Ibid., 9 Dec. 1789.
10 Ibid., 19 Nov. 1790.

Association had gained many converts, and in Orange County one of the most influential Baptist ministers in the nation, John Leland, had attracted a large following.[11] James Madison of Orange County was alert enough to recognize the value of the Baptists as political allies and beginning in 1789 he carefully cultivated their support. When Madison assumed leadership of the emerging Republican party in Congress, he attempted to persuade his Republican colleagues in the eastern, Episcopalian counties of Virginia to accede to the sale of the glebe lands in order to strengthen his alliance with the Baptists, but his efforts were unsuccessful. Republicans from the eastern counties were willing to join in his fight against the federal government, but they were not yet prepared to subordinate their own local interests for the sake of national partisan gain. As a result, the nature of the political divisions over the question of the glebe lands remained roughly constant for most of the decade. In votes on the same question in 1791, 1792, 1794, and 1795 the sources of support and opposition for the measure to divest the Episcopal Church of its lands remained stable. It was not until the end of the decade that Madison actually succeeded in persuading the eastern members of his party of the importance of the Baptists to the Republican cause.[12]

Policy toward the status and treatment of Negro slaves was similarly determined by the special interests of the members of the legislature. In 1792, the General Assembly undertook a thorough revision and consolidation of its many laws respecting the slave population. The result, an "Act to reduce into one, the several acts concerning slaves, free Negroes and mulattoes," was prompted at least in part by the recent rebellion in Haiti and by a minor and abortive slave revolt in Norfolk.[13] The act of 1792 reflected growing fears on the part

11 Hall, "A Quantitative Approach to Virginia, 1790-1810," analyzed the vote on the glebe lands question a year later, in 1791, and found a roughly similar pattern.

12 Ibid. There is disagreement between Hall and myself on the causes of the voting shift on the glebe land issue after 1795.

13 Officials investigating the planned insurrection received testimony that the slaves involved had used the recent uprising in Haiti as a model for their own

of whites of unrest among the slave population. It placed
further restrictions on assemblages of blacks and increased the
punishments for such unlawful gatherings. The Assembly also
took the final step in degrading the black man's status as a
human being. In the past, slaves had been treated either as
real or personal property as the situation dictated, but in 1792
the Assembly made the Negro personal estate, chattel, once and
for all, thus preventing him from legally owning or possessing
private property. In addition, it enabled his owner to avoid
many of the problems presented by Virginia's intricate inher-
itance laws relating to real property.[14]

Defining the Negro as personal estate could have created
problems for Virginians, since the slaveowner was held liable
for any damages or injuries caused by his personal property.
But ingenious Virginians found a way out of this potential
difficulty. The courts differentiated between inanimate and
animate chattel; although a planter might be held responsible
for damages done by a falling tree or a runaway wagon, he
was not held financially responsible for the acts of his slaves,
for they were capable of acting on their own volition.[15] Thus,
Virginians succeeded in stripping their slaves of all human
rights, yet absolved themselves of responsibility for the actions
of those slaves.

Virginians, slaveowners or not, agreed that it was necessary
to supervise the slave population closely, and few would have
quarreled with the provision making slaves personal property.
But other features of the act of 1792 worked to benefit the
slaveholders at the direct expense of the nonslaveholding pop-

---

plans. The immediate cause of the disturbance in Norfolk, which did not involve
more than ten or twelve Negroes and never went beyond the planning stage, was
the "practice of severing husband, wife and children in sales." Henry Lee to
Col. Robert Goode, Richmond, 17 May 1792, Lee to Commanding Officers of
the Norfolk Militia, Norfolk, 18 May 1792, Executive Letterbooks; William
Nelson to Henry Lee, Northampton County, 3 May 1792, Littleton Savage to Lee,
Northampton, 17 May 1792, Thomas Newton to Lee, Norfolk, 19 May 1792,
Executive Communications, VSL.

14 Shepherd, *Statutes at Large*, 1: 122-30; James C. Ballagh, *A History of
Slavery in Virginia* (Baltimore, Md., 1902), pp. 66-74.

15 Ibid., p. 73.

ulation. One section provided that "the value of a slave condemned to die who shall suffer accordingly, or before execution
of the sentence perish, to be estimated by the justices, shall be
paid by the public to the owner." Not only was the slaveowner
absolved from liability for illegal acts by his slave but also
was recompensed by the public, including those who did not
own slaves, for the value of such a slave. This provision met
strong opposition, but an attempt to knock it out of the bill
was defeated, 50-57.[16]

The interests of the delegates were much in evidence during
the vote on compensation for slaveowners. Again, there was
an east-west split, but the division was more reflective of the
pattern of slaveholding throughout the state than it was of
geography. Only seven eastern counties opposed the section
on compensation—precisely those counties that had small slave
populations. Of the western counties that opposed the provision, only two had slave populations of over 50 percent, while
over two-thirds had slave populations of less than 25 percent.
Thirty-three eastern and twelve western counties supported the
measure, and again, their support corresponded with the percentage of slaves in their population. Seven of the twelve western counties voting in favor of compensation had slave populations of 25-50 percent; the other five had slave populations of
over 50 percent. Negro slaves comprised a majority of the
population in twenty-three of the eastern counties favoring the
provision, 25-50 percent in ten of the counties, and in no
eastern county did they comprise less than 25 percent.[17]

That the slaveholding counties had a majority in the legislature and were able to pass such preferential legislation did
not bode well for those who sought a gradual end to slavery.
St. George Tucker, the only Virginian of prominence to campaign actively for emancipation, was rebuffed by the General
Assembly when he presented a mildly worded proposal to that

[16] *House Journal,* 10 Dec. 1792; Shepherd, *Statutes at Large,* 1: 127.

[17] Shepherd, *Statutes at Large,* 1: 127; "A Return of the Amount of Each
Description of Persons within the District of Virginia . . . made this Twelfth Day
of August, 1791," in *Virginia Gazette and General Advertiser,* 28 Sept. 1791.

effect in 1796.[18] As both Winthrop Jordan and Robert McColley
have noted, the gap between the egalitarian rhetoric of some
Jeffersonians and the reality of their attitudes toward the black
man was enormous. And Jordan is probably correct in stressing
the psychological pressures that caused so many Virginians to
be inconsistent in their application of Jeffersonian principles.
It seems clear, however, that the decisions regulating the year-
to-year operation of the slave system itself—such as that on the
question of compensation—were decided principally on economic grounds, with those standing to profit from a system
geared toward the interests of slaveowners voting on one side
of the question and with the representatives from counties
that were not dependent on the slave system voting on the
other.[19]

This same narrow, regionally oriented attitude predominated
in most other issues affecting the internal polity of Virginia.
Important questions on internal improvements and fiscal policy
were not decided in terms of the needs and interests of the state
as a whole, or even the needs of one section as opposed to another. Rather, the delegates from each county voted in accordance with their particular needs at a given moment, often
making large-scale reform impossible.[20] Virginia was still an
agrarian-based society and the average planter or farmer had
few external needs. It was a society admirably suited to a theory

18 St. George Tucker, *A Dissertation on Slavery with a Proposal for the Gradual Abolition of it in the State of Virginia* (Philadelphia, 1796); George K. Taylor to St. George Tucker, Richmond, 5 Dec. 1796, Tucker-Coleman Papers.

19 Robert McColley, *Slavery and Jeffersonian Virginia* (Urbana, Ill., 1964), pp. 34-57, 114-41, contends that most Virginians had no desire to eliminate, or even to ameliorate the slave system because of their almost-total dependence on slave labor as a source of economic profit. Winthrop Jordan, *White over Black: The Development of American Attitudes toward the Negro, 1550-1812* (Chapel Hill, N.C., 1968), pp. 429-565, while recognizing the importance of the profit motive, achieves a more balanced view by his thorough and incisive treatment of the intellectual and psychological attitudes of the white man toward the Negro.

20 The revenue shortage was acute. An inadequate defense system, an antiquated prison, and insufficient salaries for government officials made it imperative
that taxes be raised; they were decreased instead. The delegates were equally
oblivious to the need for internal improvements. On nearly every proposal for
improvements, the few counties which would benefit directly from the improve-
ment would vote for it, the rest would vote against it. See, for example, *House
Journal*, 13 Nov. 1789, 14, 24, 25, 27, 28 Dec. 1790, 12 Dec. 1791, 12 Oct. 1792.

of government which advocated as little interference as possible, and this was exactly the way the state government operated.

Since Virginians were not willing to allow their own state government to assume broad powers, it is understandable that they were even more reluctant to grant those powers to the federal government. There was one area, however, where it was a practical necessity to yield power to the federal government. Because of its shortsighted revenue and defense policies, the Commonwealth of Virginia was wholly incapable of defending her frontier settlements against Indian attack.[21] The supporters of the federal Constitution had won important votes in the Virginia Ratifying Convention by promising to rid the frontier of the Indian problem, and for once, Virginians looked forward to the intervention of federal power.[22] Few of the policies of the federal government promised to benefit the Old Dominion and the ability of the general government to halt Indian depredations on the frontier would therefore be a major test of its utility.

While Virginia's frontier problem was not nearly as troublesome as that faced by Georgia, the Northwest Territory, or the counties in western Kentucky, this historical fact gave little solace to residents in western Virginia who were subjected to Indian attacks. The western counties were on the periphery of two Indian wars involving the Cherokee and Creek nations on the Southwestern frontier and the Shawnee and Miami Indians in the Northwest Territory.[23] Although no major battles took place in western Virginia, the residents suffered heavy casualties from sporadic raids by all four of the Indian nations.

The policy of the United States government was to maintain peace with the Indians at almost any price; the president and his secretary of war, Henry Knox, were well aware that peace

[21] Beverly Randolph to the Lieutenants of Militia, Richmond, 31 Dec. 1788, Executive Letterbooks.

[22] Elliot, *Debates*, 3: 238-41; Main, *The Antifederalists*, pp. 229-30.

[23] Ray Allen Billington, *Westward Expansion: A History of the American Frontier*, 2d ed. (New York, 1960), pp. 221-45.

treaties could not eliminate the grievances between the Indians and the frontier inhabitants, but they hoped that a pacific policy, backed by token forces of American militiamen, would allow them to buy time until a more permanent solution could be found. Small units of militia patrolled the frontier, but were widely scattered and severely handicapped by their orders to carry out only defensive warfare.[24] Virginia's frontier residents were enraged by this cautious policy. While their anger is understandable, they would have received even less protection if their own state government had been manning the defenses. The settlers were not impressed by this line of reasoning. The proponents of the federal government had promised to eliminate the Indian menace; when success did not come immediately, those already hostile to the government were much quicker to blame the federal forces than they were to remember the inadequacies of their own militia.

Pursuant to orders from the United States secretary of war, Governor Beverly Randolph of Virginia, in June 1789, ordered the disbanding of nearly all the state troops patrolling the frontier. Within a month militia strength along the western border had been reduced to token forces in scattered counties.[25] Only a few months later the Indians began to increase the frequency and intensity of their attacks. In the southwest, Wythe, Washington, Montgomery, and Russell counties were plagued by the Creeks and Cherokees. In the northwest, the Shawnee and Miami Indians terrorized the counties of Ohio, Harrison, Monongalia, Randolph, and Kanawha.[26] The federal government's system of peace treaties was not bringing peace to the frontier settlements.

There was an endless circle of complaints over the handling of the situation. The residents of the western counties petitioned the governor, asking him to appropriate funds to bolster

24 Samuel Flagg Bemis, *Jay's Treaty: A Study in Commerce and Diplomacy* (New York, 1923), pp. 11-12.

25 Beverly Randolph to George Washington, Richmond, 1 June 1789, Executive Letterbooks.

26 Samuel McDowell to Beverly Randolph, 26 July 1789, George Clendinen to Randolph, 10 Aug. 1789, Benjamin Wilson to Randolph, 27 Sept. 1789, Executive Correspondence, VSL.

the state militia. The governor answered that it was the responsibility of the federal government to patrol the frontier; he was powerless to intervene. The governor then wrote the president, begging for more federal protection. He invariably received the answer that federal troops were overcommitted and that even if the troops were available, they could not be used, since the United States was theoretically at peace with the Indian nations and therefore could not take any offensive action. This discouraging news was relayed to the frontier inhabitants, completing the circle of evasion.[27]

The western settlers were not entirely blameless for the troubles that beset them. Governor Randolph repeatedly warned against incursions into territory legally held by the Indians, but Virginia frontiersmen continued to stir up Indian animosity by their hunger for western lands.[28] Nevertheless, most of the settlers were the unfortunate victims of the meddling of others. The machinations of James Wilkinson, intrigue by the Spanish and British, and agitation by the more unruly residents of Kentucky did much more to stir Indian hostility than did the expansionist desires of Virginia frontiersmen. Of particular concern to Governor Randolph was the shockingly unneutral conduct of Great Britain. Randolph was convinced, and there was considerable evidence to bear him out, that Great Britain was using the frontier posts, illegally retained after the Treaty of Peace, to foment Indian unrest.[29] That the United States government would condone such action was proof to all Virginians that the commercial and financial interests of the Northeast were in league with the British.

[27] Robert Johnson to Beverly Randolph, Woodford County, 2 June 1789, in William P. Palmer, ed., *Calendar of Virginia State Papers and Other Manuscripts Preserved in the Capitol at Richmond,* 11 vols. (Richmond, 1875-1893), 4: 634-35 (hereafter referred to as *Calendar of State Papers*); Beverly Randolph to Robert Johnson, Richmond, 26 Sept. 1789, Randolph to Henry Knox, Richmond, 5 May 1790, Executive Letterbooks; Henry Knox to Randolph, New York, 10 June 1790, Executive Communications, VSL.
[28] Beverly Randolph to Lieutenants of the Western Counties, 10 March 1790, Randolph to the Virginia House of Delegates, Richmond, 3 May 1791, Executive Letterbooks.
[29] Randolph to Timothy Pickering, Richmond, 4 Oct. 1793, Timothy Pickering Papers, Massachusetts Historical Society; Bemis, *Jay's Treaty,* pp. 11-20.

The situation became intolerable following the bungled efforts of General Arthur St. Clair. On November 4, 1791, St. Clair's federal forces met the Indians along the Maumee River. The result was a humiliating defeat for the American army; 630 men were lost, a devastating toll considering the paucity of American troops on the frontier.[30] The debacle gave the Indian tribes of the Northwest a great boost in morale. Their attacks increased until Governor Henry Lee was driven to circumvent the restrictions placed on him by the federal government. Lee appealed to the General Assembly to appropriate more funds to raise a special militia force to perform the job the federal troops were supposed to be doing. The Federalist governor made no attempt to defend the administration in New York. He condemned United States Indian policy as a failure and demanded that the federal government reimburse the state for any funds it spent policing its frontiers.[31]

The state militia proved no more successful than in previous years. Casualties continued to mount, prompting Governor Lee to embark on an inspection tour through the frontier counties. What he saw was not encouraging. The state militia was woefully understaffed, underequipped, and plagued with quarrels. There was bickering among the commanding officers as to the proper means of defense and politicking among the lower-ranking officers over promotions.[32] The governor eventually had to resort to the policy used by the federal government. Realizing that he did not have enough men to mount an assault on Indian outposts, he established a system of defensive patrols of ten or twelve men in scattered areas. At the same time, he pleaded with his officers to give him some kind of minor victory in order to raise morale and attract additional recruits. As a stopgap measure, he placed the burden of defense on the residents of the frontier counties themselves. He recommended that families keep a loaded gun at all times, that they barricade

---

[30] Billington, *Westward Expansion*, p. 224.

[31] Henry Lee to William Blount, Richmond, 14 Dec. 1791, Lee to Lieutenants of the Western Counties, Richmond, 12 Dec. 1791, Executive Letterbooks.

[32] John Preston to Henry Lee, 13 June 1792, 15 Aug. 1792, Preston Papers; Lee to Lieutenants of Western Counties, 15 Aug. 1792, Executive Letterbooks.

their doors day and night, and that they remain alert to repel any Indian attack.[33]

The governor's efforts were unproductive. The state simply could not afford to appropriate the necessary revenue to strengthen the militia, enlistments stayed low, and the frontier inhabitants became progressively more disillusioned with both the state and national governments. By 1793, Governor Lee was forced to admit that "at the present, the Commonwealth may be considered destitute of any legal system of defense."[34] At this juncture he tried once again to obtain more aid from the already depleted federal troops. The reply of Secretary of War Knox was not reassuring. He admitted that the pacific policies of the United States government were not working and that more vigorous action might be necessary in the future, but he added that it was impossible to increase the government's effort against the Indians because most of the members of Congress lived far from the frontier and could not be persuaded of the necessity for more stringent measures. At least for the present the United States would continue its policy of peaceful overtures.[35] Knox's judgment was sound. The policy of biding time until a sufficient force could be raised proved to be wise, but it was not easy to convince the frontiersmen of the virtue of peace treaties and patience when their neighbors were being killed.

In addition to discontent over tactical solutions to the frontier problem, all three agencies of government—county, state, and national—became embroiled in a controversy over the distribution of the expenses of the war. The state government could not afford to supply local militia companies with adequate equipment; the local commanders either had to do without or impress the necessary supplies from local merchants. Not even the merchants could meet their demands, however,

33 Ibid.; Lee to Captain Andrew Lewis, Richmond, 8 May 1792, Executive Letterbooks.

34 Lee to the Justices of the Counties of Virginia, Richmond, 19 Jan. 1793, Executive Letterbooks.

35 Henry Knox to Lee, Philadelphia, 10 May 1793, Executive Communications, VSL.

and the militia commanders continued to plead with the state government for more money and equipment. The governor sent these requests to the federal government, only to receive the answer that the president could not believe things were as bad as the governor had pictured them and that the existing federal forces could handle the problem. After receiving several such requests from Governor Lee, Secretary Knox finally told the Virginia chief executive to stop being so impatient; the United States had many other obligations and the frontier problem of Virginia was low on its list of priorities.[36] This hardly strengthened the party loyalty of an embattled Federalist governor who was already dissatisfied with the financial policies of the new government. And it provides yet another example of the difficulties faced by Federalist officials in Virginia. Although devoted to union, they were driven to oppose federal policies which threatened to work against the interests of their state.

Relations between Governor Lee and the federal government were exacerbated by the unwillingness of the War Department to reimburse Virginia for funds already spent in defense of the frontier. The War Department had agreed to pay a large part of the expense, but was being obstinate about paying the balance. Lee was irate; if the federal government was going to assume control over Indian affairs, and a very poor control it was, then it must be prepared to assume the full expense of that control. To let it shirk that responsibility would set a dangerous precedent.[37]

Not until August 1794 did the federal government succeed in getting a full force of troops. General St. Clair's successor, Anthony Wayne, won a major victory at Fallen Timbers on August 20, thereby reducing the Indian threat to Virginia's frontier for the remainder of the decade and providing a severe

36 John Preston to Lee, 13 June 1792, Preston Papers; Knox to Lee, Philadelphia, 14 Oct. 1792, 3 Nov. 1792, Executive Communications, VSL; Lee to Knox, 29 April, 11 Sept. 1793, Executive Letterbooks.

37 Lee to Virginia Representatives in Congress, Richmond, 9 Jan. 1792, Lee to Richard Henry Lee, Richmond, 1 April 1792, Lee Family Papers, VHS; Lee to the Auditor of Public Accounts, 18 April 1792, Executive Letterbooks.

blow to British hopes of using the Indians to thwart American expansion westward.[38] And the victory came at precisely the right time. The promise of federal protection from hostile Indians had been one of the few appealing proposals in the Federalist platform, but in the years prior to Wayne's victory it looked as if the federal government was not willing or able to fulfill its promise to the frontier residents. Fortunately for the supporters of the Federalist administration, the performance of the state government in the field of Indian defense during that time was even more dismal than that of the federal government and criticism of federal policy was therefore muted. Dissatisfied as they were with federal Indian policy, the frontier residents had no choice but to remain primarily dependent upon the federal government for protection. Wayne's victory at Fallen Timbers finally gave the Federalist administration a measure of positive appeal. The citizens of northwest Virginia, who tended to place most of the blame for their Indian troubles on the state government, would actually constitute a stronghold of Federalist support for the rest of the decade.[39]

The weaknesses of the state militia system, although plainly apparent to those concerned with the problem of defense against hostile Indians, continued to escape reform. The inherent defects of the militia system, and of the attitudes that produced such a system, were a result of the negative theory of government held by most Virginians. At the heart of the matter was the lack of funds—a problem that hindered Virginia's development in almost every area. When Governor James Wood informed his militia commander that it would be impossible to raise military expenditures, he voiced a common complaint: "Because of the ill-judged policy of our Legislature in reducing the taxes, we have an empty treasury."[40] The unwill-

---

38 Billington, *Westward Expansion,* pp. 225-26.

39 Federalist strength in the northwest was bolstered by other factors as well. The failure of the Republican-dominated state government to grant the northwestern counties greater representation in the legislature served to drive the representatives from those counties into the arms of the Federalists.

40 James Wood to Captain Southern, Richmond, 26 June 1794, Executive Letterbooks.

ingness of the legislature to levy taxes for anything but the most immediate needs of the state not only weakened the militia, it also hindered programs for internal improvements, education, and even delayed repair of a leaky roof on the governor's mansion for six years.[41] The existing tax rate was insufficient to meet the needs of the state, but worse, the perennial problem of tax arrears made it impossible to collect taxes that had been assessed. It was not that the tax burden was too high—few people complained of this—but that men entrusted with collection of taxes, the county sheriffs, had many other duties and could not spend the time traveling through the county to make their collections. Since the collector was legally responsible for any revenue he failed to collect, many counties were unable to find anyone to fill the post. Consequently, some counties fell as much as ten years behind in their taxes. This problem became acute at the height of the frontier warfare; Governor Lee pleaded with his revenue agents to increase efforts to collect tax arrears, but there was no appreciable change in the situation.[42]

The state militia probably could not have functioned efficiently even if it had been properly financed. In the populous eastern counties, where monthly militia musters were a pleasant diversion and service did not subject participants to immediate danger, there was no problem finding recruits. It was a mark of social distinction to be a militia officer in Virginia, and the same families that controlled the county court and served in the Assembly also held the top ranks in their county's militia unit.[43] The main problems facing these militia commanders

41 The governor, in his annual addresses to the legislature, continually pleaded for more funds for all these items. Beverly Randolph to the Speaker of the House of Delegates, 20 Oct. 1789, Henry Lee to the Speaker, 21 Oct. 1793, Robert Brooke to the Speaker, 8 Nov. 1796, James Wood to the Speaker, 4 Dec. 1797, Executive Letterbooks.

42 The legislature was engulfed with petitions from sheriff-tax collectors, asking to be relieved of their responsibilities. The petitioners usually complained that the burden of their other duties, plus the large territory to be covered in collecting the taxes, made it impossible for them to carry out their job. See, for example, Petitions of Ohio County, 23 Nov. 1796, Botetourt County, 16 Nov. 1795, Loudon County, 8 Nov. 1790, Legislative Petitions, VSL; Henry Lee to Virginia Revenue Agents, Richmond, 17 Feb. 1794, Executive Letterbooks.

were to keep the troops sober on muster day and to avoid making enemies when they appointed officers. Although the militia companies were badly disciplined (on one occasion a whole company deserted its commander for a night of revelry), it was of little consequence.[44] There was no need to be in a state of readiness.

Militia service along the frontier, however, was not a pleasant diversion. Leadership posts in the state militia were still considered an honor and remained under the control of members of prominent families, but it was much more difficult to fill the less prestigious positions. The western counties were far less populous than those of the east, and since each county constituted a separate militia unit responsible for raising its own troops, the west always had difficulty recruiting an adequate force. Moreover, militia service in the west was dangerous. It was one thing to gather every few months for a militia muster, but quite another to be fighting Indians. As a result, western residents viewed militia duty as something to avoid.

Frederick County, safely situated in the eastern portion of Virginia's Northern Neck, had a force of 2,708, while Wythe County, the subject of almost nightly visitations by the Indians of the southwest, had a force of only 494 men. Likewise, Accomac County, on the eastern shore, had a force of 1,299 men, the northwest county of Montgomery, a mere 436. This ratio held true throughout the state. This would have been of little consequence had the duties of the militia in the two regions been similar, but the vulnerability of the west to Indian attack made it all the more important that it have a strong militia.[45] Virginia's outmoded militia laws made this impos-

---

43 A study of the "Rank Role of the Virginia Militia," 15 Aug. 1794, Wilson Cary Nicholas Papers, University of Virginia, indicates that command of the militia was even more tightly controlled by Virginia's leading families than were the political positions in the state. Almost no one of social prominence was excluded from the militia role and very few people of low social standing can be found on the list.

44 Joseph Jones to William Mackin, Petersburg, 7 Sept. 1794, John Stith to Joseph Jones, Brunswick, Va., 19 Jan. 1795, Joseph Jones Papers, Duke University.

45 "Militia Role," 1798, Preston Papers.

sible. It was the responsibility of the militia in the particular county where a disturbance took place to handle the problem. Thus, the militia units of the west, which were the least equipped in supplies and men, bore most of the responsibility for policing the frontier against the Indians.[46]

The burden placed on individual counties for raising and supervising militia forces was disastrous to military efficiency, but the historical reasons for assigning the counties such a role are understandable. Aversion to large standing armies, suspicion of centralized administration—state or national—and intense pride in local government as the legitimate source of justice and protection—these all served to discourage efficient administration of military affairs. There was also a practical reason for maintaining the status quo. Those holding power in the counties had a vested interest in the old system. The county courts made all recommendations to the governor for the appointment of state militia officers, and the governor rarely refused to follow their recommendations. Since those nominated were either close friends or relatives of the county court officials, and in some cases were the officials themselves, the ruling aristocracy in the counties was understandably reluctant to relinquish power over the militia. Their control over the militia was an important ingredient in their own political power, and they would not willingly assent to any diminution in it.[47]

The militia's part in the political process varied, but occasionally it was important. The congressional elections of 1792 in the district encompassing Montgomery, Washington, Wythe, Grayson, Greenbrier, Kanawha, Lee, and Russell counties—the region where the Indian threat was the greatest—provides a dramatic example of the curious way in which the militia, the social structure, and the political process became intertwined. The opposing candidates, Abram Trigg and Francis Preston, were the two most prominent men in the region. The Trigg

[46] Hening, *Statutes at Large*, 13: 340-56.
[47] Ibid., 13: 342; Sydnor, *Gentlemen Freeholders*, p. 92.

and Preston families had dominated the affairs of their respective counties for decades. During the Revolution, William Preston, Francis's father, had been chairman of the Montgomery County Committee of Safety; Abram Trigg's father had been second in command. The families' preeminence continued into the 1790s; both had enhanced their reputations by service in the Revolution and had increased their economic standing by well-timed land speculation. In addition to being rich and socially prominent, Preston and Trigg held the same political views, both identifying with the emerging Republican party. They shared a hatred of Great Britain and a desire to defend the agrarian interests of Virginia. Nor did they differ in the way in which they ran their campaigns. They avoided major issues and relied on prominent people living within the congressional district to use their influence on the electorate.[48]

On election day events took an unusual turn. Captain William Preston, commander of the federal troops in the area, became overzealous in support of his brother's candidacy. He marched his troops into the polling place and proceeded to turn the electoral process into chaos, demanding that all his men be given the opportunity to cast ballots. This was warranted in some cases, as many men were residents of the county, but many others who voted that day lived in Kentucky. Captain Preston next marched his troops around the courthouse "to the disturbance, displeasure and terror of the voters assembled there." The soldiers began to intimidate those freeholders intending to vote for Abram Trigg. When the local justice of the peace protested, one of the soldiers knocked him down and took over his post.[49]

48 Charles W. Crush, comp., *The Montgomery County Story, 1776-1957* (Richmond, 1957), pp. 12-18; William C. Pendleton, *History of Tazewell County and Southwest Virginia, 1748-1920* (Richmond, 1928), pp. 257-58; Thomas Perkins Abernathy, *Western Lands and the American Revolution* (New York, 1937), pp. 249-50; Francis Preston to John Preston, 10 Feb. 1795, Preston Papers; Ansel Wold, comp., *Biographical Directory of the American Congress, 1774-1927* (Washington, D.C., 1928), pp. 143, 1627.

49 Francis Preston to John Preston, 1 Jan. 1793, Petition of Abram Trigg of the State of Virginia to the Speaker of the House of Representatives . . . [1793], Preston Papers.

The federal militiamen made a mockery of the election in Montgomery County. Surprisingly, Francis Preston did not deny the fact. When Trigg contested the election before a special committee of the United States House of Representatives, Preston admitted that his brother had been guilty of a breach of conduct, but claimed he would have won the election anyway. The only charge he disputed was that concerning the assault on the justice of the peace. Preston claimed that the justice was intoxicated by the time the soldiers appeared and that the justice had struck the first blow.[50]

Even more surprising than Preston's admission of his brother's guilt was the nonchalance with which Congress viewed the affair. When the matter was discussed on the floor of the House of Representatives, a few Northern members expressed surprise, but representatives from the Southern states saw nothing unusual. Samuel Smith of Maryland tried to explain to the Northern members that this sort of thing was customary in Southern elections; in the North, citizens met in small groups to cast their votes, but in the South the citizens of a county met together at once, creating great congestion, and not at all infrequently, tumult. Smith reassured his Northern colleagues that there was nothing exceptionable about one of Preston's supporters carrying a club under his coat or that drunkenness prevailed: "I suppose that five hundred of my constituents had clubs under their coats; so that if this be sufficient for putting an end to an election, the committee may begin by disallowing mine. If the committee are to break up every election whose persons are seen drunk, they will have great deal of work upon hand, sir." In regard to the charge that Captain Preston had intimidated people at the polls, Smith contended that in all Southern elections "a man of influence came to the place of election at the head of two or three hundred of his friends; and to be sure they would not, if they could help it, suffer anybody on the other side to give a vote as long as they were there." By Southern standards then,

<hr />

50 Francis Preston to William Preston, 11 April 1793, Preston Papers; *Annals of Congress*, 4: 612.

Preston's conduct was not out of the ordinary. And Smith's argument must have carried some weight, for Trigg's petition to void the election was rejected, without a division.[51]

Preston kept his seat in the House, but the controversy continued at home. For the next six years the Preston-Trigg rivalry took on the appearance of family warfare. On each succeeding election, in 1794, 1796, and 1798, Trigg and Preston opposed each other, and their campaign rhetoric became more acrimonious each time.[52] A new dimension was added to the affair when the fiery democrat Alexander Smythe, head of the Wythe County Democratic Society, joined forces with Trigg. Smythe dug up new charges, accusing Preston of land speculation and of unlawful interference in the appointment of county court officials. He claimed that Preston's large landholdings in the West aligned him with the aristocratic elements in Congress and made him unfit to serve the interests of the smaller landowners of his district.[53] Smythe became so abusive that Preston felt compelled to meet him on the field of honor. Characteristically, the duel ended with the shots going astray.[54]

Smythe's democratic rhetoric notwithstanding, the Preston-Trigg feud was not fought along ideological lines. The campaigns of 1794, 1796, and 1798, which could have centered around the important political issues of the decade, were instead contested on an intensely personal level. Both candidates were supporters of the "republican interest." While in Congress Preston had sided with the Madisonian party and in 1800

---

51 *Annals of Congress,* 4: 611-12.

52 William Lewis to Abram Trigg, 22 Dec. 1794, Francis Preston to John Preston, Philadelphia, 11 Jan. 1795, Robert Gamble to John Preston, Richmond, 23 May 1796, Circular Letter to the People of Wythe, Washington, Montgomery, Greenbrier, Kanawha, Grayson, Russell, and Lee Counties, 13 Feb. 1797, Preston Papers.

53 The democratic societies of Virginia were responsible for the most extravagant charges against the federal government. The societies had little influence however. Societies were formed in only three areas—Norfolk, Wytheville, and Dumfries, and in no cases did they survive longer than a year. Eugene Perry Link, *Democratic-Republican Societies, 1790-1800* (New York, 1942) p. 134; *A Letter from Alexander Smythe to Francis Preston* (Richmond, 1795); *The Third and Last Letter from Alexander Smythe to Francis Preston* (Richmond, 1796).

54 Benjamin Howard to John Preston, Williamsburg, 26 June 1796, Francis Preston to John Preston, Saltworks, 12 Aug. 1797, Preston Papers.

served as an elector on the Jeffersonian ticket. Trigg, though he had the support of the more radical Smythe, pursued the same policies as his predecessor when he succeeded in unseating Preston in 1798.[55] Trigg was not even able to turn Preston's record of land speculation to his political advantage. If Preston's landholdings made him unqualified to serve the interests of his constituents, then Trigg, who had also enjoyed success speculating in western lands, would have been disqualified on the same grounds.[56] Instead, Trigg continued to harp on Preston's misconduct in the appointment of county officials, while Preston asked the voters to uphold his honor in the face of the aspersions of Trigg and Smythe. Trigg's efforts finally paid off in 1798, but his victory was one of personality, not of political principles. Preston was mortified by his defeat, not because it signified a rejection of his conduct as a congressman, but because it meant the loss of his status as the most venerated man in his district.[57]

In other sections of the nation a personal rivalry such as that existing between Preston and Trigg might have created a division along ideological lines, if only out of expediency. A candidate in Abram Trigg's position might have adopted a stance in support of the Federalist administration to add substance to his personal opposition to Preston.[58] This did not, and could not, happen because of the unanimity of opinion existing between Preston and Trigg on the subject of the federal government. They both feared centralized government and detested the policies of the Federalist administration in particular. Moreover, neither candidate was accustomed to debating issues of national policy during a political campaign. Each man

55 Francis Preston to John Preston, Philadelphia, 9 Nov. 1794, Francis Preston to John Preston, 27 Feb. 1800, Preston Papers; *Annals of Congress*, 7: 1954, 9: 2721.

56 Lewis P. Summers, *Annals of Southwest Virginia, 1769-1800*, 2 vols. (Abingdon, Va., 1929), 1: 923, 925-27.

57 Francis Preston to John Preston, Philadelphia, 10 Feb. 1795, Robert Gamble to John Preston, Richmond, 23 May 1796, Francis Preston to John Preston, Philadelphia, 1 Feb. 1797, 21 March 1797, 12 Aug. 1797, Preston Papers.

58 This is the hypothesis of Robert K. Merton, *Social Theory and Social Structure* (Glencoe, Ill., 1957), 300-301.

viewed the campaigns as tests of his personal power and prestige and would have considered the manipulation of national issues for partisan gain as a breach of the etiquette of Virginia's electoral process. In many areas of the state this highly personalized view of politics was already breaking down, and the intensification of the struggles between Republicans and Federalists would cause a further decline in that kind of ethic. But for Preston and Trigg, and for their constituents, considerations of personality and prestige remained more important than public policy.

As people within Virginia began to feel the impact of federal policy, important changes were taking place in the nature of the opposition to the Federalist administration on the floor of the United States Congress. Before 1791, the loudest protests against Federalist policy had come from the members of Virginia's state government. Although these protests had not been directed by an organized political party, they were significant factors in the transformation of many of Virginia's congressmen from supporters to opponents of Federalist policy. By 1791 Virginia's congressmen had moved into the fore of the opposition and were now trying to control the sentiments that had hastened their transformation and turn them to partisan advantage. While they had formerly been captives of local interests, they were now seeking to coordinate those interests into effective opposition to Federalist policy.[59]

The leaders of the new Republican interest in Congress knew they had a ready-made constituency in Virginia. A sizable majority in the House of Delegates had criticized federal policy from the beginning and there was no sign that the strength of that opposition was declining. Moreover, the oratory of Patrick Henry and the rhetoric of the *Virginia Address to Congress*

---

[59] Noble Cunningham, *The Jeffersonian Republicans, 1789-1801* (Chapel Hill, N.C., 1957), pp. 1-32, traces the early development of the Republican party in Congress. Cunningham maintains that the impetus behind party organization came almost exclusively from the Republican members of Congress. In a technical sense Cunningham is correct, but he ignores the local pressures that made it mandatory for the congressional leaders to begin organizing in the first place.

Concerning Assumption provided them with an articulate philosophy of agrarian republicanism, well-suited to their current needs. Resistance to centralization, hatred of British influence, and a suspicion of Northern financial and commercial practices—these had already become the themes of Virginia's opposition to the national government and provided a useful weapon for Virginia's national leaders in their day-to-day opposition to Hamiltonian programs.

The new party organization in Congress promised to be much more effective than the unorganized and sporadic opposition that had appeared in the state legislature. Republican congressmen could attempt to block Federalist proposals before they became law rather than indulge in spirited, but futile, protests after the fact. There were some serious obstacles to extending party organization to include political leaders within the state. While most Virginia Republicans in Congress shared the same views on the way the government should be administered, the Republican interest on the local level was composed of many disparate elements. Their attitudes on two of the fundamental questions of the age—the proper division of power between state and nation and the value of democratic forms of government—differed significantly.

The principal division within Virginia's Republican interest on the question of sovereignty was between the old Antifederalists and the growing body of disenchanted Federalists who were drifting over to the Republican cause. The Antifederalists had joined the Republicans *en masse*. Of Antifederalist members of the Ratifying Convention whose later careers can be traced, only one man, Patrick Henry, became a Federalist, while forty joined the new Republican party.[60] This group formed the nucleus of Republican strength in Virginia and, indeed, provided the initial pressure which hastened the conversion of many of Virginia's Federalist congressmen to the Republican cause. In general, the Antifederalist wing remained unreconciled to a central government possessed with such vast power and was trying not only to block the particular policies

[60] Risjord, "The Virginia Federalists," p. 487.

of Alexander Hamilton but also to change the very structure of the government which allowed those policies to be enacted. Of the Federalists in the Virginia Ratifying Convention whose subsequent careers can be traced, thirty-eight remained supporters of the government, while twenty-three defected to the Republicans.[61] Those who joined the Republican party did so in reaction to Hamiltonian policies, but did not desire any radical changes in the structure of the government itself. Their attitudes more closely coincided with those of the Republican leaders in Congress, but they remained a minority within their party in Virginia. It was the task of Virginia's leaders in Congress, and not an easy one at that, to maintain a semblance of unity between these two wings of the party without giving in to the more radical demands of those who wished to bring about drastic changes in the structure of government. They were not always successful; often they would resort to Antifederalist rhetoric, thus giving the Federalists the mistaken impression that they too sought the destruction of the new government.

There was also a division of opinion within the Republican interest over the efficacy and desirability of democratic government. At one extreme were the wealthy gentry who, though they opposed the federal government because it threatened their own political power, were seldom in sympathy with the mildly egalitarian goals of Jeffersonian liberalism. At the other extreme was a small and disparate collection of men—consisting of radical gentrymen and yeoman farmers alike—that made up the membership of the relatively few and uninfluential democratic societies that existed in Virginia. There were of course shades of opinion between these two extremes and many special interest groups that cannot be identified with either view. The Baptist associations, which constituted another source of support for Republican policies, are an example. They distrusted all government, especially centralized government, because they had been penalized for their religious beliefs by such governments in the past. This attitude initially

61 Ibid.

aligned them with the Antifederalists, but when the Antifederalist members of the state senate attempted to strike out
the Federalist-proposed constitutional amendment guaranteeing
religious freedom, they went over to the Federalist side. When
the new Republican party emerged, led by such prominent supporters of religious liberty as Madison and Jefferson, they
changed allegiance once again. Although Baptists subscribed
to a negative theory of government, they were neither liberals
nor conservatives in the traditional sense; men both supporting
and opposing the principles of Jeffersonian democracy could be
found within their ranks. The unifying force among the
Baptists was the desire to protect and promote the liberty and
interests of their sect.[62]

It was the task of Virginia Republicans in Congress to maintain harmony among these disparate elements and channel
them into a united opposition to Federalist policy. The first
test of their ability to do this came on the issue of the Bank
of the United States. Unlike the assumption bill, when Virginia Republicans were willing to compromise to obtain the
Potomac as the permanent site of the capital, the bank bill
was opposed before and after its passage as a patent violation
of the Constitution. Jefferson's failure to convince Washington
of this fact, and Madison's inability to do the same with the
Northern majority in Congress, prompted Republican congressmen to carry the issue to the people.[63] For the first time, however, the reaction in the counties to Federalist policy did not
exceed or even equal the response in Congress. The bank bill,
though far more dubious constitutionally than the assumption
bill, did not even elicit a protest from the Virginia legislature.

James Monroe reported a "general dissatisfaction to the
measures of the Government prevailing" in Virginia, but he
advised his Republican colleagues in Congress not to press the

---

62 Gewehr, *The Great Awakening in Virginia,* pp. 189-94; Gewehr gives an
accurate account of the historical reasons for the Baptists' aversion to centralized
government, but mistakenly equates their opposition to centralism with a belief
in democracy. There is no basis in either logic or fact for the assumption that a
belief in democratic ideals and an opposition to central government were in any
way inherently related to each other.
63 Cunningham, *The Jeffersonian Republicans, 1789-1801,* pp. 8-10.

issue.[64] It was difficult to arouse any opposition because of the very nature of the Bank of the United States. While assumption threatened to do harm to Virginia's taxpayers by assessing them to pay off the debts of other states, the bank bill offered financial aid to the commercial segment of Virginia society, while threatening no adverse economic effect to those who did not stand to benefit from it. It proved impossible to stir opposition based on the bill's alleged unconstitutionality when a large segment of the population would directly benefit from it and the remainder would be unaffected.[65]

The failure of Virginia's leaders in Congress to rally public opinion at home against the Bank of the United States is indicative of the difference between the Republican movements on the national and local levels. Jefferson and Madison, although tireless in defense of state and regional interests, were nevertheless able to perceive the long-range implications of the major issues of their day. They realized that, while the bank bill might do no immediate harm to Virginians, the precedents resulting from passage of the bill might lead to more serious encroachments on the federal Constitution in the future. Their followers in Virginia, conditioned to thinking in terms of what would be beneficial to their own or their counties' immediate interests, were unable to see the consequences of such an expansion in the powers granted by the Constitution.

A few of Virginia's jurists and political theorists such as St. George Tucker and John Taylor of Caroline denounced the bank bill as a violation of the Constitution and as a device to promote consolidation, but they were men of unconventional wisdom and their views were further informed by their close association with Virginians in Congress.[66] Significantly, John Taylor's pamphlets attacking the Bank of the United States were written over a year after the passage of the bank act;

[64] James Monroe to Madison, 27 June 1792, Madison Papers.

[65] Henry Lee to Madison, 8 Jan. 1792, 17 Jan. 1792 in Hunt, ed., *Madison's Writings*, 6: 81-83.

[66] St. George Tucker to James Monroe, Williamsburg, 10 Feb. 1791, Papers of James Monroe, LC (microfilm); John Taylor to James Madison, 11 May, 20 June, 5 Aug. 1793 in *John P. Branch Historical Papers of Randolph Macon College*, 2: 253-59.

although his pronouncements on the Bank gained wide circulation and popularity, they were used not against the Bank itself, but against Federalist policy in general. By the time the pamphlets appeared, a new issue—America's relations with Great Britain—was before the people and Taylor's strictures upon the Bank served not so much to discredit the Bank as to arouse Virginians to the threat of the intrigues of "English monocrats" and Northern speculators in American foreign policy.[67]

By 1792 the Republican party in Virginia found itself in an anomalous position. It had the support of most of the state's leaders and had spoken out forcefully on the issues of constitutional amendments, assumption, and federal Indian policy. By its unrelenting agitation against the Federalist administration it had hastened the entrance of nearly all Virginia's congressional representatives into the Republican camp. Despite this strong base of support, the Republican party in Virginia had not been able to mobilize itself in an effective manner. The bank bill had not generated enough animosity to channel the diverse elements within the party into a meaningful opposition. Republicans in Congress would have to wait for an issue that would unite opinion against the general government on the local and national levels simultaneously before they could really gauge the effectiveness of their opposition.

[67] John Taylor, *An Examination of the Late Proceedings in Congress Respecting the Official Conduct of the Secretary of the Treasury* (Richmond, 1793), pp. 23-28; and Taylor, *An Enquiry into the Principle and Tendency of Certain Public Measures* (Philadelphia, 1794), passim, makes the connection between corrupt financial practices and "English influence" explicit.

CHAPTER FIVE

Federal Policy and
Foreign Affairs: I

WHILE REPUBLICANS in Congress were trying unsuccessfully to mobilize opposition to the Bank of the United States, other issues began to occupy the public mind. The judgment of the Federalist administration in foreign affairs was to be challenged at every level of political life—in Congress, in the state legislatures, and in the counties. As the Anglo-French rivalry in Europe intensified, the Republican and Federalist factions took sides in the contest, with the Federalists becoming aligned with Great Britain, the Republicans with France. In only a few cases were these attachments determined by the interests of the members of either party. Rather, they represented a set of vaguely defined emotional attitudes that existed long before the Constitution had been drafted. These loyalties might have remained dormant, even after the two major European powers had declared war on each other, had it not been for the development of party machinery in Congress which enabled them to be articulated and exploited fully. As this machinery was strengthened so were Federalist attachments to England and Republican attachments to France. This further facilitated the development of a two party political system; but unfortunately, it also wreaked havoc with American foreign policy.[1]

There were two interconnected emotional attitudes that helped shape the debate in Virginia over foreign policy. The first was a hatred for Great Britain resulting from the last

decades of colonial rule, heightened by the Revolution, and
further intensified by England's contemptuous attitude toward
America's maritime rights after the Revolution. Virginians
believed that corrupt English politicians had subverted the
liberties guaranteed by English common law and had made the
government of Great Britain a threat to the liberties of all
nations.[2] In contrast to their rather pessimistic view of the
intentions of England, Virginians viewed the French Revolution with optimism and felt a spirit of community with the
French people. They considered the turmoil in France a
natural result of their own Revolution and envisioned similar
movements by which other nations of Europe could throw off
the vestiges of their corrupt past and acquire the virtues of
America.[3] While many Federalists outside Virginia became
immediately disillusioned with the French Revolution because
of the violence attending it, most Virginia Federalists continued
to keep faith with the French commitment against corrupt,
monarchical rule.

It was much easier to support the people of France through
messages of good will than it was to commit American resources
to the French cause. When France declared war on England
in February 1793, the Federalist administration in Philadelphia
was thrown into the power struggles of Europe and Americans
were forced to take sides between England and France. It
was the intention of Washington, if not that of his secretary of
the treasury, to remain as neutral as circumstances would permit, but to most Virginians Washington's Proclamation of
Neutrality of April 22, 1793, was proof that the Federalists
sought to undermine the republican government of France.
Virginians condemned the Proclamation for its failure to reit-
erate the attachment of the United States to the French revolu-

---

[1] For the best, if also the most polemical, treatment of the relationship between
party development and foreign affairs, see Joseph Charles, *The Origins of the
American Party System: Three Essays* (Williamsburg, 1956).

[2] See, for example, Madison to Edmund Randolph, 17 Oct. 1788, in Hunt, ed.,
Madison's Writings, 5: 276; Jefferson to Richard Price, 8 Jan. 1789, in Boyd, ed.,
Jefferson Papers, 14: 420-24; Marshall, *Washington*, 2: 155.

[3] Jefferson to David Humphreys, Paris, 18 March 1789, in Boyd, ed., *Jefferson
Papers*, 14: 676-79.

tionary cause and for what they believed to be its tendency to make the United States further dependent upon Great Britain. In particular, they charged that the members of the mercantile community had sacrificed the political independence of the United States for the sake of their own pocketbooks.[4]

Affection for the French nation reached a high point soon after the Proclamation of Neutrality. Edmond Genêt, Minister of France, arrived on American shores and received a hero's welcome everywhere he visited. Even in Richmond and Alexandria, supposedly Federalist strongholds, the residents turned out in large numbers to honor the French diplomat.

Coincident with Genêt's arrival the democratic societies began to organize in Virginia to rally support for the French cause. The Norfolk and Portsmouth Society, in its first set of public resolutions, was determined to disavow any support for the Proclamation of Neutrality. Its members explicitly linked America's struggle for liberty with the French Revolution: "When we behold the Tyrants of the world combined and every engine of despotism employed in making a grand effort to crush the infant spirit of freedom, recognized by our brethern [*sic*] of France, whose virtuous exertions (in a cause so lately our own) we cannot as men and as Republicans behold with indifference, or contemplate without a mixture of sympathy and admiration." The Norfolk and Portsmouth Society then accused the Federalist administration of using the Proclamation to obstruct the French cause. The Society considered it a fact much "to be lamented, that in the bosom of our own country we have men whose principles and sentiments are opposed to all free governments, that such are just objects of suspicion."[5]

[4] *Virginia Gazette and General Advertiser*, 4 Sept., 2 Oct. 1793; see also Harry Ammon, "The Formation of the Republican Party in Virginia, 1789-1796," *Journal of Southern History* 19 (1953): 300-305. Ammon has done the most significant work to date in tracing the development of Republican party organization in Virginia. His articles, and his Ph.D. dissertation, "The Republican Party in Virginia, 1789 to 1824" (University of Virginia, 1948), are essential to an understanding of the intricacies of Republican party machinery.

[5] *Virginia Chronicle*, 8 June 1793, in Link, *Democratic-Republican Societies*, pp. 9-10.

As pro-French sentiment increased, antipathy toward the British rose. Those who desired to arouse passions against Great Britain had a solid base on which to build. The residue of bitterness from the Revolution was still present. When a young Englishman, formerly of Virginia, attempted to move back to the Old Dominion in 1790, he immediately discovered the depth of Virginia's hostility to the mother country. Severn Major had lived in Virginia prior to the Revolution, but in 1777 he joined the British army. His military service was confined to five years behind a desk, and when he left the army in 1782 he settled in New York, where he was allowed to become a citizen. Major yearned to return to his home state of Virginia, but Virginia law prohibited former loyalists from residing in the state. He petitioned the legislature, emphasizing his new loyalty to America and asking that they make an exception in his case.[6] But the House of Delegates, by a vote of 74-59, expressed its unwillingness to forgive anyone whose background was tainted by British service.[7] The war was long over, but such was the determination of Virginians to remain free from corrupt, "British influence," that the legislature persisted in strictly overseeing immigration into the state.

The activities of the federal government in its first four years of operation served only to heighten Virginians' fears about British influence. The new government was pursuing policies whose obvious design was to aid the commercial North at the expense of the agrarian South. And what was worse, the system being used to destroy the freedom and security of the agrarian section constituted "the essence of the British monopoly, and . . . is sustained by a conspiracy between the government and those who are enriched by it."[8] Thus the financial heresies of the Northern Federalists became intimately linked with the intrigues of Great Britain. Virginians were convinced that the "money-ocracy" of England was gaining control of the United States Bank in order to subvert the liberty of the South.

[6] "Petition of Severn Major," Accomac County, 6 Nov. 1790, Legislative Petitions, VSL.

[7] *House Journal,* 12 Nov. 1790.

[8] John Taylor, *Enquiry into Certain Public Measures,* p. 21.

"America," John Taylor said, "has defeated a nation, but is subdued by a corporation. . . . The Bank, without a pretense of a claim upon the community, has found the means to occupy the station precisely, which Great Britain was striving to fill."[9] This tendency to identify the financial policies of the federal government with the evils of British influence added considerable emotional emphasis to the Republican opposition to Federalist foreign policy. The complicated and intricate questions involved in the formulation of American foreign policy ordinarily held little interest to a people preoccupied with their own local problems, but in this case Federalist policy toward Great Britain became a symbol of all the dangers of consolidated government. The Republicans interpreted any sign of Federalist weakness toward Great Britain as part of a design to impose the commercial and financial systems of that nation on the agrarian South, to extend federal power, and ultimately to bring all of America under the domination of England.

A few Virginians disliked Great Britain for reasons that were not solely emotional or psychological. On the most selfish level, some people in Virginia had a vested interest in seeing that Great Britain and the United States never reached an agreement compelling Virginians to pay the ten to fifteen million dollars in debts owed to British merchants.[10] The state government, ever since the Revolution, had done everything in its power to erect legal roadblocks to the payment of those debts. In 1774, when the courts were closed, British merchants lost all chance to bring suit against Virginia debtors. This extralegal action was regularized by an act of December 19, 1776, prohibiting the recovery of all British debts. In 1787, four years after the Treaty of Peace, the legislature repealed the act prohibiting the recovery of British debts, but added a suspending clause stipulating that the act not go into effect until after Great Britain had given up her posts on America's Western frontier. This, of course, had not been done precisely because

---

9 Ibid., p. 22.
10 *Virginia Gazette and General Advertiser,* 21 Sept. 1799.

of Virginia's refusal to enforce collection of the debts. As a result, Virginians continued to avoid their British creditors.

The federal court in Virginia, dominated by Virginians, did little to encourage payment of the debts. Time and again the justices either refused to hear debt cases or instructed the jury in such a fashion as to preclude any judgment in favor of the British creditors.[11] Antifederalists, Republicans, and Federalists united in a common effort to make collection of the debts more difficult. Patrick Henry's most famous post-revolutionary cases were those in which he successfully defended Virginia debtors, and John Marshall, in a rather disingenuous argument before the Supreme Court in the case of Ware versus Hylton, was instrumental in setting the precedent which made it almost impossible for British creditors to get a fair hearing in suits for the recovery of debts owed to them by Virginians. Marshall maintained that Virginia, when it passed the law prohibiting the collection of British debts, was a sovereign nation possessed with the legal right to confiscate and sequester debts in time of war. The provisions of the Treaty of Peace guaranteeing the payment of British debts did nothing to change this, as the previous Virginia act providing for the confiscation of British debts meant that by 1783 there were in fact no British debts to be paid.[12] The cleverness, if not the fairness, of this argument, leads one to believe that it was not just Republicans who desired to avoid the payment of British debts.[13]

---

11 "Notebook of William Hay: Considerations of Various Subjects of Enquiry Arising Out of the 6th Article of the Jay Treaty . . . With an Appendix containing . . . a Variety of Acts of the Virginia Assembly which can be Considered as Lawful Impediments to the Collection of those Debts," Great Britain, Public Record Office MSS, Domestic, T79/27.

12 Ibid.; Beveridge, *Marshall,* 2: 186-98; William Wirt Henry, *Patrick Henry,* 3: 601-48.

13 Marshall, although his argument in Ware versus Hylton was instrumental in helping Virginians avoid the payment of debts, was one of the first to claim that the Republicans' hostility to Great Britain, while "cloaked in the name of patriotism," was in fact only an excuse to avoid paying their old British debts (*Virginia Gazette and General Advertiser,* 30 Oct. 1793). Although no one has yet determined whether Republicans or Federalists constituted the larger portion of debtors, it seems likely, given the similarity in the composition of the two factions, that enough members of each faction were in debt to the British to make all of them less than eager to find a solution for the payment of prewar

The number of political leaders in Virginia swayed by their own pecuniary interests was probably relatively small. More serious, because it affected both the honor and the livelihood of most Virginians, was the increasing belligerency of the British navy toward American commerce. The governor of Virginia received reports regularly from Norfolk complaining of the highhanded methods of the British navy in stopping and searching American vessels. The British were constantly impressing seamen and, of much more economic importance, slaves of Virginia merchants and shipowners.[14] Nor did they confine their activities to the high seas. The British commanders frequently sent parties ashore to search for deserters. In one case, the "deserter" arrested turned out to be the captain of the Norfolk Town Guard. The result was a chorus of complaints from Norfolk residents and increased demands for retaliation, both commercial and military, against Great Britain.[15]

No matter where Virginians turned, it seemed that the British were involved in activities detrimental to their interests. The piracy of the Algerians and the depredations of the Indians were both laid at the door of England.[16] In the absence of government action, the citizens had to be content with their own methods of reprisal. Thus, the citizens of Norfolk, who came in closest contact with the British because of their proximity to the sea, did everything possible to harass English citizens on American soil; it was reported that they performed "heroic exploits in the tar and feathers line."[17]

---

debts. A final conclusion on this question, however, must await a detailed examination into the federal court records relating to British debts and a correlation of the findings of that investigation with the partisan divisions in Virginia.

[14] Henry Lee to George Washington, 2 May 1793, Lee to Thomas Newton, 22 May 1793, Lee to Henry Knox, 3 July 1793, James Wood to John Hamilton, 10 Aug. 1793, Lee to Thomas Newton, 20 Feb. 1794, Executive Letterbooks.

[15] Robert Brooke to John Hamilton, 22 April 1795, Brooke to the Secretary of State, 18 May 1795, Executive Letterbooks.

[16] Circular Letter of John Page to the Citizens of the District of York in Virginia, 12 May 1794, Broadsides Collection, VHS.

[17] Fisher Ames to Thomas Dwight, Philadelphia, 6 May 1794, in Ames, *Works*, 1: 143-44.

It is not surprising, given the hostility toward Great Britain, that French Minister Edmond Genêt was so well received. By the late summer of 1793, however, Genêt's popularity had begun to go to his head. He traveled throughout much of the United States attempting to enlist American privateers to carry out hostile action against British ships. Although Genêt's activities in Philadelphia and Charleston were the most widely reported, he also had enlisted the aid of many of the residents of Norfolk.[18] The mayor of Norfolk, Thomas Newton, was also the president of the Norfolk and Portsmouth Democratic Society and was enthusiastic in his support for Genêt. He stood by while anglophobic Virginians fitted out their vessels to capture British ships until finally both Secretary of State Jefferson and Governor Lee had to rebuke him for condoning such partisan activities.[19]

Republican leaders in Congress were beginning to suspect that Genêt was more of a liability than an asset to their cause. The activities of some of his more radical supporters in America were exposing the Republican party to the charge of being the tool of a foreign power. While moderate Republicans sympathized with the French cause, they had no intention, at least not at this early stage, of being dragged into a foreign war with the British. Even Jefferson, one of Genêt's most ardent admirers, was beginning to have misgivings; it was apparent that the Republican interest could not control his actions and imperative that its members disassociate themselves from "this intermeddling by a foreigner."[20]

Genêt's indiscretions created a major opportunity for the Federalists to bolster their flagging support. For the first time, a political faction in Virginia made an appeal to the populace, and the group to do so was that faction which was supposedly

[18] Minnigerode Meade, *Jefferson, Friend of France, 1793: The Career of Edmond Charles Genêt* (New York, 1928), pp. 217-44.

[19] George Hammond to Foreign Office, 12 May 1795, Foreign Office, 5, IX, PRO Transcripts, LC; Jefferson to the Governor of Virginia, Philadelphia, 21 May 1793, in Albert E. Bergh, ed., *The Writings of Thomas Jefferson*, 20 vols. (Washington, D.C., 1903-1905), 9: 98-99.

[20] Jefferson to Madison, 25 Aug. 1793, in Ford, ed., *Jefferson's Writings*, 6: 7.

fearful of the passions of the people, the Federalists. The first public meeting of real significance was held in Richmond on August 17, 1793.[21] The Federalists planned the meeting masterfully. George Wythe, the law professor of both Jefferson and Marshall and the most eminent jurist in Virginia, was persuaded to preside over the meeting. He had remained aloof from the bickering over funding, assumption, and the Bank of the United States and his presence did much to obscure the partisan character of the meeting. Wythe's eminence, combined with the behind-the-scenes planning of Marshall, assured the passage of a set of resolutions friendly to the Federalist administration. The assembled freeholders unanimously endorsed the Proclamation of Neutrality as the best means of avoiding conflict with the European powers and praised President Washington for his devotion to peace. Finally, they took direct aim at Genêt, and at least an indirect shot at the Republicans who supported him. They proclaimed that "any interference of a foreign minister with our internal government or administration; any intriguing of a foreign minister with the political parties of this country would be at once a dangerous introduction of a foreign influence, and might too probably lead to the introduction of foreign gold and foreign armies, and their fatal consequences, dismemberment and partition."[22]

Republicans in Congress, after hearing of the Federalist success in Richmond, began to organize in earnest. Madison, writing to his friend Archibald Stuart, diagnosed the political climate in Virginia and then prescribed a course of action:

It seems little doubtful in my opinion what the sense of the people is. They are attached to the Constitution; they are attached to the French nation and Revolution. They are attached to peace as long as it can be honorably preserved. They are averse to monarchy and to a political connection with that of Great Britain, and will readily protest against any known or supposed designs that may have this change in their situation for their object. Why then can not the sense of the people be

21 *Virginia Gazette and General Advertiser*, 21 Aug. 1793.   22 Ibid.

collected on these points, by the agency of temperate and respectable men who have the opportunity of meeting them.[23]

Madison was trying to accomplish two objects: he was hoping to regain some of the support that the Federalists had captured at the Richmond meeting, and he was attempting to persuade "temperate and respectable men" to take the leadership of the republican interest away from the more radical members of the democratic societies.

Madison enlisted his former political rival, James Monroe, in implementing his plan in the counties. He then drew up a list of resolutions to be sent to prominent Republicans throughout the state. Madison hoped these resolutions would be offered in the counties as a rebuttal to the Federalist position.[24] The first was aimed directly at those who initiated the meeting in Richmond. It deplored the "prevailing practice of declaring resolutions, in places where the inhabitants can more easily assemble and consult than in the Country at large, and where interests, views and political opinions different from those of the great body of people may happen to predominate."[25]

After a few perfunctory statements of affection for President Washington, the resolutions moved on to the subject of Franco-American relations. They claimed that the Federalists' attempts to weaken America's ties with France in effect amounted to an assault on "the free principles of our own government." This was to be particularly lamented, since it came at precisely the time "when such vast efforts are making by a combination of Princes and Nobles to crush an example that may open the eyes of all mankind to their national and political rights." Madison ended the section with a passage that would soon become a standard theme for the Republicans. If the United States ignored its obligations to France, it "would obviously tend to forward a plan connecting them with Great Britain, as one

23 Madison to Archibald Stuart, 1 Sept. 1793, Archibald Stuart Papers, VHS.
24 For the backstage manoeuverings of the Republicans at this time see Ammon, "Republican Party in Virginia, 1789-96," pp. 284-310.
25 Madison to Jefferson, 2 Sept. 1793, in Hunt, ed., *Madison's Writings*, 6: 192-93n.

great leading step towards assimilating our Government to the form and spirit of the British Monarchy." The Republican tactic was to characterize those who refused to aid the French, even those who desired strict neutrality, as tools of the "British monocrats." It was nearly impossible to find anyone in Virginia who would admit to an affection for the British, but one only had to voice the slightest dissatisfaction with the violent course of the French Revolution to be accused of it.[26]

Finally, Madison was careful to separate the cause of Edmond Genêt, who had just been recalled, with the more general cause of revolutionary France. The Norfolk and Portsmouth Democratic Society—the only society of its kind in Virginia at that time—had been discredited because of its unwavering commitment to Genêt, and Madison wanted the Republican party to avoid that pitfall.[27]

Madison sent copies of his resolutions to Edmund Pendleton and John Taylor to be used in a meeting in Caroline County.[28] Adoption of the resolutions was a certainty, since the combined influence of Pendleton and Taylor, both opponents of administration policy, was powerful enough to gain support for almost any measure which they advocated. Taylor wasted no time. On September 23, 1793, he wrote to Madison informing him that he had already succeeded in persuading a meeting of Caroline citizens to adopt a set of resolutions similar to Madison's. He added, however, that he had made some changes from Madison's originals in order "to avoid suspicion of their being coined from the same mint."[29]

That Taylor was able to get results so quickly was testimony to his enormous prestige within his county. This same prestige also allowed him to deviate from the resolutions proposed by Madison. The Caroline Resolutions contained, nearly word for word, the ideas suggested by Madison, but the few extra sentences that Taylor had added were not simply intended to mask Madison's role in the affair. Taylor's efforts rendered the

---

[26] Ibid.   [27] Ibid.   [28] Ibid.

[29] John Taylor to Madison, Bowling Green, 25 Sept. 1793, in *The John P. Branch Historical Papers of Randolph-Macon College*, 2: 259-60.

Caroline Resolutions substantially more radical than Madison's. The resolutions linked the men responsible for the Proclamation of Neutrality with those who "desire a closer union with Britain and desire to alter the government of the United States to a monarchy." Moreover, Taylor, and the citizens whom he persuaded to pass the resolutions, refused to repudiate the conduct of Genêt.[30] Taylor's determination to avoid being dominated by the dictates of the Republican leaders in Congress was shared by many prominent Republicans within Virginia. This independence of attitude, although characteristic of Virginia politics, was often a source of anguish to those party leaders who hoped to develop a unified, national party organization.

The Federalist meeting in Richmond and the Republican-sponsored meeting in Caroline County prompted a series of gatherings throughout the state. The citizens of York and King William counties and the town of Williamsburg followed the pro-administration example of the Richmond meeting.[31] The residents of King William County, taking note of the Republicans' increased opposition to the policies of President Washington, avowed "that all attempts hitherto made to wound his character, so far from tarnishing the lustre of his political fame, have only stamped indelible disgrace on those who have made the attempt."[32] This became a standard tactic for the Federalists. Not only would they defend the Proclamation on the grounds that it was in the nation's interest, but they would also attack any questioning of government policy as an expression of disloyalty to Virginia's only demigod, George Washington.

At this stage, all the Republican-sponsored meetings carefully avoided any direct censure of Washington. Even those most hostile to the president's foreign policy prefaced their criticism with at least a perfunctory bow to the "wisdom and integrity" of the chief executive.[33] In Staunton, Virginia, where the Re-

30 *Virginia Gazette and General Advertiser,* 25 Sept. 1793.
31 Ibid., 4 Sept., 9 Oct. 1793.
32 Ibid., 4 Sept. 1793.

publican meeting was organized by Madison's confidant Archibald Stuart, the resolutions adopted were nearly identical with those in Madison's rough draft. The assembled citizens vowed to maintain their friendly ties with France, to avoid falling under the influence of Great Britain, and they made it clear that they disapproved of Genêt's conduct.[34]

In Amelia County, where the Republican leaders were much more radical than Madison or Monroe, the anti-administration resolutions went further in their denunciation of Federalist policy. After the usual tribute to Washington, the Republican leaders of Amelia launched into a conspiratorial interpretation of the events leading up to the Proclamation of Neutrality. It was impossible for them to "avoid thinking, but that our own funded debt, from its imitative construction and operation with that of Britain, had its effect in impelling this dangerous conduct." Thus, the connection between Hamiltonian financial measures and English influence, which John Taylor had scored in his attack on the United States Bank, was now being applied to the conduct of American foreign policy. The Amelia Resolutions, like those of Caroline County, refused to censure Genêt and instead blamed the Federalist press for distorting the facts concerning his conduct while in the United States.[35]

In counties where Republican leadership was weak, or where the Federalist spokesmen had enough political power to offset the prestige of the Republican leaders, Madison found that he was unable to turn public opinion against the Federalist administration. In Fredericksburg, Republicans James Mercer and Mann Page tried to persuade a town meeting to adopt resolutions critical of the Proclamation, but an equally promi-

---

33 Meetings unfavorable to the Proclamation were held in Caroline, Augusta, Amelia, Albemarle, New Kent, Norfolk, and Frederick. Ibid., 4, 25 Sept. 2, 30 Oct., 6, 23 Nov. 1793; Washington to the Mayor of Norfolk, 9 Sept. 1793, Washington to Alexander White, 23 Nov. 1793, in Fitzpatrick, ed., *Washington's Writings*, 33: 19-92, 154-55.

34 *Virginia Gazette and General Advertiser*, 2 Oct. 1793; Monroe to Madison, Albemarle, 25 Sept. 1793, in Hamilton, ed., *Monroe's Writings*, 1: 277.

35 The most prominent Republican in Amelia County was Joseph Eggleston, a former Antifederalist and a leader of the radical, anti-administration faction in the House of Delegates. *Virginia Gazette and General Advertiser*, 6 Nov. 1793.

nent Federalist, Edward Stevens, was present at the meeting and succeeded in blocking the adoption of the resolutions. The meeting finally disbanded, taking no action.[36] Much the same thing happened in Rockingham County. Republican leaders, at the request of Monroe, attempted to organize a meeting to condemn the Proclamation, but because of lack of interest and poor communications, few people appeared at the appointed hour and the meeting was cancelled.[37]

Madison had taken an important step in organizing the Republican interest within Virginia, but he had picked the wrong issue. Most Virginians in positions of political power, including some who were friendly to the Republican cause, supported the administration's Proclamation of Neutrality. When the General Assembly discussed the Proclamation in November 1793, Federalist Governor Lee urged them to adopt a resolution praising it as a "politic and constitutional measure, wisely adopted at a critical juncture." The Republicans, knowing that Genêt's conduct had caused many of their members to support the Proclamation, attempted to forestall the measure by introducing another resolution excluding any discussion of foreign policy by the legislature. For once, the opponents of the government failed to muster enough votes and the Federalist resolution was passed, 77-48.[38]

The inability of Virginia's Republicans to bring censure upon the Proclamation indicated weaknesses both in their ideology and in their organization. Before Genêt's arrival they could have expected near-unanimous support for any reasonable measure designed to aid the French, but Genêt's indiscretions put a temporary end to the pro-French phase of Virginia politics. Virginians were not so devoted to the French revolutionary cause as to allow them to support France at the expense of their own self-interest. Although they were gradually diversifying their markets, Virginians were still dependent

---

[36] Ibid., 16 Oct. 1793; Monroe to Jefferson, 14 Oct. 1793, in Hamilton, ed., *Monroe's Writings*, 1: 278.

[37] Monroe to Madison, Albemarle, 25 Sept. 1793, in Hamilton, ed., *Monroe's Writings*, 1: 277.

[38] *House Journal*, 1, 15 Nov. 1793.

upon Great Britain for the sale of tobacco and, to a lesser extent, flour and could not afford to lend their aid to France if it meant the disruption of that trade.[39] Genêt's privateering activities threatened to do just that. Madison and Jefferson realized the damage that Genêt had done to their cause and were quick to disassociate themselves from him, but Republican leaders in the counties were much slower to abandon the French minister. By the time the full story of Genêt's activities had been revealed, they were too committed to retreat, and much of the resulting reaction fell on their shoulders.

The organizational failure of the Republicans is not surprising. Up until the time of the Federalist meeting in Richmond, it had never been necessary for the Republicans to organize themselves within the state; they could always be assured of a majority in the legislature without the necessity of building a party structure. The decision of the Federalists to appeal directly to the people through the county meetings changed this. When James Madison attempted to meet the Federalist challenge by organizing the Republican forces in the counties, he found that he was successful only in those areas where he had close friends who were themselves in full agreement with him and who were in positions of undisputed local leadership. In Albemarle and Staunton counties, where Archibald Stuart and Wilson Cary Nicholas held sway, events went exactly as planned. In Amelia and Norfolk counties, where popular sentiment was with the Republicans, but where the leaders were not disposed to follow the advice of leaders in

---

[39] Norman Risjord, in his article "The Virginia Federalists," pp. 486-517, argues that the Federalists monopolized the increasing trade in wheat and flour and thus had a vested interest in a powerful, commercially oriented government. The evidence supporting this hypothesis is inconclusive, however. Most of Virginia's flour was shipped to France and Southern Europe. If the Federalists relied on this trade as heavily as Risjord claims, they would undoubtedly have sided with France, not Great Britain during the foreign policy disputes of the 1790s. Evidence that both Republicans and Federalists were taking advantage of the new markets can be found in Robert Gamble to Wilson Cary Nicholas, 24 Feb. 1794, John Nicholas to Wilson Cary Nicholas, 30 April 1794, Wilson Cary Nicholas Papers; George Hammond to Foreign Office, 29 Aug. 1794, Foreign Office, 5, V, PRO Transcripts, LC; "Petition of Westmoreland Co.," 16 Nov. 1795, Legislative Petitions, VSL.

Congress, the resolutions passed were of such a radical nature that the Republican position was discredited. Finally, there were many areas, particularly in the far west, where poor communications and the apathy of the citizens made organization impossible.

The activities of the democratic societies, both in the Genêt affair and later in the Whisky Rebellion, also proved an embarrassment to Republicans. The members of the Norfolk and Portsmouth Society were enthusiastic in their support of Genêt, and their enthusiasm led to conduct which served to bring censure upon the pro-French faction as a whole.[40] Federalist publicists wasted no time in exploiting the excesses of these radical Republicans. They raised the specter of anarchy, claiming that the democratic societies intended to rule the country through the threat of "tar and feathers, a guillotine, or riots." According to these Federalist propagandists, the Republicans in Congress were responsible for this shocking behavior; while the Republicans had not openly advocated violence, their opposition to government policies greatly encouraged the growth of the democratic societies.[41]

The Federalists' dire predictions about the intentions of the democratic societies gained some credence after the Whisky Rebellion. The backcountry residents of Virginia showed no desire to aid the insurgents in neighboring Pennsylvania, but the Virginia Federalists were nevertheless able to score propaganda points against both French "meddling" and the democratic societies. The apparent machinations of Joseph Fauchet, Genêt's successor, and the undeniable role played by members of Pennsylvania's democratic societies in the Rebellion provided the Federalists with good ammunition to use against their opponents. They took every opportunity to publicize Washington's letter to Governor Lee, which declared: "I consider this insurrection as the first *formidable* fruit of the Democratic Societies. . . . That these societies were instituted

40 George Hammond to Foreign Office, 8 May 1794, Foreign Office, 5, IV, PRO Transcripts, LC.
41 "Distinctions between a Republican and a Democrat of the Present Day," in *Virginia Gazette and General Advertiser,* 20 Aug. 1794.

by the *artful* and *designing* members . . . primarily to sow the seeds of jealousy and distrust among the people, of the government, by destroying all confidence in the Administration of it; and that these doctrines have been budding and blowing ever since, is not new to anyone, who is acquainted with the characters of their leaders, and has been attentive to their manoeuvres."[42]

Republican leaders in Virginia did not make the same mistake with the Pennsylvania insurgents as they had with Genêt. They denounced all attempts to oppose the policies of the government by force. Republican Congressman John Page, who just a month before had praised the democratic societies as patriotic organizations designed to preserve the true principles of the Constitution, immediately broke off all connection with them. He joined the Continental Army under the command of Virginia Governor Lee and vowed: "I obey the call of my General with Alacrity. I defend freedom of speech, of the press, and of clubs examining the measures of government, but I will oppose as the deadly enemy of the Republic the man who will oppose the execution of our laws by Force of Arms."[43]

The Republicans were quick to condemn the Pennsylvania insurgents, but they were still disposed to find fault with the manner in which the Federalist administration handled the affair. Characteristically, the issue revolved around the question of national versus local control. Although the Virginia General Assembly unanimously passed a resolution praising the Virginia

---

[42] Washington to Henry Lee, Germantown, 6 Aug. 1794, in Fitzpatrick, ed., *Washington's Writings*, 33: 474-79. Jefferson was furious when he heard of Washington's denunciation of the democratic societies. He described the members of these societies as republicans and patriots and charged that the Federalists "are themselves the fathers, founders, and high officers" of the most dangerous organization in America, the Society of Cincinnati. Jefferson to Madison, 28 Dec. 1794, in Ford, ed., *Jefferson's Writings*, 6: 517. Lisle A. Rose, *Prologue to Democracy: The Federalists in the South, 1789-1800* (Lexington, Ky., 1968), pp. 19-23, 39-40, has attempted to document Jefferson's charge and has himself concluded that the Society of Cincinnati was one of the major bases of organization for the Federalist party. This may have been true in some states, but an examination of the Society of Cincinnati Papers, VSL, indicates that Republicans played as active a role in the Virginia Society as did Federalists.

[43] John Page to St. George Tucker, Rosewell, 9 Aug., 22 Sept. 1794, Tucker-Coleman Papers.

state militia for its role in quashing the Rebellion, it remained critical of the intervention of federal troops into the local affairs of Pennsylvania.[44] The matter came into the open during debate on a resolution concerning Lee's conduct. Proponents of the resolution claimed that Lee, by accepting the post of commander of the United States forces during the Rebellion, had violated the statute prohibiting men from holding offices in the state and federal governments simultaneously and had thus lost title to his position as governor. During the debate on Lee's status, it became apparent that he was not the only person being judged. Many members of the House of Delegates believed that the president "had exceeded his power in calling out the militia of the neighboring states before it was sufficiently proved that the militia of the state where the insurrection arose, was incompetent to the task of quelling it."[45]

The outnumbered Federalists maintained that Lee was serving only in his capacity as head of the state militia and that his post as commander of the combined forces was an unofficial one awarded to him by the other state militia commanders with the consent of the president. Federalist delegate Thomas Evans charged that the Republican "endeavor seems to have been aimed to obstruct the General Government rather than harmonize the interests of the two."[46] The Republicans held the necessary votes, and the House declared the office of governor vacant. They next used their majority to elect their candidate, Robert Brooke, by a 90-60 margin over James Wood, a political neutral.[47]

Brooke's election marked the beginning of a qualitative change in the structure of politics in Virginia. For the first time, a major state official had been selected on the basis of his stand on national issues. Prior to the foreign policy debates of the 1790s, state and local officeholders had been accustomed to operating independently of the controversies surrounding

44 House Journal, 12 Nov. 1794.
45 Thomas Evans to John Cropper, 30 Nov. 1794, John Cropper Papers.
46 Ibid.
47 *House Journal*, 14 Nov. 1794; Madison to Monroe, 5 Dec. 1794, in Hunt, ed., *Madison's Writings*, 6: 225.

the activities of the federal government. The unseating of Governor Lee, and the subsequent election of Robert Brooke, constituted a break in this tradition. Most state officials would continue to be appointed or elected on a nonpartisan basis, but the episode was indicative of an increasing interrelation between local and national affairs.

In spite of the generally adverse effects of Genêt's visit and of the Whisky Rebellion, the Republicans, by the fall of 1794, were in control of the state legislature. Although many Republican members of the House of Delegates were disposed to acquiesce to Washington's Proclamation of Neutrality and to join with the Federalists in condemning Genêt, their anglophobic spirit continued unabated. And events since the Proclamation of Neutrality had shown that there was much basis for that spirit. British confiscations of American commodities on the high seas mounted steadily; hardly a day went by when the governor did not receive at least one complaint from a Norfolk citizen regarding the highhanded conduct of the British navy. Nor were the complaints confined to Norfolk. Crop failures in Europe had created an unusually large demand for American grain, and Virginia's commercial farmers, who were increasingly dependent on flour rather than tobacco as their principal export crop, were being hurt by England's seizure of American ships bound for France.[48] No single faction had a monopoly on this trade, and, as a result, even the Virginia Federalists were turning against the British. No one in Virginia was more devoted to the nationalist goals of the Federalist program than John Marshall, yet even he was forced to declare: "The man does not live who wishes peace more than I do, but the outrages committed upon us are beyond human bearing."[49]

In Virginia, the fundamental difference separating Federalists and Republicans lay in their solutions to the British threat. The

[48] Robert Brooke to John Hamilton, Richmond, 22 April 1795, Brooke to the Secretary of State, Richmond, 8 May 1795, Executive Letterbooks; *Columbian Mirror*, 19 June 1794.

[49] John Marshall to Archibald Stuart, Richmond, 27 March 1794, Archibald Stuart Papers.

Republicans believed that a firm alliance with France and strict discriminatory duties against English imports were the minimum conditions which would convince Great Britain that the United States would not tolerate her interference. The radical, Antifederalist wing of the Republican faction wished to take more drastic steps: they wanted a declaration of war.[50] But the Federalists realized that Americans, especially Virginians, were too dependent upon English markets to risk either war or a tariff battle. Although they had no affection for the British, they did not believe that the French were any more trustworthy and thought the Republicans naive in claiming that there was any natural basis for an alliance with France. The Virginia Federalists were convinced that the mere existence of a common revolutionary heritage could not change the fact that "interests and convenience are the principal directors of the conduct of European nations," and they were certain that France would treat American commerce with the same contempt as Great Britain when it was in her interest to do so.[51]

The immediate result of increasing anti-British sentiment was the revival of agitation for the passage of discriminatory legislation against Great Britain. It was the threat of such legislation, barely averted by the tie-breaking vote of Vice President Adams, that prompted England to receive an American envoy to discuss terms for a commercial treaty.[52] The man chosen Envoy Extraordinary to Great Britain, Chief Justice John Jay, possessed as much diplomatic skill and experience as any man in America. To many Republicans the choice was less than ideal. They reminded their fellow citizens that "the general character of Mr. Jay is that of being at least *very friendly* to the British interest."[53] Virginians in particular could not forget that he was the man who had attempted to barter away their right to navigate the Mississippi in 1784 and that he had defended the right of England to maintain her military posts on the nation's Northwest boundary.[54]

50 Bemis, *Jay's Treaty*, pp. 192-96.
51 William Lee to Henry Tazewell, 1 Dec. 1794, Tazewell Family Papers.
52 Bemis, *Jay's Treaty*, pp. 199-202.
53 *Columbian Mirror*, 19 June 1794.

While Jay carried on negotiations, Republicans predicted dire consequences. They accused him of being taken in by the flattery of the wily British diplomats. "It is feared," said a Republican publicist, "that if the business is to be settled at convivial entertainments, that some of our poor countrymen will be choused out of their rights."[55] After Jay returned, in March 1795, the Treaty was discussed in secrecy by the United States Senate. This served only to heighten suspicion. Republican opponents likened the procedure to the "darkness of a conclave or a seraglio" and declared the whole business to be incompatible with republican government. When Senator Steven Thomson Mason of Virginia defied the administration by giving a copy of the Treaty to the *Philadelphia Aurora,* the leading Republican newspaper in the nation, public debate on the merits of the Treaty began in earnest. One Virginia Republican exclaimed: "The negociator must have been intoxicated; the charms of royalty must have bewitched him."[56] Another went even further, giving vent to his anglophobic ire:

To be dragooned onto a treaty with barbarians, who the other day were laying this Country to smoke and ashes—and are at this day committing every Species of piratical depredation that robbers can suggest—For the citizens of America to be degraded by an instrument, obtained by British influence and calculated to make this Republic a party with the coalesced monsters against a nation which has so lately saved us from gibbets and confiscation. . . . To submit to this and to become the felons of our own constitution, would be synonymous terms. It would be on the one hand, a tyranny unread in the annals of the most despotic government, and on the other, a passive obedience unfound among our African slaves.[57]

The Jay Treaty was not nearly as bad as its Republican opponents claimed. Although Great Britain did not make any unnecessary concessions to America, the young nation did

---

54 Ibid.
55 *Virginia Gazette and Richmond Chronicle,* 3 Oct. 1794.
56 *Columbian Mirror,* 20 June, 1 Aug. 1795.
57 W. Wilson to Joseph Jones, Portsmouth, 14 Sept. 1795, Joseph Jones Papers.

derive some benefit from the few commercial privileges that the English granted her. The Treaty temporarily provided the peaceful climate between the two nations that was vital to American commercial expansion. Indeed, considering England's overwhelming commercial and military superiority over America, it is surprising that Jay accomplished as much as he did. Few people in America were blessed with the necessary foresight to appreciate the ultimate value of the Treaty, and as a consequence, it met a storm of criticism when it first appeared. The Treaty's failure to protect against the capture and impressment of Negro slaves and its acceptance of the highly restrictive "Rule of 1756," which stipulated that trade prohibited in time of peace could not be opened in time of war, overshadowed English concessions for the abandonment of the western garrisons and for the opening of certain of the West Indian Islands to American trade.[58]

The fight over the Treaty in Virginia was carried out on two fronts. In the counties, Republican and Federalist leaders called meetings either to denounce the repugnant articles of the Treaty and to castigate the "monocrats" who had perpetrated it or to defend the administration against the "gross calumnies" of the opposition. While these meetings had a marginal effect on the United States Senate's decision on whether or not to ratify the Treaty, they served to publicize the respective positions of each of the two parties. In the Virginia House of Delegates, the discussions were aimed at more constructive attempts to persuade Congress to reject the Treaty. By the time the text of the Treaty reached the House of Delegates the legislators realized that it could be defeated only by contesting its constitutionality, and they directed their efforts at this point.

During the late summer and early fall of 1795, both parties held meetings in counties throughout the state. In the early stages, nearly every meeting was dominated by those opposed to the Treaty.[59] The effectiveness of these opposition meetings

---

58 Bemis, *Jay's Treaty*, p. 270.

59 At this early stage, meetings were held to denounce the Treaty in Richmond,

varied according to the leadership available. When the organizers of the meeting were tied closely to the Republican leaders in Congress, the resolutions adopted were usually moderate in tone and reasoned in their criticism. In other counties, where knowledge of the issues was not so widespread and where the leaders of the opposition were not controlled by the moderate wing of the party, the result was often a set of resolutions that were marked by hysterical anglophobia and charges of conspiracy.

The citizens of Amelia County, unfettered by control from congressional Republicans, were not content with a mild statement of disapproval. As in the Genêt affair, they saw the whole negotiation as one more step in an anglo-monarchical conspiracy. They charged that the Treaty was "wholly calculated for the aggrandizement of Great Britain and . . . the extension of her commerce, to the destruction of American property, and eventually, her independence."[60] The message was similar in many counties throughout the state: a coalition of self-interested merchants and Englishmen seemed to be bent on destroying the natural alliance existing between Republican France and America, thus bringing about the destruction of American liberty.[61]

The Amelia County Resolutions were mild compared to those of Clarke County in Kentucky. The citizens there warned the president that "should he concur with the Senate in the signature of the Treaty, our prognostication is that

---

Petersburg, Norfolk, Mecklenburg, Lunenburg, Brunswick, Greensville, Amelia, Culpeper, and Caroline counties. *Virginia Gazette and General Advertiser*, 1, 8, 12, 15 Aug., 15 Sept. 1795; *Columbian Mirror*, 13 Aug. 1795; "Petition of the Citizens of Mecklenburg, Lunenburg, Brunswick, and Greensville Counties to the President . . . , 25 Aug. 1705, Petition of Culpeper County, 27 Aug. 1795, Washington Papers. Westmoreland County passed a resolution praising the surrender of the Western garrisons, but made no other mention of the Treaty. The few remaining pro-administration counties were content with an expression of confidence in the personal integrity of the president. Joseph Pierce to George Washington, 29 Sept. 1795, Washington Papers.

60 For the text of the Amelia Resolutions, and a sampling of Virginia opinion on the Treaty, see *The American Remembrancer; or an Important Collection of Essays, Resolves, and Speeches Relative, or Having Affinity to the Treaty with Great Britain*, 4 vols. (Philadelphia, 1795), 2: 43-45.

61 Ibid.

Western America is gone forever—lost to the union."[62] One Northern newspaper had even heard the rumor that "in case the Treaty entered into by that *d — d* Arch Traitor J..N J.y with the British tyrant should be ratified—a petition will be presented to the next General Assembly of Virginia at their next session, praying that the said state may secede from the union and be left under the government and protection of ONE HUNDRED THOUSAND FREE AND INDEPENDENT VIRGINIANS."[63]

Such talk was not confined to newspaper propagandists. Littleton Waller Tazewell, soon to become a member of the House of Delegates, remarked to his father Senator Henry Tazewell: "Do you seriously believe that . . . disunion would be an event injurious to the Southern Interests? For my part, I have considered . . . it is more to be apprehended than its affects ought to occasion—A country like the U.S., so extensive, so difft. in wealth, manners, temper and the real situation of its inhabitants, can not hope for the long continuance of Republican govt. . . . The friends of this form of govt. should rather desire than fear an event of this sort."[64] Even so respectable a man as Judge John Tyler was led to speculate in the same vein. He maintained: "Tempers, customs, manners and a thousand things more [should have] been well-weighed before union had taken place. Every circumstance of our life (both civil and political) prove how unfit the states were for such an union as ours."[65] President Washington was convinced that these were not isolated sentiments. As Tyler was speculating on the future of the union, Washington was warning United States Attorney General Edmund Randolph of the possibility of "a separation of the Union into Northern and Southern."[66]

More helpful to the Republican cause than threats of dis-

---

[62] *Lexington Kentucky Gazette,* 19 Sept. 1795, quoted in Thomas J. Farnham, "The Virginia Amendments of 1795: An Episode in the Opposition to Jay's Treaty," *Virginia Magazine of History and Biography* 75 (1967) : 81-82.

[63] *Hartford Connecticut Courant,* 31 Aug. 1795, in ibid.

[64] Littleton Waller Tazewell to Henry Tazewell, 3 Jan. 1797, Tazewell Family Papers.

[65] John Tyler to St. George Tucker, 10 July 1795, John Tyler Papers, LC.

[66] Farnham, "The Virginia Amendments of 1795," p. 82.

union were those county meetings planned and controlled by the moderate Republicans in Congress. The most important of these, both in the prestige of those who organized it and in the attention it attracted, was held in Richmond on July 29, 1795. The meeting owed much of its success to George Wythe, who agreed to serve as chairman. Wythe had been a key figure in the 1793 Richmond meeting defending the Proclamation of Neutrality, and his switch to the Republican camp was hailed as a great victory.[67] There was little that the Federalists could do in response. Except for one gathering in Westmoreland County, where the residents praised the surrender of the Western garrisons, there were no Federalist attempts during the summer and fall of 1795 to rally support for the Treaty. The Republicans were well aware of their advantage. Jefferson gleefully reported to Madison that none of the Federalists dared raise his voice in support of the administration.[68]

When Washington, on August 18, 1795, signed the Treaty into law, he put a temporary halt to the Republican opposition in the counties. The Virginia Republicans discovered that it was more difficult to rouse the citizenry once the Treaty had become an accomplished fact. John Guerrant, a leading Republican member of the House of Delegates, tried to organize a meeting in Goochland County, but was thwarted by the apathy of his constituents. He reported to Wilson Cary Nicholas, overseer for Madison and Jefferson of Republican interests at the local level, that the residents of Goochland would no longer protest the Treaty now that the president had assented to it.[69]

The Republicans obviously needed a new strategy. Consequently, they turned their efforts away from the counties to the floor of the state legislature. In late October 1795, one of

[67] *Virginia Gazette and General Advertiser,* 1 Aug. 1795.

[68] Joseph Pierce to Washington, 29 Sept. 1795, Washington Papers; Jefferson to Madison, 3 Aug. 1795, in Ford, ed., *Jefferson's Writings,* 7: 23.

[69] John Guerrant to Wilson Cary Nicholas, Goochland County, 11 Sept. 1795, Wilson Cary Nicholas Papers, LC; Jefferson to Madison, Philadelphia, 2 June 1795, in Ford, ed., *Jefferson's Writings,* 6: 278; Madison to Jefferson, Orange, 17 June 1795, in Hunt, ed., *Madison's Writings,* 6: 133.

Madison's informants in Virginia, Joseph Jones, outlined the plan of attack. He saw "no impropriety" in the General Assembly "declaring their opinion of the late Treaty, confining themselves to the truly exceptionable parts. With equal propriety may they propose an amendment in the Constitution to prevent a similar inconvenience in the future."[70] The plan was to reopen the debate on the Treaty, but this time on grounds of its constitutionality. If enough doubts were raised on that score, there was a chance that the Congress would be forced to reexamine it.[71]

Edward Carrington kept President Washington informed of the climate of opinion in his home state. A few days before the legislature convened, Carrington assured Washington that the "spirit of dissatisfaction" over the Treaty had abated and predicted that "a question put on this day for making the Treaty a subject of conversation would be negative."[72] Only a week later he was proved wrong. On a motion by Mann Page and Joseph Eggleston to approve the conduct of Senators Tazewell and Mason in voting against the Treaty, the subject came before the House of Delegates. The Federalists, led by Charles Lee, Robert Andrews, and John Marshall, immediately proposed a counterresolution stating that the Virginia legislature had no authority or reason to pass upon the action of the two senators. Their argument rested on the assumption that the state and federal governments were separate and distinct and that the state government therefore had no right to censure those acts which were properly in the sphere of the federal government.[73] With these proposals before the House, the

70 Joseph Jones to James Madison, 29 Oct. 1795, in *Massachusetts Historical Society Proceedings* 25 (1901-1902): 150-51.

71 Farnham, "The Virginia Amendments of 1795," pp. 83-88, argues that the Virginia legislature acted on the Treaty in order to persuade Congress to reopen discussion on it the following year. He attempts to refute the hypothesis of Stephen G. Kurtz, *The Presidency of John Adams: The Collapse of Federalism, 1795-1800* (New York, 1961), pp. 24-25, that the Republicans in the legislature were using the amendments to promote the candidacy of Thomas Jefferson for the presidency. It seems likely that both of these were factors.

72 Edward Carrington to Washington, 10 Nov. 1795, Washington Papers.

73 Joseph Jones to Madison, 22 Nov. 1795, Madison Papers.

merits of the Treaty were "warmly agitated three whole days."[74]

The debate began with another move by the Federalists to postpone discussion of the issue. The Federalists argued that any approval of the Virginia senators' conduct would amount to a censure of the president. Miles King, a Federalist from Elizabeth City, attempted to persuade the Republicans to drop their opposition to the Treaty by reminding them that the president "was incapable of acting against the true interests of his country." Washington's name was losing its magic, and the motion for postponement of the resolution was voted down, *viva voce*.[75]

The Republicans took the offensive. As expected, their opposition to the Treaty centered around its alleged unconstitutionality. The principal objection was that the Treaty dealt with many items that were connected with the commerce power, a power given to both Houses in Congress, not to the Senate alone. The Treaty also involved naturalization, the levying of imposts, and the expenditure of money—all the concern of the entire Congress.[76] Most galling was the Treaty's usurpation of the power of the United States judiciary. The assessment of debts was taken out of the hands of the United States courts and put under the control of a commission composed of both British and Americans, with a provision insuring that the Americans would never constitute a majority on the commission.[77]

The Federalists, outnumbered, did not even try to defend the Treaty on its merits. Instead, they used evasive action. John Marshall argued that the House of Delegates could not pass judgment upon the Treaty while the House of Representatives was debating its commercial provisions. He contended that it was more in the spirit of the Constitution for the House of Representatives to render the Treaty inoperative by refusing to appropriate the necessary funds for its implementation than

---

[74] Edmund Randolph to Jefferson, 22 Nov. 1795, in Ford, ed., *Jefferson's Writings*, 7: 197n.

[75] Jones to Madison, 22 Nov. 1795, Madison Papers.

[76] Beveridge, *Marshall*, 2: 133.   [77] Bemis, *Jay's Treaty*, p. 259.

it would be for a state government to denounce the Treaty before it had officially been put into operation.[78] In short, he was asking for a delay, hoping that the Federalists in the House of Representatives would have enough strength to silence the opposition.

Carrington was so impressed with Marshall's defense that he advised Washington that "on the point of constitutionality, many conversions were acknowledged."[79] But Carrington's judgment was once again overshadowed by his desire to please the president. The resolution denying the authority of the House of Delegates to pass judgment on the Treaty was defeated 52-98 and the resolution praising the Virginia senators for voting against the Treaty was passed, 100-50.[80]

The Federalists could take some small comfort from the fact that the legislatures of the other states did not follow Virginia's lead. Although the Virginia Delegates "supposed there was nothing unconstitutional in a state legislature speaking its opinion on any public measure," many states condemned the action as an attempt to "diminish the confidence of the people in the President."[81] Virginians, of course, did not share this view. The legislature, acting in its official capacity, had denounced the acts of the federal government since the Constitution had been ratified and it would continue to do so whenever the situation warranted.

The Republicans in the Virginia legislature were not content with a simple show of disapproval of the Treaty. The Committee of the Whole House on December 12, 1795, proposed four amendments to the United States Constitution. Although the amendments did not mention the Jay Treaty by name, their intent was obvious. The first would have made it necessary for both houses of Congress and not the Senate alone to approve any treaty affecting the commerce power. The next

[78] Edmund Randolph to Jefferson, 22 Nov. 1795, in Ford, ed., *Jefferson's Writings*, 7: 197n.

[79] Carrington to Washington, 20 Nov. 1795, Washington Papers.

[80] *House Journal*, 20 Nov. 1795.

[81] *Columbian Mirror*, 15 Feb. 1796; Jones to Madison, 17 Feb. 1796, Madison Papers.

two amendments were aimed at weakening the power of the Federalist-controlled Senate. They proposed that a tribunal other than the Senate be responsible for impeachments and that senators' terms be limited to three years. The fourth amendment would have prevented United States judges from holding other offices at the same time. This last was directed at John Jay, the most recent judge to hold another office while serving on the bench. The Federalists attempted to delay discussion of the amendments for a year, or until after the House of Representatives had acted on the Treaty, but they failed in their effort, 57-79. The resolution proposing the amendments was then passed, 88-32.[82]

At least one of the purposes of the amendments was to give Congress, and particularly the Republican-dominated House of Representatives, another chance to debate the merits of the Treaty. The stratagem was successful in that it helped persuade the members of the House of Representatives to demand that the president send the Treaty to the lower house for approval, but in doing so the Republican delegates suffered a setback with some of Virginia's most prominent citizens. Many Virginians remained dissatisfied with the Treaty, but they saw little merit in the Republican argument that it needed the approval of the House of Representatives before it could become law. They thought the House of Delegates had overstepped its bounds in challenging the legality of a federal law not in the sphere of the state government.

The most illustrious convert to this point of view was Patrick Henry. The staunch Antifederalist of 1788 was far from pleased with the actions of the federal government since that time, but he was even more upset with those Federalists of 1788 who were now controlling the Republican opposition in Congress. Henry thought that the Treaty was "a very bad one indeed," but he had no doubt about the right of the Senate to approve it. He had pointed to the dangers of the treaty-making power in the Virginia Ratifying Convention, and he probably took

[82] *House Journal,* 12 Dec. 1795.

satisfaction in seeing some of his old opponents trying to deny the existence of that power which they had been instrumental in creating. He did not like the treaty-making provision, but it was the law of the land; he could only see disorder and possible disunion if the Republicans continued their opposition on those grounds.[83]

The Republicans had also gone too far in their attacks on Washington and had inadvertently given the Virginia Federalists a cause for which they could fight with real conviction. It had even been reported that one Virginia Republican, after a county meeting denouncing the Jay Treaty, had proposed a toast to "a speedy death to General Washington."[84] The Federalists, although not fond of the Jay Treaty, were deeply concerned with this increasingly strident rhetoric of the Treaty's opponents. Reacting to Republican criticism of the president, the Federalists made one last attempt to rally support for the Treaty which he had so recently endorsed. As usual, the most important appeal to the people came in Richmond. The meeting, held in April 1796, succeeded in winning over many of the people who had opposed the Treaty in the 1795 meeting.[85] Again, the Federalist tactic was not to argue the merits of the Treaty itself, but to defend the constitutional right of the president and Senate to enact the Treaty. The address adopted by the gathering in Richmond was almost apologetic about past Federalist policy. It reviewed the events of the past year, admitting that the memorialists of 1795 were perfectly right in asking the president to withhold his signature from the Treaty on the grounds that it was injurious to American interests. Once the Treaty had been signed, however, it became a matter

83 Patrick Henry to his daughter, Red-hill, 20 Aug. 1796, William Wirt Henry Papers.

84 Fisher Ames to Christopher Gore, 10 Jan. 1795, in Ames, ed., *Works,* 1: 161-62.

85 Henry Banks, an organizer of the earlier meeting in Richmond, was one of those who changed his mind. "He observed on this occasion, that while the treaty was unratified, disliking some of its parts, he thought himself justifiable in opposing it, but after it had received all the constitutional sanctions of a law of the land, he conceived it to be a violation of the national faith to defeat its operation." *Columbian Mirror,* 30 April 1796.

of national honor to carry it into effect. Not to do so would "be productive of war; and what is worse—of dishonor."[86] The citizens of Richmond, like their counterparts in similar meetings in Frederick, Prince George, Fairfax, Loudon, King William, and Westmoreland counties and in the cities of Fredericksburg and Alexandria, also decried the slandering of the president during the whole controversy.[87]

The Richmond meeting of 1796 was the first such gathering where the organizers did not have complete control of the proceedings. Both Republicans and Federalists were given an opportunity to argue their case—a radical departure from the traditional one-sidedness of most county meetings. John Marshall spoke for the Federalists, and Arthur Campbell presented the Republican argument. There was considerable debate, and even disorder, over who should be allowed to cast a vote at the meeting. The Federalists, with the Republicans protesting vehemently, managed to push through a resolution allowing nonfreeholders to participate. No sooner had the Federalists succeeded in passing the pro-administration resolutions than the Republicans issued a minority report claiming that the operation of the Jay Treaty would cause the retention of the Western posts by the British, the resumption of Indian warfare, and a renewal of British depredations on the high seas.[88]

The historic significance of the Richmond meeting is to be found not in the pro-administration resolutions adopted, but rather in the structure of the meeting. For the first time, free-holders and nonfreeholders listened to both sides of an argument instead of being presented with a set of resolutions to approve. This was the first important attempt to conduct a political campaign squarely on the issues, and it would spread to other counties as the competition for support increased. There were few areas so politically aware as Richmond, though, and in most counties those who initiated the meetings remained

[86] Ibid., 3 May 1796.

[87] Ibid., 19 Jan., 23, 28, 30 April, 3, 10, 14 May 1796; *Virginia Gazette and General Advertiser*, 4 May 1796.

[88] Edmund Randolph to Madison, 25 April 1796, Madison Papers; *Virginia Gazette and General Advertiser*, 27 April 1796.

in full control from beginning to end. In the winter and spring of 1796 those in control were usually Federalists, since there were few attempts to oppose the Treaty once the president had signed it. The Republicans were unable to persuade the people to protest a measure that had already become the law of the land.

Unable to revive opposition in the counties, the Republicans made one last attempt to defeat the Treaty in Congress. When Federalists in the House of Representatives sought to secure the appropriations necessary to put the Treaty into effect, the Republicans tried a new tactic. They directed their arguments at the danger of unchecked executive authority, claiming that in signing the Treaty, the president had usurped the power of the House of Representatives.[89] Senator Henry Tazewell feared that ratification of the Treaty was a signal that "there may be yet something behind the curtain, that perhaps may authorize the President and Senate to convert our government into a monarchy and totally annihilate the state governments."[90] Few members of Congress shared that conspiratorial view, and the House of Representatives, by the slim margin of 51-48, agreed to appropriate the funds to put the Treaty into operation. In spite of the strong Federalist showing in the county meetings, the Virginia delegation to Congress was not swayed in its determination to block the Treaty. All Virginia's congressmen, with the sole exception of George Hancock, a Federalist from Hanover County in Eastern Virginia, refused to vote for the necessary appropriations.[91]

Nothing more could be done to block the Jay Treaty, so Republicans in the state legislature vented their anger on the man who had signed it into law. Prior to the close of the 1796 session, after Washington had announced his decision to step down from the presidency, the Virginia General Assembly decided to draft an address to present to him upon his retire-

---

[89] Samuel Shield to Henry Tazewell, York County, 20 March 1796, Tazewell Papers; Francis Preston to Thomas Madison, Philadelphia, 16 April 1796, Preston Papers.

[90] Henry Tazewell to John Ambler, 4 April 1796, Tazewell Papers.

[91] *Annals of Congress,* 5: 1291.

ment. Two separate addresses were drawn up and presented to the House for approval. The address proposed by the Federalists was a long and laudatory document praising the President for his wisdom and for his attempts to "check the destructive contest of party spirit." It was defeated, 70-76. The next day the Republicans proposed a new address, much shorter and less complimentary. The Federalists then attempted to amend the Republican version by adding a sentence praising his administration as one "marked by wisdom in the Cabinet, by valor in the field, and by the purest patriotism in both."[92] This move, according to John Marshall, provoked a debate in which "the whole course of the Administration was reviewed, and the whole talent of each party brought into action."[93] The Washington administration evidently came out on the short end of the debate, as the Federalist amendment was defeated, 67-75, and the Republican address passed, *viva voce*.[94]

The tone of the second address differed so strikingly from that proposed by the Federalists that it could only reflect the decline of Washington's popularity in his home state. Federalists and Federalist-inspired measures were never popular in predominantly Republican Virginia, but the figure of George Washington had always served to blunt the force of the opposition. By 1796, in his final days in office, Washington's stature at home had so diminished that he was unable to obtain a full vote of confidence for himself, let alone for the measures of his administration.

The voting behavior of the members of the House of Delegates further indicates the extent of dissatisfaction with the policies of the general government. Of the sixty-one delegates serving all three terms during 1794-1796, thirty-seven voted with the Republican interest with a consistency of 75 percent or greater, seventeen voted with the Federalists, and only seven were unaligned. There was no pattern of economic or

---

92 *House Journal*, 9, 10 Dec. 1796.

93 John Marshall to Joseph Story, n.d., in John F. Dillon, *John Marshall: Life, Character and Judicial Services*, 3 vols. (New York, 1903), 3: 355.

94 *House Journal*, 10 Dec. 1796.

regional interests which can wholly explain this division. Both factions were dominated by planters, most of them at least moderately wealthy, and nearly all of them slaveowners.[95]

Some regional voting patterns on national issues are discernible, but these are not sufficiently pronounced to permit any broad generalizations about the determinants of voting behavior throughout the state as a whole. On the November 20, 1795 vote affirming Virginia's opposition to the Jay Treaty the delegates from the northwest and the Eastern Shore voted predominately Federalist while those from the southern and central Piedmont areas voted overwhelmingly Republican. Voting patterns in other regions of the state, however, were considerably more mixed, with the Republicans nevertheless commanding majorities. Comparing the geographic divisions over the Jay Treaty to those occurring over the issues involving ratification of the federal Constitution and Hamilton's financial policies, one finds that the northwest remained consistently Federalist and that the southern and central Piedmont for the most part remained opposed to Federalist proposals. And perhaps most significant, the residents of the Tidewater seem to be moving out of the Federalist camp and into the Republican[96] (see maps on pages 244, 245, and 247).

95 The divisions listed in the second part of Appendix 2 are based on an analysis of the voting behavior, on national issues, of the sixty-one men who served in the House of Delegates every year between 1794-1796. A rate of 75 percent agreement was set as the minimum requirement for inclusion within either voting bloc. The larger sample of national issues during these years permitted the rate to be lowered from the 80 percent requirement used to calculate the Federalist-Antifederalist blocs.

The Republican preponderance in the United States House of Representatives was even greater than that in the Virginia lower house. By 1796 all Virginia's delegates to the House of Representatives voted more often with the Republicans than with the Federalists. In fact, all but three of the nineteen representatives from Virginia voted with the Republicans with a frequency of at least 80 percent. The three men who did not—George Hancock, John Heath, and Robert Rutherford—seem simply to be more independent than Federalist in their inclinations. They represented three entirely different regions within Virginia and do not seem, at least at this time, to have been closely attached to either of the two parties. A detailed analysis of congressional voting behavior during this period can be found in Manning Dauer, *The Adams Federalists* (Baltimore, Md., 1953), p. 292.

96 *House Journal*, 20 Nov. 1795. I have selected the vote on the Jay Treaty as the basis for this analysis because it seems to be the one that was most crucial in

Factional alignments, however, were shaped not so much by strict economic or regional interests as by the emotional attitudes of the members of Virginia's ruling elite. Although Federalist foreign policy, and particularly the Jay Treaty, provided the focus for the Republicans' attack against the general government, the sources of antagonism to federal policy ranged far beyond the immediate issue of Anglo-American relations. The Republican attitude was a direct continuum of Antifederalism, and all the Antifederalists' fears about "consolidated government" were aroused once again during the debate over the Jay Treaty. Their antipathy toward Great Britain and of what they believed to be the corrupt British system of government, their distrust of any extension of central authority, particularly executive authority, and their determination to defend the agrarian way of life against the machinations of the mercantile community of the North—all these emotions became entangled with the more complicated problem of the proper conduct of American foreign policy. Moderate leaders in the Republican party tried to tone down some of these sentiments, but they were for the most part unsuccessful. In the end, they too relied on Antifederalist rhetoric to condemn the Federalist administration.

The federal government was doing exactly what the Antifederalists had warned against. With its excessive power it was moving toward a consolidation of the states and pursuing policies whose design was to aid the commercial North at the expense of the agrarian South. Hamilton's financial programs were the first signs of this trend, but by 1793 the term consolidation began to take on a broader and more dangerous meaning. It was now not only the North which was profiting at Virginia's expense but also the British nation. When the Jay Treaty appeared, Virginia Republicans viewed it as another example of the treasonous collaboration between the commer-

---

determining a delegate's position on a whole range of foreign policy issues during the period under discussion. Similar analyses of the vote can be consulted in Risjord, "The Virginia Federalists," pp. 495, 502, and Hall, "A Quantitative Approach to . . . Virginia, 1790-1810."

cial North and England. The Treaty's many concessions to Great Britain only served to strengthen their conviction that the "monocrats" of both nations were trying to "draw over us the substance as they have already done the forms of the British Government."[97] The fact that the names of Alexander Hamilton and John Jay were those most closely associated with the Treaty seemed to many to be conclusive evidence that this was the case.

The Republicans were hypocritical in attacking the aristocratic leanings of the Federalist administration. What they objected to was not the hostility of Alexander Hamilton or John Jay to democratic government, but rather, the Federalists' British sympathies. It could not have been otherwise, for Virginia's Republican leaders showed no greater love for democratic procedure than did the Federalists. When the results of the Richmond meeting of 1796 were revealed, the Republicans were the ones to complain that the Federalists had packed the meeting with propertyless supporters and to denounce those without a "shadow of a freehold." The party of Jefferson and Madison was not made up of democrats, but rather of wealthy lawyers, planters, and merchants who wanted to preserve local control over their own affairs.

The philosophy of agrarian Republicanism constituted one of that party's greatest obstacles to effective organization, particularly at the state level. Virginia Republicans were more anti-Hamilton, anti-Treaty, and anti-British than they were pro-Republican. In Congress, Virginia Republicans at least attempted to block Federalist proposals and to formulate alternatives. Yet on the state level, they were strictly an *ex post facto* organization whose task was to alert the people after the danger was already present. Republican sentiment would lay dormant until the Federalists in Congress committed some new act to rouse them. The citizens in the counties were often uninformed of the day-to-day contests in the nation's capital. Jefferson, in temporary retirement at Monticello, wrote in

[97] Thomas Jefferson to Phillip Mazzei, 24 April 1796, in Ford, ed., *Jefferson's Writings*, 7: 75.

exasperation at the apathy of his fellow citizens: "I could not have supposed, when at Philadelphia, that so little of what was passed there could be known even at Kentucky, as is the case here. Judging from the rest of the Union, it is evident to me that the people are not in a condition either to approve or disapprove of their government, nor consequently influence it."[98]

The behavior of Virginia's voters bears out Jefferson's assessment. Despite the introduction of foreign affairs into the debate between Republicans and Federalists, few Virginia voters bothered to exercise their option, and of those that did, only a small number showed any awareness of the divisions developing in the nation's capital. They continued to elect the same candidates to office regardless of party loyalties. In those counties for which there are complete records of the elections for Congress and the state legislature, voter turnout remained abysmally low, averaging roughly 25 percent of the eligible voters and occasionally dipping below 15 percent. Most representatives to Congress and the House of Delegates were elected by overwhelming majorities and in many cases, ran without opposition.[99] Since the Virginia Republicans were able to maintain such strength in their congressional delegation and in the state legislature, and therefore could always be sure of a majority of votes on any critical issue, they saw no reason to change from their traditional, elitest style of campaigning to the newer, partisan methods that were being used in other states. While John Beckley was making frantic efforts to get the names of every pro-Republican voter in Pennsylvania and to organize them into a smoothly running party machine, the Virginia Republicans continued to rely on personal prestige and convivial entertainments.[100]

[98] Jefferson to Madison, 15 Feb. 1794, Madison Papers.

[99] For figures on voter participation compare Greene and Harrington, *American Population*, pp. 154-55, with the poll lists for 25 March 1795, 27 April 1795, and 23 April 1796, in Brunswick Election Records, VSL; poll lists for 18 March 1793, 30 April 1793, 29 April 1794, in Westmoreland County Records and Inventories, Vol. 7, VSL; and poll lists for 18 April 1796, 23 April 1796, in Essex County Deed Book, no. 34, VSL.

[100] Cunningham, *The Jeffersonian Republicans, 1789-1801*, pp. 102-6.

The Federalists, although always in a decided minority in the legislature and rarely elected to Congress, nevertheless profited from the continuation of the old style of Virginia politics. The Republicans, true to a tradition which judged people on their prestige and their record of public service, allowed prominent Federalists to continue to occupy important positions within the state government. The speakership of the Virginia lower house was occupied by a Federalist every year from the ratification of the federal Constitution until 1799, when the Republicans in Congress, led by James Madison, imposed rigid party discipline and purged most Federalists from positions of power. Federalist Henry Lee was governor of Virginia from 1792 until November 1794, when the Republicans in the legislature expressed their dissatisfaction with Lee's role in quashing the Whisky Rebellion by removing him from office. Partisan feelings cooled, and James Wood, a political neutral, served as chief executive from 1797 to 1799.[101]

The Republicans probably would not have been willing to allow the Federalists to maintain their power in state affairs had their opponents been Federalists in the Hamiltonian sense. For the most part, the supporters of government in Virginia were Federalists in name only. The vast majority of them opposed funding and assumption and only undertook to defend those policies on the grounds of their constitutionality. Similarly, they did not like the Jay Treaty, but defended the constitutional right of the administration to enter into it. They were not opposed to the policies of Jefferson and Madison nearly so much as they were to the excesses of their partisans in the counties.[102] This attitude was both the Federalists' greatest strength and their greatest weakness. On the one hand, their moderation obscured the differences between themselves and the Republicans on the state level and enabled them to be elected to important statewide offices. On the other hand, when important national issues did come up, they rarely could

---

101 Swem and Williams, *Register of the General Assembly*, pp. 41-50; *House Journal*, 2 Dec. 1799.

102 Thomas Evans to John Cropper, 6 Dec. 1796, John Cropper Papers.

defend them with conviction. The only success the Federalists enjoyed was their defense of the Proclamation of Neutrality. Not coincidentally, this was the only administration policy which they in good conscience could endorse without reservation.

Why, if Virginia's Federalists were so lukewarm in their attachment to the policies of the administration, did they remain Federalists? They had no love for the British, they distrusted the North, and had precisely the same interests as their Republican neighbors. Nor does it seem that a faith in national rather than local control was a central part of Federalist ideology. John Marshall was virtually the only Virginia Federalist who could see beyond the immediate issues and view the struggle as one of national versus local, parochial interests; most of his Federalist colleagues in Virginia were as anxious as the Republicans to maintain the locally based power that they had so long held. The only beliefs that Virginia's Federalists seemed to share was their abiding faith in the ability and integrity of President Washington and their fear of disorder should the effects of party spirit go unchecked. As overzealous Republican orators continued to criticize Washington in county meetings, the Federalists were pushed into a defense of administration policies.[103] While their concern for Washington's reputation may have often been only a tactic to disarm their opponents, the tone of outrage running through nearly all the Federalists' responses to the Republican attacks indicated their concern for more than the reputation of one man. They were beginning to believe that the whole direction of Republican criticism would ultimately lead to civil war and disunion. They envisioned America's experiment in liberty degenerating in the same fashion as that of revolutionary France. When Federalists described their opponents as "jacobinical," they were not merely using a popular epithet; they were drawing an explicit parallel between the dangerous factionalism and violent mobism attending the French Revolution and the current

[103] *Virginia Gazette and General Advertiser,* 24 Jan. 1796. See also *Columbian Mirror,* 23, 28, 30 April, 3, 10, 14 May 1796.

opposition of the Republican party to the federal government.[104]

Patrick Henry admitted that this fear of disorder was the decisive factor in his decision not to aid the Republican party. In October 1795 he informed Washington: "I have bid adieu to the distinction of federal and anti-federal ever since the commencement of the present government, and in the circle of my friends have often expressed my fears of disunion amongst the states from collision of interests, but especially from the baneful effects of faction."[105] Henry's fear of disunion was based on his knowledge of the sectional differences within the nation. He too was suspicious of the power of Northern commercial interests and saw that entrance into the union, far from lessening those tensions, had only exacerbated them. His fear of the "baneful effects of faction," more pronounced every day, caused him to view the Federalist administration with some sympathy.

Neither order nor a quieting of party spirit was in the offing. Divisive issues would appear more frequently, party lines would harden, and the leaders of both the Federalist and Republican factions, unwillingly, would begin steps to include the mass of Virginia's citizenry in their expanded party organizations. The Federalists, soon to be deprived of the services of George Washington, would find it even more difficult to remain a force in Virginia politics.

104 See, for example, the writings of "Bradford" and of "A Friend to the Present Administration of Government," in the *Columbian Mirror,* 1 Oct., 1 Nov. 1796.

105 Patrick Henry to George Washington, 16 Oct. 1795, in William Wirt Henry, *Patrick Henry,* 2: 558.

CHAPTER SIX

Federal Policy and Foreign Affairs: II

THE INTENSE DEBATE over the Jay Treaty and the impending retirement of President Washington combined to make the 1796 presidential election the most bitterly contested in the nation's brief history. For the Republicans, it was a matter of reversing the dangerous trends toward consolidation and alliance with Great Britain; for the Federalists, it was a means of vindicating Washington and putting a halt to the attempts by the opposition to bring about anarchy and disunion.

In Virginia, preparations for the election began much earlier than usual. As early as May 1796, four months before Washington had officially announced his intention to retire, William Munford, author of *The Candidates,* announced his own candidacy for presidential elector. Munford noted: "A suggestion has generally gone forth that the President who now fills the chair intends to decline the office. If this should be the case, every true Republican must wish that the virtuous and philosophic Jefferson may succeed him. I candidly avow my resolution, if I am honored by the suffrages of my Countrymen, to give my voice in his favour, provided Washington declares in a solemn manner that he will not accept the place."[1] Munford took great pains to assure the voters that his loyalty would always be to Washington, and when Republican leaders in Congress picked their candidate they followed the same tack. They had lost considerable support during the controversy over the Jay

Treaty because of the attacks made on Washington by some of their more intemperate followers. Consequently, nearly all Republican candidates for elector stated that they would support Jefferson only if Washington decided not to seek a third term; privately they were confident Washington would retire.[2]

Only a few weeks after Munford's announcement, Republican congressmen informally agreed to back Jefferson for the presidency. A caucus, probably the first of its kind in American politics, was held in Philadelphia to choose a vice presidential nominee, but it broke up before any choice was made. Nevertheless, when Congress adjourned in June 1796, Jefferson had become the official candidate of the Republican party and it was recognized that the Republican members of Congress would be entrusted with primary responsibility for promoting his candidacy in their respective states.[3]

The Republican congressmen met varying success in organizing campaigns within their home states. In Pennsylvania, where presidential electors ran on a single statewide ticket, it was relatively easy to build a unified party organization.[4] In Virginia, where each elector was chosen in a separate district, it was more difficult to control the campaign. In all states, the Republicans were handicapped because they could not start their campaigns in earnest until Washington had announced his retirement. And the Federalist candidates used this delay to every possible advantage. They continued to act as if Washington would be their candidate, refused to disclose their second choice should the chief executive decline to seek reelection, and pretended to view Republican speculation about Washington's retirement as disloyal.

When Washington's Farewell Address was published on September 19, 1796, it was, as Fisher Ames described it, "a signal, like dropping a hat, for the party racers to start."[5] Virginia Republicans unanimously supported Jefferson: their

---

[1] William Munford to Joseph Jones, 18 May 1796, Joseph Jones Papers.

[2] Cunningham, *The Jeffersonian Republicans, 1789-1801*, pp. 89-91,

[3] Ibid., p. 91.   [4] Ibid., pp. 98-115.

[5] Fisher Ames to Oliver Wolcott, 26 Sept. 1796, quoted in Cunningham, *The Jeffersonian Republicans, 1789-1801*, p. 93.

principal problem was coordinating the campaigns in the Old Dominion's twenty-one separate electoral districts. The Federalists faced more difficult obstacles. They knew that John Adams was not likely to win any popularity contests in Virginia and were themselves not overly sympathetic with his political views. They could not dispel the notion, contained in Adams's writings, that the testy New Englander was a partisan of the monarchical government of Great Britain.

The Virginia Federalists, to avoid the burden of campaigning for a man they did not like, attempted to lure Patrick Henry out of retirement. Whether they thought he had a chance of winning the presidency or were merely using him to draw enough votes away from Jefferson in Virginia to assure Adams's victory is not clear, but their alliance with the old Antifederalist was not built on cynicism alone. When members of the Federalist administration in Philadelphia heard of Henry's disenchantment with the tactics of the Republican opposition, they offered him his choice of a position as minister to Spain, chief justice of the United States, or secretary of state. Although he had declined all three offers, Henry assured Washington that he was no longer a foe of the federal government.[6] Whatever the drawbacks to Henry's candidacy, not least of which was the uncertainty of his acceptance, the Federalists desperately needed a candidate who could rally support. And Henry could certainly do that. His personal popularity in Virginia was far greater than that of Jefferson, Madison, or any other candidate the Republicans had to offer. Henry, not Jefferson, was regarded as the patron saint of the Revolution in Virginia. His fellow citizens continued to honor him during the two decades after the Revolution by offering him every statewide office imaginable, including the governorship and a seat in the United States Senate, even though they were virtually certain that he would decline them.[7]

---

[6] Edmund Randolph to P. Henry, Philadelphia, 28 Aug. 1794, William Wirt Henry Papers, VHS; George Washington to Patrick Henry, Mt. Vernon, 9 Oct. 1795, Henry Lee to Washington, 26 Dec. 1795, in Fitzpatrick, ed., *Washington's Writings*, 34: 334-35, 421.

[7] William Wirt Henry, *Patrick Henry*, 2: 553.

The Federalists contended that Henry would "unite all parties and do away with that spirit of contention which at present rages with so much violence amongst us and threatens the destruction of the Union." While recalling Henry's heroism during the Revolution, they leveled their most serious charge against Jefferson, one from which he could never completely escape: cowardice during the American Revolution. They disclosed details of his midnight retreat from the capital at Richmond in 1781 in the face of a British invasion and hinted that Jefferson's resignation as secretary of state after the Genêt Affair stemmed from the same lack of fortitude. The Federalists argued that both actions "shew him to want a firmness; and a man who shall once have abandoned his helm in the hour of danger, or at the appearance of a tempest, seems not to be trusted in better times, for no one can know how soon or from whence a storm may come."[8] Nor did the Federalists fail to exploit Jefferson's other political liabilities. They noted his deism, warning the voters against casting a ballot in favor of a man "whose Christian principles are much in question."[9] Jefferson's attachment to France and his role as the philosophical leader of the opposition party also left him open to criticism. The Federalists predicted that if Jefferson were elected, "government itself may be destroyed and give place to sweet chaos and confusion." They claimed that soon after Jefferson took office taxes would be abolished, the arbitrary rules of the democratic societies would become the law of the land, and debts would be forfeited.[10]

The Republicans were not particularly bothered by the charges that Jefferson was an atheist and an anarchist—Federalists had been trying unsuccessfully to capitalize on those for years—but the personal attacks on Jefferson's courage during the Revolution necessitated a careful reply. Jefferson remained aloof from the controversy, but Daniel Brent, a Republican

8 *Columbian Mirror,* 8, 29 Sept. 1796; *Virginia Gazette and General Advertiser,* 8 Sept., 12 Oct. 1796.
9 *Virginia Gazette and General Advertiser,* 12 Oct. 1796.
10 *Columbian Mirror,* 1 Oct. 1796.

elector in the midst of a close race with his Federalist opponent in Alexandria, undertook to disprove the accusation by making public a resolution of the 1782 session of the General Assembly exonerating Jefferson from the charge of cowardice. In a speech to his constituents, Brent admitted that Jefferson had dropped in popularity after the incident and had been forced to resign his office as governor, but he noted that the public later realized its error in judgment and within a year had fully endorsed the Assembly's resolution. In answer to the charge that Jefferson had also resigned as secretary of state under fire, Brent pointed out that Jefferson had decided to retire a full year before the Genêt Affair and that the effective date of his retirement just happened to fall at a time when he was in disfavor.[11]

Jefferson, for all his liabilities, was at least reasonably popular in his home state. And as it became obvious that Henry would not agree to become a candidate, the Federalists were unable to find anyone with even that advantage working for them. They were forced to back John Adams, but did so as unobtrusively as possible. Charles Simms, the Federalist candidate who initiated the charges against Jefferson for his conduct during the Revolution, stoutly maintained that Henry was his first choice; when pressed about Henry's unwillingness to run, he grudgingly admitted that he would vote for Adams if necessary, but continually tried to evade the subject by renewing his attacks on Jefferson.[12] Levin Powell, candidate for elector in Loudon and Fauquier counties, would not even go that far in defense of Adams. He continued to list Henry as his first choice, adding that if Henry refused to run he would vote for either Adams or Jefferson.[13]

As the election drew near, the Federalists found it impossible to maintain the fiction of Henry's candidacy. Both Charles Simms and Levin Powell, the only two Federalist electors in the state who had any chance, were forced to defend Adams

11 "Address to the Freeholders of Prince William, Stafford and Fairfax Counties," ibid., 18 Oct. 1796.
12 Ibid., 29 Sept. 1796.
13 Ibid., 1 Oct. 1796; *Virginia Gazette and General Advertiser,* 12 Oct. 1796.

against the accusations that he was a partisan of monarchy and an enemy of Southern interests. Republicans maintained that Adams's *Defense of the Constitutions of . . . the United States* was irrefutable proof that the New Englander had aristocratic leanings. The Federalists tried to explain that Adams, in his *Defense,* was making a subtle distinction between the kind of government that would be best for the people of corrupt, European nations and that which was best for virtuous America, but Adams's political philosophy was consistently misinterpreted by his Republican opponents, who insisted that he preferred the monarchical forms of Europe to the republican features of the American government.[14]

More damning was the publicity given to a conversation between Adams and John Taylor of Caroline on the floor of the Senate in 1794. According to Taylor, there was some disagreement between the senators on whether a democratic government could survive in France:

> Mr. Adams urged the ignorance, vices and corruptions of Europe, to prove that such a government could not exist there. Upon its being observed, that same argument he used would extend to America, after admitting, that the greater degree of virtue existing here, from the circumstance of our being a young country, would have a temporary effect, and enable us to go on some time longer as a popular government, he subjoined "that he expected or wished to live to hear Mr. Giles & Myself acknowledge, that no government could long exist, or that no people could be happy, without an hereditary first magistrate, and an hereditary senate, or a senate for life."[15]

Adams was not advocating a monarchy for the United States, but was merely ruminating on the possible results of the declining virtue of the American people. The people of Virginia could not be expected to make that fine distinction and Jeffer-

14 Criticisms of Adams's "monarchical" prejudices appeared almost daily. See, for example, *Virginia Gazette and General Advertiser,* 12, 26 Oct., 2 Nov. 1796; and *Columbian Mirror,* 18, 25 Oct. 1796.

15 John Taylor to Daniel C. Brent, Caroline, 9 Oct. 1796, in *John P. Branch Historical Papers of Randolph-Macon College,* 2 (1908): 267.

son's supporters did everything in their power to see that they did not. As a result, Adams was forever accused of being a "monocrat."

This was not John Adams's only handicap. As one of Jefferson's partisans noted, "Mr. Jefferson is a Virginian. The eastern people will vote for Mr. Adams. . . . The Southern people . . . ought to do the same for Mr. Jefferson. The local interests of the two parts of the union are known to be different, and as it is natural for every man to respect his own in preference to those of others, so I think that the electors of Virginia ought to vote for Mr. Jefferson."[16] Virginia Republicans predicted that the South would lose the Potomac as the site of the capital if Adams were elected. There had already been too many signs that the Northern states were planning to renege on the agreement of the location of the capital, but Jefferson's election, they claimed, would put an end to any plans to change the site.[17]

It was difficult for Virginia Federalists to find any quality in their candidate that would offset those disadvantages. The recurring theme in their defense of Adams was that he had been in agreement with President Washington while vice president and it was incumbent upon Virginians to uphold Washington's policies.[18]

This last argument was not persuasive, for the election in Virginia was a disaster for the Federalists. In only one district, which included Loudon and Fauquier counties, was an Adams elector victorious. And much of Adams's success there was due not to his own popularity, but to the campaign that the Federalist elector Levin Powell conducted against Jefferson's record as a war governor. The only other area where a Federalist candidate came even close was in neighboring Alexandria, where Charles Simms was narrowly defeated by his Republican opponent, Daniel Brent. Even the counties in northwest Virginia, whose representatives to the state legislature seemed to

[16] *Virginia Gazette and Central Advertiser,* 26 Oct. 1796.
[17] *Columbian Mirror,* 20 Sept. 1796.
[18] Ibid., 20, 27 Oct., 1 Nov. 1796.

be leaning toward Federalism, chose Republican electors.[19]

Thomas Griffin of York County and Ralph Wormley of Middlesex, two Federalist candidates for elector, simply refused to declare a preference for either Jefferson or Adams in hopes that a nonpartisan appearance would obscure their Federalist attachments. The voters were unimpressed by this approach, however, and the two men were defeated along with the other Federalist candidates for elector in the state.[20] It would appear that the failure of the nonpartisan approach used by Griffin and Wormley signified that Virginia's voters were becoming more aware of the new party alignments in the nation's capital and less inclined to follow traditional, deferential voting patterns. This is to some extent true, but the importance of the Republican and Federalist party labels in the presidential campaign of 1796 should not be overestimated. For example, Wormley, the thinly disguised Federalist candidate from Middlesex County, would have had a difficult time gaining election had Jefferson himself campaigned for him. Except for his immense wealth, Wormley had little working in his favor. In addition to being a partisan of Adams, he was suspected of toryism during the Revolution and had suffered a long string of defeats in elections for local office during the past decade. His opponent, Benjamin Temple, had beaten him in previous contests where the Republican and Federalist labels were not a factor and there is little doubt that his victory over Wormely in 1796 was a continuation of this preeminence.[21]

Similarly, Thomas Griffin could hardly blame his defeat in the electoral districts encompassing Henrico, Charles City, New Kent, and York counties on a smoothly running Republican party machine. The Republicans in those counties were either so confident, or so ill organized, that they allowed two Jeffer-

19 Ibid., 12 Nov. 1796. Unfortunately, it is impossible to make further generalizations about voting patterns in the 1796 election in Virginia. Since electors were chosen by the voters of individual electoral districts, no one felt it necessary to collect the vote totals for the state as a whole. As a result, only scattered returns for a few counties have survived.

20 Ibid.; *Virginia Gazette and General Advertiser*, 12, 19 Oct., 7 Dec. 1796.

21 Main, "The One Hundred," pp. 363-83.

sonian candidates to enter the race, thus running the risk of splitting the pro-Jefferson vote and permitting Griffin to gain a plurality. One Jeffersonian candidate, Nathaniel Wilkinson, was a former Antifederalist who was now loyal to the Madisonian wing of the Republican party; the other, John Mayo, was a Federalist who nevertheless preferred Jefferson to Adams.[22] Wilkinson narrowly triumphed, with Mayo finishing a close second and Griffin a poor third. Voter turnout was no higher than in most elections for local offices. In Charles City County it was 25 percent of the free adult white males, in New Kent County 20 percent, and in Henrico only 18 percent.[23]

The inability of the Republicans to persuade many pro-Jefferson voters in the district to cast their ballots for Wilkinson rather than the Federalist Mayo offers further evidence of the weak state of their party organization. Nor does it appear that Mayo's support of Jefferson was merely a Federalist ploy to draw votes away from Wilkinson. Everyone, including Wilkinson's supporters, was convinced of Mayo's sincerity in supporting Jefferson. That Mayo chose to stand for election as a Jeffersonian elector is itself indicative of the principal reason why the presidential campaign of 1796 in Virginia was not conducted solely in terms of Republicans versus Federalists. It was, above all, a contest between Thomas Jefferson, a popular Virginian, and John Adams, a crotchety New Englander. It cannot be ascertained just how many Federalists deserted their party to vote for the Republican candidate, but Thomas Evans, a loyal Federalist from Accomac County, made it clear that a Virginia-born Republican president would not be viewed as a catastrophe. He predicted that if Jefferson were elected in 1796 "he will support the measures which have been pursued, and will soon be obnoxious to those violent partisans who are willing to go any lengths in his favor, whilst his administra-

22 For Wilkinson's and Mayo's party affiliation see the *Virginia Gazette and General Advertiser*, 9, 12, 19 Oct. 1796.

23 The election returns for Charles City, New Kent, and Henrico counties are printed in the *Virginia Gazette and General Advertiser*, 9 Nov. 1796. The results in Richmond and York counties, which also fell within the bounds of the electoral district, are not extant.

tion may probably be supported by those who seem now unfriendly."[24] Those were hardly sentiments that could be expected from the Hamiltonian wing of the Federalist party, but Virginia's Federalists were never enthusiastic for the nationalistic programs of the New York lawyer and financier. In spite of Jefferson's sympathy for France and his opposition to Washington's policies, he was after all a Virginian; he would surely look after the interests of the Old Dominion.

Not until December 1796 did Virginians hear the results of the presidential election in their home state; it was another month yet until they heard of Adams's victory throughout the nation as a whole.[25] The Virginia Republicans accepted the news of Jefferson's defeat with surprising equanimity, at least in part because the months between the election and the inauguration in March 1797 were ones of conscious and well-publicized conciliation between the leaders of the opposing parties. Adams, increasingly alienated from Hamilton's wing of the party, proved willing to cooperate with Jefferson and other moderates in the Republican party. Jefferson was content to play along, since he earnestly desired an untroubled term as vice president. Even the Federalist and Republican newspapers did their part. They stressed the differences between Hamilton and Adams and publicized the cordial relations between the new president and vice president.[26]

Unfortunately, the foreign powers of Europe were at the same time taking steps to destroy this sudden harmony. The French Directory, on March 2, 1797, announced that it would treat all American seamen serving on British ships as pirates and would henceforward confiscate goods on neutral ships laden in whole or in part with enemy goods. This was in contradiction to the "free ships free goods" provision of the

24 Thomas Evans to John Cropper, 6 Dec. 1796, John Cropper Papers.

25 *Virginia Gazette and General Advertiser,* 7 Dec. 1796; Jefferson to Edward Rutledge, 27 Dec. 1796, in Ford, ed., *Jefferson's Writings,* 7: 93-94.

26 For the best account of Hamilton's attempts to dump Adams in favor of the more pliant Thomas Pinckney and of the brief reconciliation between the moderate Republicans and Federalists, see Kurtz, *The Presidency of John Adams,* pp. 209-38.

Franco-American Treaty of 1778 and was even more strict in its application than the much-hated British "Rule of 1756." At the same time, the Directory refused to receive American Minister Charles Cotesworth Pinckney, presumably in retaliation for the recall of the previous American minister, James Monroe, who was considered by the Federalist administration to be too attached to the French cause to carry out his job effectively.[27] President Adams informed Congress of the new French directives and recommended a series of steps to be taken should France attempt to interfere with American commerce. He proposed that a navy be created, that coastal defenses be strengthened, and that a provisional army be raised in case France attempted a land invasion.[28] The ensuing reaction both in Congress and in Virginia brought an end to any hope of reconciliation between Republicans and Federalists.

Most Virginia Republicans blamed the sudden hostility of the French on the errors of the previous Federalist administration. In a Republican-sponsored meeting in Richmond in April 1797, they admitted that the French had become an "annoyance to our commerce," but claimed that the Federalists' pro-British policies, and particularly the Jay Treaty, had forced France to protect herself. Republicans present at the meeting reaffirmed their confidence in France as America's only republican ally and vowed to maintain their friendship toward the French people.[29] The Virginia Federalists were not so impressed with France's republican principles. The incursions of the French, following similar action by the British, convinced them that it was imperative to remain free from any connection with the European powers. They saw the need for a stand against future French aggression and thus supported Adams in his attempt to strengthen American defenses, but were not in favor of a precipitous war with any of the European nations.[30]

---

27 Samuel Flagg Bemis, *A Diplomatic History of the United States*, 4th ed. (New York, 1955), p. 114.

28 *Annals of Congress*, 7: 54-59.

29 An account of the meeting is in the *Columbian Mirror*, 22 April 1797.

30 See, for example, the argument of "A Friend to Peace," in the *Virginia Gazette and General Advertiser*, 12 April 1797.

The radical, pro-French wing of the Republican party was in the ascendant. John Marshall noted "the insidious attempt which is made to ascribe the aggressions made on us by France to the British Treaty" and lamented that the Republican "party has laid such fast hold on the public mind in this part of Virginia that an attempt to oppose [French influence] sinks at once the person who makes it. The elections for the state legislature go entirely against the federalists, who are madly and foolishly as well as wickedly styl'd a british party."[31] Marshall's diagnosis of the political climate in Virginia was correct. The Republicans had become so committed to France, or more important, so hostile to Great Britain, that they undertook to defend the French Directory even when it was threatening their interests.

Republicans in the state legislature, with a two-to-one majority, waited for the proper moment to record their opposition to the Adams administration. Federalist Judge James Iredell, presiding over a grand jury presentment in Richmond, gave them their opportunity. In the course of a judicial hearing Iredell lashed out at a number of unnamed public officials, who by their allegedly seditious writings had earned the judge's scorn. Although no indictment was, or legally could have been, brought against the offenders, the jury presented "as a real evil the circular letters of several members of the late Congress, and particularly letters with the signature of Samuel J. Cabell, endeavouring at a time of real public danger to disseminate unfounded calumnies against the happy government of the United States."[32]

This attack by the federal judiciary on a Virginia congressman provoked an immediate outcry from the Republicans. At issue were both Cabell's constitutional right to speak out against the Federalist administration and the wisdom of the pro-French policy he had been advocating. Cabell, along with several other Virginia representatives, immediately wrote a

[31] John Marshall to Charles Lee, Richmond, 20 April 1797, Adams Family Papers, Massachusetts Historical Society.

[32] Iredell's charge to the jury and the jury's presentment were published in the *Virginia Gazette and General Advertiser*, 24 May 1797.

circular letter defending his conduct and condemning the judiciary for meddling in the affairs of Congress.[33]

For the first time since the new government went into operation, Thomas Jefferson took the lead in formulating strategy for the opposition party. Previously reluctant to oppose Federalist policy publicly, he now struck out on a course independent from that of the administration. He drafted a petition for the counties encompassing Cabell's congressional district condemning the grand jury presentments as "a great crime, wicked in its purpose and mortal in its consequences." He denounced the action as both a violation of the principles of free speech and as an unlawful interference with the affairs of Congress by the judiciary.[34] There was some uncertainty as to where the petition should be sent—to county meetings, to the Virginia House of Delegates, or to Congress. The county meetings often failed to exert enough influence and there was no certainty that the Federalist-dominated Congress would look favorably on the petition, so Jefferson, with the advice of Madison and Monroe, decided to lay the petition before the state legislature.

This marked the first time that either Jefferson or Madison had placed their faith in the state government for a redress of their grievances; in the past they had been content to fight their battles in the halls of Congress, but with the tide rising against the Republicans in the nation's capital they had no alternative but to turn to the states.[35] The decision to rely on the state legislature rather than Congress as a base of political operations had far-reaching implications. From this point on the importance of the state's rights argument became paramount for both Jefferson and Madison. Reliance on the state legislature rather than Congress would mean that they would occasionally have to deviate from their moderate constitutional

[33] Circular Letter of Samuel J. Cabell to his Constituents, Philadelphia, 31 May 1797, in ibid., 14 June 1797; Henry Tazewell to John Ambler, 3 June 1797, Tazewell Papers, LC; John Clopton to Francis Ferguson, John Clopton Papers, Duke University.
[34] Dumas Malone, *Jefferson and the Ordeal of Liberty* (Boston, 1962), pp. 334-37; Jefferson's petition is printed in Ford, ed., *Jefferson's Writings*, 7: 158-64.
[35] Ford, ed., *Jefferson's Writings*, 7: 158-64.

positions to win support from the many factions within the Republican party in Virginia.

The House of Delegates took immediate action on Jefferson's petition. The Republicans proposed that the House demonstrate its approval of the petition by ordering a thousand copies printed and distributed at public expense. In effect, they were asking the legislature to subsidize their campaign against the Federalist-dominated judiciary. The Federalists used every parliamentary maneuver to block the proposal, but failed. They first contended that it was the duty of Congress, not the House of Delegates, to pass judgment on a petition concerning a federal representative. A motion to this effect was defeated, 56-94. They then brought forward a resolution denying the authority of the House to define the powers of the grand juries. This too met defeat, 54-93. Finally, they asked that the matter be left to the courts. This also met the disapproval of the House; the Republican-sponsored resolution passed, 92-53.[36]

Nothing ever came of the Cabell case; no formal charge was brought against Cabell, but Virginia Republicans managed to gain considerable propaganda benefit from it. The two combatants seemed to represent in microcosm the struggle that was taking place throughout the nation. Cabell, a popular Virginia congressman, was speaking out courageously against policies aimed at increasing United States dependence on Great Britain at the expense of republican France and agrarian Virginia. The federal court, composed at least in part of judges living outside Virginia, was attempting to curb the inalienable right of free speech, hoping that an unwary electorate would not perceive the dangers inherent in the policy of the Adams administration.

The highhanded action of the grand jury insulted nearly everyone in Virginia, and the Republicans took advantage of the reaction. Yet they were not able to turn their attachment to France to similar advantage. By January 1798, French depredations on American shipping were exceeding even those of Great Britain; moreover, England, contrary to the Republi-

---

36 *House Journal*, 27 Dec. 1797.

cans' expectations, was beginning to live up to its obligations under the Jay Treaty.[37] Worse, it was apparent that France was not even willing to enter into serious negotiations with the United States. Throughout the first months of 1798 rumors reached American shores that the American diplomatic team composed of John Marshall, Elbridge Gerry, and Charles Cotesworth Pinckney were being treated with a good measure of contempt by the French. When President Adams presented the details of the XYZ Affair before Congress in April 1798, the Republicans were thrown off balance. The Federalist majority in Philadelphia, its numbers increased by the sudden popular revulsion against France, adopted a decidedly militant posture.[38]

The Republicans in Congress were powerless; they could only sit back and watch while the Adams and Hamiltonian wings of the Federalist party struggled with one another for supremacy. Unable to influence the course of events in Congress, Virginia's political leaders looked homeward for support. But even there the Republicans found that their strength had eroded. The Federalists in Virginia took advantage of the anti-French sentiment generated by the XYZ Affair and for once they had both the numbers and the strength of conviction to give the Republicans a good fight.

At about the same time that Adams announced the details of the XYZ Affair, Monroe distributed a defense of his conduct while minister to France in 1795 and 1796. By this time, public

[37] Alexander DeConde, *The Quasi-War: The Politics and Diplomacy of the Undeclared War with France, 1797-1801* (New York, 1966), pp. 8-12; Bemis, *Diplomatic History*, p. 114. The editors of the *Virginia Gazette,* on hearing news of the evacuation of the Western posts by the British, exclaimed: "What think you of the Treaty now? The posts are taken and not one drop of blood shed. Eternal praises to the God of Peace and Negociation. Thanks to his servants, the President, Vice-President, Messrs. Jay, Hamilton, Knox, Wolcott and Pickering— Thanks to the majority in both Houses of Congress—and let all people say AMEN." *Virginia Gazette and General Advertiser,* 17 Aug. 1796.

[38] Although all the Federalists in Congress advocated a firm stand against France, there were differences of opinion as to the means to be used. Alexander Hamilton and his wing of the party desired a strong army, presumably to put down domestic as well as foreign opposition, while Adams placed a higher priority in building the navy. For an excellent account of the intrigues within the Federalist party in the nation's capital see Manning J. Dauer, *The Adams Federalists* (Baltimore, Md., 1953), pp. 225-45.

opinion was so polarized that Monroe's *View of the Conduct of the Executive* served only to reinforce the existing loyalties of the members of each of the two parties. To diehard Republicans, it offered conclusive proof that the United States had always been slavishly dependent upon Great Britain and that the Federalist administration had never been sincere in its desire for peace and friendship with France.[39] The Federalists saw in the *View* irrefutable proof of Monroe's shockingly unneutral conduct while in France and were convinced that he had willfully disobeyed his instructions in order to sabotage the Jay Treaty. They were certain that much of France's current hostility toward the United States could be blamed on the false picture of American affairs given to the French Directory by Monroe.[40]

Party rivalry in Virginia had reached such heights that passion and partisanship, not reason, became the principles behind the discussion of American foreign policy. It mattered little what was in America's interest: Republican leaders were too committed to the French cause to back down at such a late date and the Federalists, forgetting that they had urged restraint when Great Britain had been the aggressor, were now urging stern measures against the new enemy. The only people in Virginia who seemed to have a clear view of the situation were the residents of Norfolk. They voted and acted according to their interests. When the British were harassing their shipping, they denounced Great Britain; when the French began their depredations in 1797, they quickly switched allegiance and supported the Federalist administration in its attempt to bring pressure on France.[41] If everyone in Virginia had pos-

---

[39] One of the best-publicized defenses of Monroe by a Virginian was that by "Thrasybulus," *Virginia Gazette and General Advertiser*, 21, 28 Feb. 1798.

[40] The most violent attack on Monroe was that by "Scipio," who was evidently Federalist Charles Lee. Monroe to Jefferson, Richmond, 27 Jan. 1798, in Hamilton, ed., *Monroe's Writings*, 3: 98.

[41] Norfolk was the most violent center of anti-British activity in 1795. Not only did the residents hold county meetings protesting Great Britain's conduct, but they also took matters into their own hands by harassing British seamen at every opportunity. When the French became belligerent, the Norfolk residents gave them the same treatment. See the *Virginia Gazette and General Advertiser*, 15 May, 10 July 1798.

sessed such a clear understanding of his own interests, the debate over foreign policy might have been more rational and productive. Unfortunately, the propagandists of both political parties made this impossible.

Denunciations of Federalist policies became more strident than ever. Senator Henry Tazewell was convinced that "the great political object of our govt. has from the beginning been to assimilate it to that of G. Britain . . . if war is declared I shall instantly return home—for I can no longer be a fit representative to conduct and measures which I believe to be so big with calamities to my country."[42] Tazewell, according to one Federalist congressman, had even threatened to fight on the side of France should that nation become involved in a land war against the United States.[43] Major General Richard Meade of the state militia was court martialed for voicing similar sentiments. If the French army invaded America he was prepared "to repair to their standard with the black people who he could enlist."[44] Bishop James Madison, not always as moderate as his cousin in Congress, thought it would be an act of "self defense on the part of the Southern states to break the Union," should the Federalists continue their warlike aims.[45] Daniel Brent, Republican congressman from Virginia's Northern Neck, vented his anger on Adams. When asked if he would support the idea of a national holiday in honor of Adams's birthday, he replied that "he would not fast a day 'to save John Adams from an apoplectic fit'—and repeated the assertion that he would on that day rather introduce a dance."[46]

The Federalists, after years of being on the defensive, were able to defend Adams's policies with conviction. They blamed the Republicans for encouraging the French to believe they could expect preferential treatment from the United States and

---

42 Henry Tazewell to John Ambler, Philadelphia, 9, 20 May 1798, Tazewell Papers.

43 Testimony of Thomas Evans, reported in *House Journal*, 11 Dec. 1798.

44 James Wood to Captain Archibald McRae, Richmond, 16 July 1798, Executive Letterbooks.

45 Bishop James Madison to Henry Tazewell, 31 May 1798, Bishop Madison Papers, Duke University.

46 *Virginia Gazette and General Advertiser*, 24 April 1798.

claimed that the recent acts of war by France provided final proof that none of the nations of Europe could be trusted. They asked: "Will we even now learn that to make ourselves, our country respected, & to obtain that justice we are entitled to from other nations and powers—is to respect ourselves, our Country—to cling to our Government and descry the more childish folly, the belief that foreign nations ever will act toward us with any views but as it accords their own interest."[47] This had been the position of the Virginia Federalists throughout the decade. They liked neither the British nor the French and thought the Republicans naive to believe that their friendship toward the people of France could affect the actions of the self-interested French diplomats with whom they had to deal.

More important than the Federalists' approval of Adams's policy toward France was their abhorrence of the Republican opposition to those policies. Federalists viewed the statements of people like Henry Tazewell and Daniel Brent as disloyal and urged their fellow Virginians to "Banish my friends from your confidence those designing hypocrites who delight in painting the power and wisdom of France—who declaim against the President and government as subservient to British influence. . . . Be assured they have their ends to answer."[48]

The commitment of the Virginia Federalists to the policies of the federal government, or at least their distaste for the Republican opposition, had never been stronger. The civic-minded citizens of Norfolk were so eager to aid the Adams administration that they raised a private fund of over $16,000 to help build and equip ships to be loaned to the United States government to carry out an attack on the French navy.[49]

Soon after the details of the XYZ Affair were announced, Republican and Federalist leaders, in what was becoming standard practice, organized county meetings to rally support to their banners. Although the Republicans enjoyed some success

[47] Robert Gamble to Timothy Pickering, Richmond, 20 March 1798, Timothy Pickering Papers.

[48] *Virginia Gazette and General Advertiser*, 24 April 1798.

[49] Robert Gamble to John Cropper, Richmond, 11 July 1798, John Cropper Papers.

in the counties, their efforts were seriously handicapped by the continuing belligerency of France. The arguments used by the Republicans paralleled those of the Federalists of 1795 and 1796. They lamented the actions of the French, but maintained that the United States was in no position to go to war with such a powerful European nation.

At a meeting in Richmond, Republican William Foushee proposed a set of resolutions condemning Adams for his unwarranted exercise of executive power and asking that peace with France be preserved at all costs. He was immediately opposed by Federalist Bushrod Washington who called for a statement affirming America's determination to defend the national honor against all aggression. Both sides claimed that a majority of the people present supported their resolutions and as a result, the meeting ended with two sets of resolves.[50] In Caroline County, where Edmund Pendleton and John Taylor controlled the electorate, the citizens agreed on a petition to Congress containing a violent denunciation of Federalist policy. The petition was in keeping with Taylor's agrarian philosophy, claiming that "war makes individuals richer, by making the people poorer," and blaming the current desire for war on those who wanted to protect British commerce. The petitioners from Caroline saw no way in which agrarian Virginia could benefit from the protection of British trade and therefore vowed to maintain their friendly ties with republican France.[51]

The freeholders of Albemarle County gathered not only to listen to opposing arguments regarding Federalist foreign policy but also to witness the beginnings of a bitter family quarrel. Wilson Cary Nicholas, the leading Republican in the General Assembly, sponsored a series of resolutions condemning the foreign policy of the Adams administration, while his cousin, John Nicholas, attempted to defend the Federalists.[52] Although

[50] *Virginia Gazette and General Advertiser,* 3 April 1798.
[51] Ibid., 10 April 1798.
[52] Ibid., 12 June 1798. There were two John Nicholases, both living in Albemarle County, and, as a result, there has been confusion as to which deserted the Republican cause. Manning J. Dauer, "The Two John Nicholases," *American Historical Review* 45 (1940); 338-53, has cleared up much of the misunderstand-

the views of Wilson Cary Nicholas prevailed, the young Republican leader was dismayed by the political heresy in his family. He confided to his father, George Nicholas, the former governor of Kentucky:

> J. Nicholas has taken the side of the administration. He has been constantly disgraced when he has made a public effort, but such is his zeal or pique, that he has been unwearied in his personal applications to the people—But the great body of people are right; it is a mortification to me that a man of our name should take part against the liberty of his Countrymen. I have frequently pressed John to let me get an Act of Assembly to change his name. Next to this reputation of being honest men, I am most anxious that our family should be distinguished for their love of country and the rights of man.[53]

Not all Federalists were as unsuccessful as John Nicholas. On the whole, they gained more support in the county meetings than at any previous time. Resolutions praising Adams's conduct were passed in Norfolk, Alexandria, Fairfax, Boutetourt, Frederick, Portsmouth, Lancaster, and Rockbridge.[54] Most followed the form of those passed in Norfolk, where the citizens reaffirmed their attachment to the initial stages of the French experiment with republicanism, but rejected "with honest indignation her inadmissable demands." As in all cases, the meeting closed with a statement deprecating war, but refusing to "purchase peace at any price."[55]

The annual celebration of Independence Day, always an occasion for patriotic speeches, gave the Federalists another opportunity to drum up popular support. With the threat of war on the horizon, they were able to use the holiday to

---

ing. The John Nicholas who became a Federalist was the cousin of Wilson Cary Nicholas and a county clerk in Albemarle County. The other John Nicholas was Wilson Cary Nicholas's brother and a Republican congressman. It is important to keep the two men straight, as each played important parts, on opposing sides, during the controversy over the Alien and Sedition Acts.

53 Wilson Cary Nicholas to George Nicholas, Warren, 21 Sept. 1798, Wilson Cary Nicholas Papers.

54 *Virginia Gazette and General Advertiser*, 15 May, 12 June, 10 July 1798; *Columbian Mirror*, 17, 19, 29 May 1798.

55 *Virginia Gazette and General Advertiser*, 15 May 1798.

advantage. In towns and counties throughout the state, the citizens drank toasts to President Adams and the burgeoning United States military establishment. The order in which the toasts were given provided a clue as to the current popularity of the men and policies of the period. In Richmond, honors went to the "People and Government of the United States . . . Not to be separated by the diplomatic skill of France."[56] In Albemarle County, Jefferson's home, the vice president was at the bottom of the list, with the warning: "may those who dispose to slight the voice of the majority of their fellow citizens, in the choice of the rest of our officers of government, learn to respect that voice as we do."[57]

The high point of Federalist sentiment in Virginia was reached during the weeks that John Marshall traveled through Virginia on the way home from his mission to France. On June 18, 1798, Marshall entered the capital city of Philadelphia and received a hero's welcome unsurpassed by any except that given to Washington. As he set out for Virginia, he was honored at every stop on the way.[58] The Federalists were overjoyed. They had an issue capable of attracting public support and, at the same time, a popular leader who was capable of capitalizing on that support. In his hometown of Richmond, Marshall made an impressive speech to an enthusiastic audience where he castigated the French diplomats for their duplicity and warned his fellow citizens not to become attached to any foreign powers. His speech was followed by a series of toasts to Northern Federalists.[59] This burst of enthusiasm for Northern Federalists was unprecedented in Virginia, but such was the popular reaction against France, and to the Republican attachment to France, that even the men surrounding Alexander Hamilton were temporarily in public favor.

One side effect of this resurgence of the Federalist party in Virginia was the beginnings of a political system where decisions

---

56 Ibid., 10 July 1798.
57 Ibid., 28 Aug. 1798.
58 Beveridge, *Marshall*, 2: 344.
59 The text of Marshall's address is printed in ibid., 2: 571-73; *Virginia Gazette and General Advertiser*, 14 Aug. 1798.

were made on the basis of issues and not on the personalities of the respective candidates. In many of the county meetings during the winter and spring of 1798 there were debates between the members of the two opposing parties, and as a result, the electorate was beginning to play at least a small role in influencing public policy. Even the state legislature, which for almost two centuries had been the private reserve of the wealthy and well-born, was beginning to feel the democratizing pressures of party politics. For the first time on record, candidates for the legislature were running as Republicans or Federalists.[60] Not coincidentally, the only areas where this occurred were those where Federalist policy was popular with a large portion of the electorate; in most parts of the state, where influential Republicans and Federalists commanded the respect of the voters for reasons other than their political ideology, the political structure remained unchanged. If the Federalists could continue to formulate policies capable of winning wide popular support, the system of deferential politics would be subject to its most severe test.

On the negative side, there is no doubt that the tightening of party lines around complex questions of American foreign relations was disastrous to the conduct of foreign policy. At one extreme, Alexander Hamilton and his coterie were using the crisis with France to advance their plans to raise a provisional army to quell domestic as well as foreign opposition. At the other, some Virginia Republicans were threatening disunion and even offering to fight on the side of the French. Virginia, for the first time, was beginning to experience the divisive quarrels between Republicans and Federalists that were troubling so many other states in the union.

Partisanship was not the sole cause of the profound division of opinion within Virginia, however. To be sure, the increasingly heated contests for political power between Republicans

60 The candidates did not call themselves "Republicans" or "Federalists," but rather, "opponents" or "supporters" of the "present Administration." Although it cannot be ascertained how many counties felt the impact of this sudden burst of partisanship, it is certain that the campaigns in Alexandria, Hanover, Chesterfield, Gloucester, York, and Fauquier were at least partially affected by the divisions over foreign policy. *Columbian Mirror*, 14 April, 12 May 1798.

and Federalists caused each faction to take a more extreme and inflexible stand toward the nations of Europe than they would have under ordinary circumstances. The Republicans surely would not have gone to such lengths to defend the belligerent French if they had not already committed themselves to a pro-French position during the debates on the Proclamation of Neutrality and the Jay Treaty. Nor would the Federalists have advocated such stern measures against the French if they had not seen in such a policy a means of discrediting the Republicans' attachment to that nation. But this does not explain either the nature or the depth of the loyalties of the members of both parties. The Republicans sincerely believed that their predictions about the threat of consolidation had been confirmed. The Virginia state legislature had proved itself powerless to halt the dangerous trend of government policy. Even more alarming was the ascendancy of the executive branch over Congress within the federal government. Everything the Republicans detested—funding, assumption, the Bank of the United States—had been initiated by the executive branch. At least Congress had added its sanction to these measures. In foreign affairs the House of Representatives was unable to check the actions of the president and his advisers. In all parts of the world Federalist diplomats of known British sympathies were now trying to barter away America's political and economic independence, for the sake of a small, self-interested minority of Northern merchants. The Republicans believed that France and the United States were partners in an attempt to eliminate this kind of corruption from the world—the only reason that France was temporarily hostile to America was because of the Federalists' collaboration with the British. The Adams administration's warlike posture toward France was only one more step, they claimed, in the attempt to bring America permanently under the influence of the British.

The Republicans were uncharitable in assessing the motives of the Federalists and excessively optimistic in their faith in France. The French, for their part, had no illusions about any natural alliance with America. The new French minister to America, Pierre Adet, summed up the attitude of France toward

America while discussing the character of the leader of the
Republican interest: "Jefferson, I say, is American and, as such
he cannot be sincerely our friend. An American is the born
enemy of all the European peoples."[61] If only the Republicans
could have been aware of that attitude. America, despite the
turmoil of her internal affairs, was fast becoming one of the
major powers of the world, a potential rival to both Great
Britain and France. The French minister could see that self-
interest, not republican loyalties, would be the force that would
guide the country's conduct with the rest of the world.

The Federalists were every bit as unrealistic as the Republicans. Everywhere they saw conspiracy. They charged the French,
who had meddled in American politics to gain advantage over
Great Britain in the power struggles of Europe, with attempting
to undermine and eventually overthrow the American government and they accused the Republicans of materially aiding
the French in their treasonous activities. Most of this hysteria
was connected with the Federalists' growing concern for order
and with their alarm over the direction and tone of the Republicans' criticism of federal policy. The Virginia Federalists, far
more than their Republican opponents, were unable to realize
that disagreement with government policy was not equivalent
to disloyalty. Both Republicans and Federalists felt distinctly
uneasy about the growth of party in America, but the Federalists complained more about the partisan rhetoric that party
warfare engendered. It does not seem likely that the Federalists
were by nature any more intolerant or illiberal than their
Republican opponents; they simply happened to be the ones
who were most often on the receiving end of those partisan
attacks.

At least two of Virginia's political leaders were able to rise
above the animosities generated by his party warfare. In the
summer of 1798, John Marshall and Wilson Cary Nicholas
exchanged letters in which they discussed the political situation
in America. Marshall, writing while he was in Europe, gently
urged his Republican opponent to give up his attachment to

[61] Quoted in Malone, *Jefferson and the Ordeal of Liberty*, pp. 289-90.

France. Nicholas, who just a few months later would take the responsibility for guiding the Virginia Resolutions through the General Assembly, replied in a tone which indicated that the gentlemanly style of Virginia politics was not a thing of the past:

> Your letter gave me infinite satisfaction, for there is not a man whose esteem I value more, whose friendship I reciprocate with more sincerity. I sincerely lament the difference of opinion that has existed between us as to some of the great political events, but I flatter myself that you will give me full credit when I assure you, that my confidence in you, my affection and regard for you, has not been for one moment in the smallest degree impaired. I have myself consciously pursued that course which seemed to me best calculated to promote the happiness and secure the liberty of my countrymen. I am confident that your motives are equally pure, and your only object the public good.

Nicholas then explained his reasons for opposing war with France and asked only that Marshall accept the sincerity, if not the wisdom, of his position. He was confident that "however we may differ about the means, our objects are the same." Nicholas could foresee the difficulties and crises that were to come in the years ahead and saw the necessity of joining with Federalists of good faith, like Marshall, to discourage the radical members of both parties. He was well aware that he and Marshall would never be able to agree on all matters of public policy, but he hoped that they could both use their wisdom and moderation to see that future disagreements would be kept within responsible limits.[62]

Events were moving too fast to allow the two Virginia statesmen to continue their efforts toward conciliation. As Nicholas was replying to Marshall, Federalists in Congress were putting the finishing touches to the Alien and Sedition Acts. The resulting uproar would not recede until the election of Jefferson two and a half years later.

[62] Wilson Cary Nicholas to J. Marshall [Summer] 1798, Wilson Cary Nicholas Papers.

CHAPTER SEVEN

Party Politics and Political Theory

In the summer of 1798 the Federalist majority in Congress enacted measures to organize a provisional army, to suspend trade with France, to capture and punish French privateers, to regulate the activities of aliens, and to punish anyone guilty of seditious writings against the federal government.[1] The citizens of Virginia were enraged—not since the Revolution had the actions of the central government so threatened their liberties. The establishment of a sizable peace-time army—which many Virginians feared would be used to crush domestic opposition to administration policy—and passage of the Alien and Sedition Acts raised new questions regarding the civil liberties of American citizens and the proper balance of federal-state authority. The division caused by these measures was widened by rifts within the Federalist party and by a marked increase in party spirit in general. As both Federalists and Republicans stepped up their efforts to win support from the electorate, it became increasingly difficult for the two parties to place the public interest above partisan gain.[2]

The most controversial of the Federalist measures, and the one at which Republicans decided to direct their attack, was the second section of the Sedition Act, which provided a fine of up to two thousand dollars and a prison sentence not exceeding two years for anyone who wrote, printed, published, or even spoke "false, scandalous, and malicious" statements against any member or branch of the federal government.[3] The Federalists maintained that the federal courts had assumed common law jurisdiction over seditious libel, and that the Act only codified what had been accepted procedure. Indeed, they claimed that the Sedition Act was a liberalization of the English Libel Law of 1792, since it permitted anyone charged with libel to give evidence of the truth of his statements as a defense. The Republicans believed it a patent violation of the first amendment and a blatant attempt to silence opponents of the Federalist administration.[4]

If the members of either party had been capable of a dispassionate examination of the Act, they would have discovered no clear precedents defining the limits of the federal government's power to punish seditious libel. John Marshall, the only prominent Federalist to oppose the Alien and Sedition Acts publicly, gave his tentative opinion on the question in 1794, long before it had become such an explosive issue: "Whether the truth of the libel may be justified or not is a perfectly unsettled question. . . . The principle which seems now to prevail, tho' it is scarcely to be found in print, is that where words are said to be maliciously spoken & to be injurious to the plaintiff & the verdict has established them to be so, they are to be considered as actionable unless it is plain that they could not be slanderous."[5]

While the right of the federal government to punish seditious libel was unclear, there was no uncertainty as to the right of the state to take such action. The state was explicitly given

---

1 *Annals of Congress,* 9: 3729, 3733, 3738-39, 3744, 3754, 3776.

2 For a discussion of Federalist policy, and of the division within the Federalist party during this crucial year, see Dauer, *The Adams Federalists,* pp. 225-45.

3 *Annals of Congress,* 9: 3776.

4 The modern equivalents of the Republican and Federalist positions on this question can be found in the recent historiography of the Alien and Sedition Acts. The Republican position is taken by James Morton Smith, *Freedom's Fetters: The Alien and Sedition Laws and American Civil Liberties* (Ithaca, N.Y., 1956); Leonard W. Levy, *Legacy of Suppression: Freedom of Speech and Press in Early American History* (Cambridge, Mass., 1960), argues persuasively that the Alien and Sedition Laws were actually a step forward toward a more liberal interpretation of the first amendment.

5 John Marshall to Archibald Stuart, Richmond, 28 May 1794, Archibald Stuart Papers.

the power to punish seditious libel, and moreover, the accused was not allowed to offer proof of the truth of his statements as a defense. The framers of the Virginia libel law reasoned that "the party grieved ought to complain for an injury done to him in the ordinary course of law and not by any means to revenge himself, whether by the odious course of libelling or otherwise."[6]

The Virginia Republicans carried out their fight against the Alien and Sedition Acts on three different fronts. They continued, as they had done in the past, to call county meetings where memorials and petitions were drafted denouncing the laws. Of much greater importance than these meetings were the highly secret plans of Jefferson and Madison to persuade the legislatures of Virginia and Kentucky to lodge formal protests against the Alien and Sedition Acts. And finally, in a number of campaigns for seats in the state legislature and in Congress, the Republican candidates subjected the merits of Federalist policy to the closest scrutiny. The Republicans used these channels of protest not to condemn the Alien and Sedition Acts alone, but to link them to a more systematic design, manifested in both the Federalists' foreign and domestic policy, to rob Virginians of their liberties.

At a meeting in Powhatan County, the citizens mixed partisanship with political theory. First, they resumed a theme that had been debated since ratification of the Constitution—the degree to which British influence guided Federalist policy. They denounced the Federalists' attachment to the British, claiming that "such connections have an evident tendency to corrupt our own, and subject us to a participation of those evils, which the pride, ambition, and avarice of Monarchical and Aristocratical Governments naturally produce."[7] The Powhatan residents then labeled the Alien and Sedition Acts "tyrannical and unconstitutional" and in their final resolution, turned to the more complicated problems of the relationship between

[6] William Walter Hening, *The New Virginia Justice, Comprising the Office and Authority of a Justice of the Peace* . . . (Richmond, 1796), pp. 313-17.
[7] *Virginia Gazette and General Advertiser,* 25 Sept. 1798.

a representative and his constituents and of the proper mode of seeking repeal of unjust laws. They claimed that ultimate sovereignty rested with the people and, when the people discovered that their will had been subverted, it was their right "to resist the usurpations, extirpate the tyranny, to restore their sullied majesty and prostituted authority; to suspend or abrogate those laws, to punish their *unfaithful* and *corrupt* servants."[8]

This last resolution suggests some fundamental changes in the concept of representation. As the activities of the two political parties increased, so too did the awareness of the electorate. Some voters were no longer content to give their representative a free hand to decide what policy was best for them and now demanded that he act as their direct agent in all dealings with the government. Nearly a quarter of a century after the Revolution, some Virginians were beginning to ask for the kind of constituent power that most New Englanders had been exercising for over a century. The Powhatan residents were less successful in defining the way in which an unconstitutional law could be abrogated. They were certain the people had the right to disallow any law which violated the Constitution, but they were not able to define the procedure for doing so.[9]

Not all the memorials from the counties were as restrained or as well reasoned as that of Powhatan. Secretary of State Timothy Pickering, when he received a copy of the Address of the Citizens of Prince Edward County to the President of the United States, refused even to deliver it to Adams on the grounds that it was personally insulting to the chief magistrate. Pickering maintained that the publication of the Address in the newspapers was proof that it was meant as a device "to

---

8 Ibid.

9 In one respect, the resolutions adopted in Powhatan were more sophisticated in their theory of sovereignty than were the Virginia Resolutions passed by the General Assembly two months later. The Virginia Resolves never clearly identified where ultimate sovereignty rested; they implied that the state legislature might have the right to claim it. The Powhatan resolutions, on the other hand, explicitly vested the people with the ultimate sovereign power.

inflame the minds of the people," rather than a sincere remonstrance. The Republicans, of course, made much of the fact that the Secretary of State was suppressing the document, and cited it as one more example of the government's determination to destroy all civil liberties, even the right "to petition the Government for a redress of grievances," a freedom specifically guaranteed by the first amendment.[10]

Republican leaders were beginning to realize that county meetings alone could not exert enough influence to change Federalist policy. Wilson Cary Nicholas, the man entrusted by Jefferson and Madison with the advance preparations for the Virginia and Kentucky Resolutions, was convinced that "the disease has gained too much strength to be destroyed by anything they [the county meetings] can do" and predicted that "if no other effort is made, we are undone."[11] At that very moment, Jefferson, Madison, John Taylor, John Breckinridge of Kentucky, and Nicholas were taking steps to guarantee that some other effort was made.

The Kentucky Resolutions were drafted by Jefferson sometime before October 4, 1798.[12] He gave them to Wilson Cary Nicholas and instructed him to send them to the North Carolina legislature for approval. Nicholas instead turned them over to John Breckinridge of Kentucky and asked Breckinridge to steer them through the Kentucky legislature. Jefferson was happy with this scheme, since the Kentucky legislature was friendly to the Republican cause and Breckinridge's participation would help obscure his own role in the affair. When Madison drafted the Virginia Resolutions, he had with him a

10 Timothy Pickering to P. Johnston, Trenton, 29 Sept. 1798, Johnston to Pickering, Prince Edward County, 20 Oct. 1798, Timothy Pickering Papers.

11 Wilson Cary Nicholas to George Nicholas, Warren, 12 Sept. 1798, Wilson Cary Nicholas Papers.

12 Madison's role in the drafting of the Virginia Resolutions did not become public knowledge until 1809; it was not until 1814 that Jefferson's participation was revealed. The exact details of Madison's and Jefferson's effort remained obscure throughout the nineteenth and early twentieth centuries, and only recently has the sequence of events been discovered. See Adrienne Koch and Harry Ammon, "The Virginia and Kentucky Resolutions: An Episode in Jefferson's and Madison's Defense of Civil Liberties," *William and Mary Quarterly*, 3d ser., 5 (1948): 145-76.

copy of Jefferson's resolves. Jefferson, again using Wilson Cary Nicholas as an intermediary, suggested some last minute changes in Madison's draft and then sent the Resolutions to John Taylor of Caroline, who was to introduce them in the Virginia House of Delegates.[13]

Although they were not aware of the backstage maneuverings of Jefferson, Madison, Nicholas, and Taylor, the members of both parties knew that the 1798 session of the Virginia General Assembly would be crucial. As early as July 1798, almost five months before the legislature convened, the Federalists were speculating that the Republicans would use the assembly session to pass resolutions critical of the general government. The Republican members of the Governor's Council, to insure an even greater majority for the opponents of the federal government in the legislature, attempted to push through a measure calling the General Assembly into session early in order to prevent the Federalists from faraway western Virginia from attending. They nearly succeeded, but at the last minute one Council member changed his vote, giving a majority to those who wanted the legislature to convene at the usual time.[14]

When the General Assembly convened on December 3, 1798, the Republicans tried to displace John Wise as Speaker of the House. The Speaker ordinarily voted only in the case of a tie, and while Wise had never officially cast his vote with either party, it was common knowledge in the state capital that he had been a supporter of the Federalist faction ever since ratification. Yet he had been elected Speaker by the predominantly Republican House of Delegates every year since 1794, when his predecessor, Thomas Mathews, also a Federalist, retired.[15] The speakership had never before been an object of partisanship, but some Republicans were intent on gaining every advantage possible and accordingly nominated Wilson Cary Nicholas to

13 Ibid., pp. 155-60.

14 Robert Gamble to Timothy Pickering, Richmond, 12 July 1798, Timothy Pickering Papers; William Radford to John Preston, Richmond, 21 July 1798, Preston Papers.

15 Thomas Jefferson to John Wise, 12 Feb. 1799, in *Virginia Magazine of History and Biography* 12: 257.

oppose Wise. Although they possessed a substantial majority in the legislature, the Republicans were unable to persuade their members to abandon their traditional mode of selecting a presiding officer. While Wise was a Federalist, he was also an experienced and respected legislator; some Republicans were not willing to carry partisanship to such an extreme and they joined with the Federalists in reelecting Wise.[16] Thomas Jefferson was incensed at this lack of discipline in the Republican ranks. He denounced Wise as a tory and "roundly abused those of his followers who had forgotten their party allegiance at such a time."[17]

Jefferson had little to complain about, for Wise's victory was the only setback suffered by the Republicans during the entire session. On December 10, John Taylor introduced the Virginia Resolutions into the House of Delegates.[18] In the first two resolutions the Republicans paid their obligatory homage to the Constitution and the union. The third resolution analyzed the nature of the compact between the states and the federal government, declaring "that in the case of a deliberate, palpable and dangerous exercise of power not granted by the said compact, *the states . . . are in duty bound to interpose for arresting the progress of evil.*" If the states did not take these steps to limit the exercise of federal power, "the inevitable result . . . would be to transform the present republican system of the United States into an absolute, or at best, a mixed monarchy." The fourth resolution dealt explicitly with the Alien and Sedition Acts, claiming that they were a "palpable and alarming" violation of the Constitution.[19]

Up to this point, the wording of the Resolves was nearly identical to Madison's rough draft. The final resolution was introduced at the suggestion of Thomas Jefferson. It declared the Acts unconstitutional and pronounced them *"not law, but*

[16] *House Journal,* 3 Dec. 1798.
[17] Jefferson to John Wise, 12 Feb. 1799, *Virginia Magazine of History and Biography* 12: 257.
[18] *House Journal,* 10 Dec. 1798.
[19] Italics mine. *Resolutions of Virginia and Kentucky . . . and Debates in the House of Delegates of Virginia . . .* (Richmond, 1832), pp. 174-76.

utterly void, and of no force or effect."[20] In this form, the Virginia Resolutions were not a mere statement of opinion, but an explicit defiance of federal law.

During the next two weeks of debate, both Federalists and Republicans demonstrated that they were as much concerned with advancing the cause of their respective parties as they were with the constitutionality of the Alien and Sedition Acts. John Taylor opened the debate. He maintained that the Alien and Sedition Laws violated every principle of civil liberties contained in the bill of rights and "deemed it a sacrilege for Government to regulate the mind of man." Taylor and his Republican colleagues may have believed that the Alien and Sedition Laws were a threat to civil liberties, but the Federalists had a devastating rejoinder. If the Republicans were so concerned with preserving human rights, why had they enacted laws similar to the Sedition Act within their own state? "An act against divulgers of false news," passed by the Virginia General Assembly in 1792, specifically excluded from protection under the Bill of Rights anyone accused of spreading defamatory propaganda. Under the Virginia statute the accused was not even allowed to offer proof of the truth of the statement in his defense. The Federalists were able to point to an old letter from Thomas Jefferson to Henry Lee to reinforce their argument. In this letter the indefatigable champion of freedom had ventured that "in preventing the abridgment of the freedom of the press, punishment for uttering falsehoods, ought not to be inhibited."[21]

The Federalists' arguments, however disingenuous, were technically correct. The Republicans realized this and did not rely on the civil liberties issue after the Federalists had made their counterattack. They turned instead to the problem of the proper division of authority between the state and federal governments, arguing that the federal government derived its

---

[20] Italics mine. Ibid., p. 166; Jefferson added this statement just before the Resolutions were sent to John Taylor. Jefferson to Wilson Cary Nicholas, Monticello, 29 Nov. 1798, in Ford, ed., *Jefferson's Writings,* 7: 312-13.

[21] *Resolutions of Virginia,* pp. 7, 70, 110.

power from the states alone, and that nowhere in the Constitution was there mention that the states had relinquished power to regulate the conduct of aliens or of the press.[22] The Federalists challenged the Republicans' reliance on the states. The phrase "We the states" was purposely deleted in favor of "We the people" in the preamble of the Constitution. Hence, a state legislature surely would not disobey a law passed by men representing a majority of the people of the United States. The attempt by the Republicans to coerce Virginia into unlawful behavior was the more odious, the Federalists charged, because the Republicans who controlled the state legislature had systematically denied to some sections of the state adequate representation in the affairs of government and thus did not even have a legitimate claim to representing the will of the people of Virginia.[23] This wrangling over the locus of sovereignty continued throughout the two weeks of debate. Most of the arguments were similar to those used during the first half of the nineteenth century. Tragically, the difficult question of ultimate sovereignty was not settled by words; it would have to be settled by force.

The Federalists, after defending the constitutionality of the Alien and Sedition Laws, turned to the area where their Republican opponents were most vulnerable: they enthusiastically supported the Enemy Alien Act and used that Act as a platform from which to launch their attacks on French influence. Federalist George K. Taylor claimed:

> attempts . . . had already been made, by French emigrants, to excite our slaves to insurrection. Suppose then, they were to attempt the thing again, and an insurrection should accordingly take place, what would be the consequence? . . . The inexorable and blood-thirsty negro would be careless of the father's groans, the tears of the mother, and the lamentation of the children. The loudest in their wailings would be their wives and daughters, torn from their arms, with naked bosoms, outstretched hands and dishevelled hair, to gratify the brutal passion of a

22 Ibid., pp. 26-34, 43-50, 118-19.
23 Ibid., pp. 71, 133-36.

ruthless negro, who would the next moment murder the object of his lust. [How was] . . . all that to be prevented? By vesting the General Government with the power to remove such aliens, which it already so generously exercised for the purpose, in the law under consideration; a law particularly calculated for the protection of the Southern States.[24]

Somehow the issue had clouded; while John Taylor talked of human rights, George Taylor warned of "naked bosoms." But Taylor's rhetoric, however partisan, played upon some real fears. Concern over slave violence, particularly sexual violence, was constant in Virginia; it was only natural, and unfortunate, that at least one of the two political parties would discover a way to exploit that concern.

The Republicans did not match George K. Taylor's demagoguery, but they rarely missed an opportunity to attack the Federalist administration. They conceded that Adams had somehow received a majority of the votes in the presidential election of 1796, but claimed that "it was well known that the majority was produced by artifice and coalition of Federal officers, persons deeply concerned in funding and banking systems, refugees, foreigners (whose life has been but a life of warfare against the principles of free government), bankrupt speculators, and to complete the groupe all those who could profit by change and convulsion."[25]

This exchange of abuse continued throughout the debates, but the legislators ultimately had to face the central issue presented by the Virginia Resolutions. Jefferson's contribution to the Resolves had been the one phrase in the last resolution declaring the Alien and Sedition Acts "utterly null, void, and of no force or effect." The implications of this single phrase were frightening to both Federalists and moderate Republicans. They feared that "the old Republican maxim that the majority must govern" would be destroyed if a single state legislature was vested with the power to declare a law null and void. While Virginians might be morally justified in defying a law

[24] Ibid., pp. 20-21.
[25] Ibid., p. 56.

they thought to be a clear violation of the Constitution, other legislatures at other times might use the precedent set by Virginia to sow the seeds of anarchy and disunion.[26]

This coalition of Federalists and moderate Republicans, fearful of the consequences of Jefferson's doctrine, succeeded in deleting the nullification provision from the Virginia Resolutions.[27] The radical Republicans were disappointed. John Taylor thought its inclusion in the Resolves "would have placed the State and general governments at issue" and would therefore have necessitated the calling of a new constitutional convention to resolve the problem. It was Taylor's hope that such a convention would completely change the structure of the federal government and give back to the states much of the power they had lost in the Convention of 1787.[28] Taylor could not convince enough of his colleagues to embrace his radical doctrines, and the Virginia Resolutions, without the nullification provision, as passed by the House on December 21, 1798, by a vote of 100-63, merely declared the Alien and Sedition Acts unconstitutional and asked that "necessary and proper measures" be taken to repeal them.[29]

The Virginia Resolutions, because of their kinship with John C. Calhoun's nullification doctrine, have received the close attention of historians, but the Resolves were but one item in the Republican program during the legislative session of 1798. The Republicans also proposed a series of resolutions commenting once again on the conduct of American foreign policy. The growing body of evidence attesting to French hostility toward the United States made it necessary for the Republicans to retreat from their position of unqualified support for France, but they remained adamant that "our security from invasion, and the force of our militia, render a standing army unnecessary." The Federalists countered with a set of resolutions vigorously condemning the French for their con-

26 Ibid., pp. 154-57.
27 *House Journal*, 21 Dec. 1798.
28 John Taylor to Jefferson, Richmond, 1798, in *John P. Branch Historical Papers of Randolph-Macon College* 2 (1908): 277.
29 *House Journal*, 21 Dec. 1798.

duct in the XYZ Affair and for their attacks on American shipping, and finally, praising the administration's proposal for a provisional army. In votes nearly identical to the one on the Virginia Resolves, the Federalist resolutions were defeated, 68-97, the Republican ones passed, 103-58.[30]

The Republicans next drafted and passed, 80-58, a lengthy *Address to Congress from the General Assembly.*[31] The *Address,* which was to be distributed to the public at government expense, was in many ways more inflammatory than the Virginia Resolutions. Madison, the author of the *Address,* unquestionably meant it as a campaign document for future elections. In it he warned that the "acquiescence of the states under infractions of the federal compact, would either beget a speedy consolidation, by precipitating the state governments into impotency and contempt; or prepare the way for a revolution, by a repetition of these infractions."[32] The only alternative to consolidation or revolution was, in his opinion, the speedy installation of a Republican administration in the nation's capital.

The *Address* sought to demonstrate how the Federalist administration had subverted the liberties of Americans. The first steps on the road to consolidation were "the fiscal systems and arrangements, which keep an host of commercial and wealthy individuals, embodied and obedient to the mandates of the Treasury." Next came the dangerous alliance with Great Britain, which could only corrupt America's republican institutions. The Republicans deplored the creation of an army and navy, which was obviously intended to "employ the principle of fear, by punishing imaginary insurrections under the pretext of preventative justice." Warming to his partisan task, Madison claimed that the Federalist administration was composed solely of "swarms of officers, civil and military, who can inculcate political tenets tending to sovereignty and monarchy." The *Address* closed with a denunciation of the Alien

---

30 Ibid., 4 Jan. 1799.
31 Ibid., 22 Jan. 1799.
32 Ibid.

and Sedition Acts similar to that contained in the Virginia Resolves.[33]

The Federalists, aided by the pen of John Marshall, drafted an *Address from the Minority*.[34] Like the Republican *Address*, it was a partisan document. The Virginia Federalists not only defended the Alien and Sedition Acts but also embarked on a belated, yet vigorous defense of the entire Federalist program over the past decade. They lauded President Washington for his wise decision to avoid the power struggles of Europe, but noted that "unfortunately, for America, and for Republican government, a few openly, and more secretly, lifted their voice against the country's will." They lamented the fact that Citizen Genêt, with the help of the more radical opponents of the government, was able to stir up "acrimony against the constituted authorities of the nation."[35] Turning their attention to Anglo-American relations, the Federalists admitted that the Treaty of Peace had not eliminated America's grievances against England: "The unjustifiable conduct of our late foe, especially on the ocean, rekindled our ardor for hostility and revenge." Fortunately, the brilliant diplomacy of John Jay had averted war and resolved most of America's differences with Great Britain. In spite of these efforts, a coalition of dissatisfied Americans and self-interested Frenchmen persisted in their attempts to undermine America's relations with England.[36]

There was of necessity some hesitation in the Federalists' justification of administration policy toward Great Britain, for they had misgivings about the wisdom of that policy themselves. But when they turned to President Adams's policy toward France they were able to speak with more conviction. They

33 Ibid.

34 Ibid. According to Albert J. Beveridge, *Marshall*, 2: 402, 575-77, the style and language of the *Minority Report* indicate that it was the handiwork of Marshall. If Beveridge is correct, then Marshall, who had initially opposed the Alien and Sedition Acts, was either playing both sides of the political fence or was facing extreme pressure from his fellow Federalist legislators to support the administration measures. For further proof of Marshall's authorship of the *Minority Report*, see Theodore Sedgwick to Rufus King, Stockbridge, 29 March 1799, in King, *Life and Correspondence*, 2: 581.

35 *House Journal*, 22 Jan. 1799.

36 Ibid.

condemned the French demand for tribute from America and vowed to put an end to French military encroachments. The only way America could maintain her independence, claimed the Federalists, was by supporting the policies of the present administration.[37] The most recent of those policies was, of course, the Alien and Sedition Acts. The Enemy Alien Act was relatively easy to justify; it was a fundamental weapon in America's fight against "French influence." The Sedition Act was necessary because "government cannot be secured, if, by falsehood and malicious slander, it is to be deprived of the confidence of the people. It is vain to urge that truth will prevail and that slander, when detected, recoils on the calumniator. The experience of the world, and our own experience, prove that a continued course of defamation will at length sully the fairest reputation and throw suspicion on the purest conduct."[38]

To make certain that virtue was recognized, the Federalists felt it necessary to punish anyone who attempted to question the virtues of their leaders. Thus, the Virginia Federalists, who in the past had given only grudging support to Alexander Hamilton's financial measures and the Jay Treaty—policies which later proved to be in the nation's best interest—were now actively defending the most unpopular and illiberal of all administration measures, the Alien and Sedition Acts.

The harsh rhetoric of both the Republican and Federalist Addresses was due at least in part to the fact that each was meant to constitute an unofficial party platform. The Republicans concentrated on Hamilton's detested financial policies, the threat of English influence, and the menace to civil liberties and states' rights posed by the Alien and Sedition Acts. These were the issues which promised to win them the most votes. Similarly, the Federalists tried to avoid discussion of the secretary of the treasury's financial schemes and the administration's close ties with Great Britain because they knew that they could not make a case for them with the electorate; instead, they

37 Ibid.
38 Ibid.

resumed their persistent theme—the need to combat French influence and Republican disloyalty.

The legislative session had dragged into January 1799, but the Republicans still had one more item on their agenda. Although in no way connected with the Alien and Sedition Acts, or with any matter of national concern, it was nevertheless a valuable weapon in their campaign against the Federalists. In January 1798, Madison had lamented that Republicans had not rallied behind the recent attempts to divest the Episcopal Church of its glebe lands and hinted that he hoped that they would do so in the future.[39] The Baptists and other dissenting sects had come close to victory in the legislative session of 1797, but at the last minute the state senate had vetoed the House proposal to sell the church lands.[40] In 1798, the Republicans lined up solidly with the Baptists and pushed their plans to completion. On January 19, 1799, at the close of the session, the General Assembly finally agreed to a measure divesting the Episcopal Church of its lands.[41]

Party spirit had worked a revolution in the attitude of the assembly toward what had earlier been a purely local issue. On all previous occasions, the dominant division on the church land issue had been that between the east and the west; Federalists and Republicans could be found in equal proportions on both sides of the question. The predominantly Episcopalian east, because it had more representatives than the Baptist-dominated west, had always been able to rebuff any attempts to sell the church lands. By 1798, party loyalty had become more important than religious persuasion. Of those who voted for the proposal, sixty-seven were Republicans, only seventeen were Federalists. Predictably, all seventeen Federalists were from western counties. Thirty-three Federalists and only twenty-

---

39 Hamilton, ed., *Monroe's Writing*, 2: 97n. The glebe lands issue did not suddenly reappear in 1799. The House of Delegates had voted on, and rejected, petitions calling for the sale of the glebes nearly every session between 1790 and 1799. The most detailed treatment of the voting pattern in the House during the decade of the 1790s on the glebe lands issue is Hall, "A Quantitative Approach to . . . Virginia, 1790-1810."

40 *House Journal*, 5 Jan. 1798; *Senate Journal*, 20 Jan. 1798.

41 *House Journal*, 19 Jan. 1799.

one Republicans opposed the bill; nearly all the opponents from both parties represented the eastern part of the state. The three areas most affected by the increasingly partisan character of the glebe lands issue were the Southeastern Piedmont and the Central Neck, previously heavily Republican and opposed to the sale of the lands, and those counties lying in the Shenandoah Valley, which had formerly been leaning toward Federalism and had favored sale of the glebes. In each of these areas the respective positions on the glebe lands question shifted as partisan divisions tightened.[42]

The legislative history of the glebe lands proposal provides an excellent example of the way in which national politics and local interests were beginning to play upon one another. Madison, working to strengthen the position the Republican party in national affairs, recognized the importance of this strictly local issue in bolstering Republican support in Virginia. The Baptists, less concerned with national politics than with their own special interests, were more kindly disposed to the Republicans after receiving their aid in the church land struggle. The culmination of this alliance would come in the presidential election of 1800, when the Republican ticket would reap the rewards of Madison's efforts.

The assembly session of 1798 was momentous. Never before had opposition to federal policy been so persistent and never before had partisanship affected such a variety of legislative business. But it would be unfair to judge the actions of the legislature solely on the quality of the political theory it espoused. The Virginia Resolves and the Republican and Federalist Addresses were not abstract, political treatises, but were campaign documents aimed at attracting popular support for the respective parties. The Republicans, because they were fighting to maintain their advantage over the Federalists within Virginia and to set an example for Republicans elsewhere,

---

[42] Again, the best discussion of voting patterns on the issue is Hall, "A Quantitative Approach to . . . Virginia, 1790-1810." For the specific votes on the question see *House Journal*, 9 Dec. 1789, 13 Nov. 1790, 6 Dec. 1791, 25 Nov. 1794, 27 Nov. 1795, 5 Jan. 1798, 19 Jan. 1799.

resorted to much stronger rhetoric than they would have under ordinary circumstances. This was certainly the case in Jefferson's attempt to nullify the Alien and Sedition Laws. But the doctrine advanced by Jefferson cannot be ignored because it was proposed at the height of partisan rivalry. As a leader of the Republican party and as one of the most gifted political thinkers of his day, Jefferson had a special obligation to keep the methods of opposition to the Federalist administration within reasonable bounds.

Was Jefferson justified, then, in using the nullification doctrine to promote civil liberty and victory for the Republican party? Did the evils of the nullification doctrine, which were apparent even to Jefferson's contemporaries, outweigh any good that might be obtained by its use?[43] In assessing Jefferson's conduct, it is not fair to compare his attempt to nullify the Alien and Sedition Laws with those of John C. Calhoun three decades later. The circumstances were different. When the Virginia Resolves were proposed, the bonds of union were new and uncertain; the Supreme Court had not yet asserted its authority as the final arbiter of the constitutionality of federal statutes. Furthermore, in the absence of any clear precedents as to where sovereignty ultimately rested, it was not unreasonable to assume that it resided with the states. Indeed, the Articles of Confederation, upon which the Constitution was based, clearly made the states the final source of sovereign power. If the states possessed ultimate sovereignty, then it was only logical, from the viewpoint of a political theorist in 1798, that the states should also possess the power to declare a federal law unconstitutional.

Even in its proper historical context, however, the nullifica-

---

43 Most of the leading Jeffersonian scholars have maintained that Jefferson was justified in this particular case in resorting to the nullification doctrine. Their reasoning has been best summed up by Douglass Adair: "Jefferson and Madison in advancing their theory of States' Rights were not defending the abstract authority of the states as an end in itself, but as a practical means to protect the civil liberties of living persons." *William and Mary Quarterly*, 3d ser., 5 (1948): 146. One of the few dissenters from this viewpoint is Leonard W. Levy, *Jefferson and Civil Liberties: The Darker Side* (Cambridge, Mass., 1963), pp. 42-70.

tion doctrine advanced by Jefferson was dangerous. Both Federalists and moderate Republicans in the Assembly warned that if a single state legislature attempted to disallow a federal law either anarchy or forceful repression would shortly follow.[44] Jefferson, John Taylor, and those who supported nullification had no way of knowing that the means they advocated would be the same as those used by South Carolina nullifiers and Southern segregationists, but they should have recognized that the act of defying established laws and institutions, no matter how noble the ends, was fraught with danger. A great many Republicans were aware of the implications of nullification even if their leaders were not, for without their support the Federalists would never have succeeded in deleting the passage from the Virginia Resolutions.[45]

One aspect of the proceedings in the Virginia legislature of 1798, seemingly unrelated to the controversy over the Virginia Resolutions, has remained under a cloud of suspicion. During the session in which the members of the Assembly debated the constitutionality of the Alien and Sedition Acts, they also passed legislation to reorganize the militia, to purchase additional arms, and to erect an armory in Richmond. The legislature also raised taxes by 25 percent, presumably to pay the cost of these increased defense expenditures.[46] Historians writing in the nineteenth and early twentieth centuries maintained that the increase in the defense establishment was intended to provide for armed resistance against enforcement of the Alien and Sedition Acts.[47] The basis for this conclusion

---

[44] *Resolutions of Virginia*, pp. 76-78, 111-13, 154-57.

[45] *House Journal*, 21 Dec. 1798. As a political weapon, the Virginia Resolutions at least partly failed in their objective. The Republicans had hoped that other states would join in their protest over the Alien and Sedition Acts, but the exact opposite was the case. None of the other states concurred with Virginia and Kentucky, and the legislatures of Delaware, Rhode Island, Massachusetts, New York, Connecticut, New Hampshire, and Vermont condemned the Resolutions as an unwarranted exercise of power. Even in Staunton, Virginia, when the Resolutions were presented for distribution, "the court, without any deliberation, tore them to pieces and trampled them under foot." *Resolutions of Virginia*, pp. 5-16; *Columbian Mirror*, 23 April 1799.

[46] Shepherd, *Statutes at Large*, 2: 141-47, 151.

[47] Among those who have repeated the story are Beveridge, *Marshall*, 2: 406; and Henry Adams, *John Randolph* (Boston, 1887), p. 27.

has previously rested on a few, isolated pieces of evidence. John Nicholas, the heretical member of the predominately Republican Nicholas family, published an open letter in the *Virginia Argus* on March 29, 1799, accusing the Republicans of gathering a store of arms in Richmond as part of their plans for rebellion.[48] In 1817, John Randolph of Roanoke openly boasted of these plans for resistance in a speech on the floor of the United States House of Representatives.[49] And William Branch Giles, reminiscing before the Virginia legislature in 1825, again kindled the suspicion that the Republicans' opposition to the Alien and Sedition Acts was not meant to be confined to peaceful remonstrances.[50] All these sources are highly suspect. Nicholas had already been involved in an abortive attempt to incriminate Jefferson by stealing his mail from the Albemarle County Post Office, and his Republican opponents believed him to be so embittered against them that he would easily stoop to lying.[51] Randolph's testimony is also open to question, since it is impossible to know whether the mentally unstable Virginia congressman was enjoying one of his lucid moments at the time he made his statement. Twenty-seven years had passed when Giles recalled the event in the Virginia legislature; he might have mistakenly passed off as absolute fact the rumors he had heard from people like Randolph.

It is possible to reject a conspiratorial interpretation and to view the strengthening of the militia as just one step in a campaign begun as early as 1792 to improve Virginia's defenses against Indian attacks and foreign intrigue. The need for additional armaments was apparent as early as 1796, and in September of that year Governor James Wood began negotiating for the purchase of additional arms. These activities, initiated long before the passage of the Alien and Sedition Acts, may

48 *Virginia Argus,* 29 March 1799.
49 *Annals of Congress,* 30: 794-95.
50 William B. Giles, *Political Miscellanies* (Richmond, 1830), p. 146.
51 The letter that Nicholas stole contained statements highly critical of President Washington. It actually belonged to Jefferson's nephew, Peter Carr, but Nicholas tried to make Washington believe that Jefferson wrote it in order to damage Jefferson's political career. Malone, *Jefferson and the Ordeal of Liberty,* pp. 309-11.

have been part of a long-range plan to guard against outside aggression and may have had no connection with the Republican opposition to federal policy.[52]

There are some pieces missing from the puzzle. Accusations regarding plans among Republicans to resist the federal government were not confined to John Nicholas, John Randolph, and William Branch Giles. After the legislature adjourned in January 1799, similar charges were circulated by Federalists throughout the state. One Republican, Augustine Jennings, was reported to have declared openly that "the object of the last Virginia legislature in increasing the taxes upon the people to twenty five per cent is to purchase arms to put in the hands of the people of this state for the purpose of enabling them to oppose the government of the United States." Other Federalists maintained that it was common knowledge that "the people were encouraged most openly to make resistance" during the controversy over the Alien and Sedition Acts.[53]

More important than the partisan and self-serving testimony of the Federalists was the way in which the members of the House of Delegates reacted to the proposals for a larger defense establishment at the various times during the decade at which they were discussed. The Virginia legislature had been notorious in its failure to provide funds for defense. At the height of the Indian warfare, when physical danger to Virginians was greatest, the legislature had refused to increase taxes to provide more troops and material.[54] The General Assembly continued to procrastinate on matters of defense during every session until 1798. Furthermore, on all occasions prior to 1798, the vote on whether or not to increase defense expenditures had been nonpartisan; Federalists and Republicans were evenly divided on the question. In the 1798 session, however, the Federalists specifically asked that the "act to authorize the Executive to

---

[52] This is the argument of Philip Davidson, "Virginia and the Alien and Sedition Laws," *American Historical Review* 36 (1931): 336-42.

[53] *Columbian Mirror*, 23 April 1799; *Virginia Gazette and General Advertiser*, 29 Jan. 1799, 26 Feb. 1799; Alexander Hamilton to Jonathan Dayton, 1799, in *The Works of Alexander Hamilton*, ed. Henry Cabot Lodge, 9 vols. (New York, 1885-1886), 8: 518; *Resolutions of Virginia*, p. 11.

[54] See *House Journal*, 13 Nov. 1789, 2 Dec. 1793, 24 Dec. 1794.

procure arms for the defense of the Commonwealth" be suspended for twelve months. This request was denied, 73-81.
Fifty-four Federalists supported the motion to delay the purchase of the arms, only one opposed it.[55] Thus, although it
may have been only coincidental that the efforts to improve
Virginia's military establishment occurred at the same time
that Republican opposition to federal policy was greatest, it
is evident that the Federalists were well aware of the possible
consequences of such an unfortunate accident of timing. Republicans in positions of authority probably had no intention of
using the newly strengthened militia to resist federal enforcement of the Alien and Sedition Laws, but the Federalists almost
certainly believed they did.

Many Virginians thought that the Republicans had gone
too far in their opposition to the federal government. There
had been altogether too much talk about disunion and secession
during the legislative session of 1798, and the Federalists took
advantage of the reaction that followed. Although the Virginia
Federalists had on the whole approved of the Alien and Sedition
Acts they had played, by necessity, an essentially defensive role
when faced with the Republican attacks on government policy.
Once the Virginia Resolves were adopted, however, the Federalists were able to take the offensive. With considerable gusto,
they turned from their defense of the Alien and Sedition Acts
to attack the Virginia Resolutions as an unwarranted exercise
of power by the state legislature.

The major testing ground for the Federalists' strategy was
the congressional district encompassing Richmond. John Marshall, the Federalists' strongest possible candidate, was running
against the Republican incumbent, John Clopton. Although
the election was not held until April 1799, the campaign began
as early as September 1798 when one of Marshall's supporters
(possibly Marshall himself), signing himself as "Freeholder,"
publicly inquired about Marshall's qualifications for office.[56] A

55 Ibid., 15 Jan. 1799.
56 Beveridge, *Marshall*, 2: 386-87.

week later, on September 20, Marshall replied to "Freeholder" in the newspapers. His remarks with respect to signs of party division and French influence within America paralleled the sentiments of Federalists everywhere. In replying to the query regarding the Alien and Sedition Acts, however, Marshall differed sharply with many of his Federalist colleagues. He declared: "I am not an advocate for the alien and sedition bills; had I been in Congress when they passed, I should, unless my judgment could have been changed certainly have opposed them. Yet, I do not think them fraught with all those mischiefs which many gentlemen ascribe to them. I should have opposed them because I think them useless; and because they are calculated to create unnecessary discontents and jealousies at a time when our very existence as a nation, may depend on our union."[57]

Some Northern Federalists were particularly upset at Marshall's statement and denounced him for his cowardice.[58] But it was moderation that kept Federalism alive in Virginia. Unfortunately, most Virginia Federalists, by deciding to support the Alien and Sedition Acts, were in the process of abandoning their moderation.

Soon after Marshall had published his "Answers to a Freeholder," John Clopton's supporters published some questions for their own candidate. Clopton unequivocally opposed the Alien and Sedition Laws, would continue to fight all attempts to draw America under the influence of Great Britain, and, although continuing to champion the cause of revolutionary France, would never work for her interests at the expense of those of the United States.[59]

"Buckskin," a supporter of Marshall, was the next to speak out. He accused Clopton of calling President John Adams "a traitor to the United States."[60] This was a serious charge; Secretary of State Timothy Pickering began plans to prosecute

---

57 Marshall's "Answers to a Freeholder" are printed in full in ibid., 2: 575-77.
58 Fisher Ames to Christopher Gore, 18 Dec. 1798, in Ames, ed., *Fisher Ames,* 1: 246-47.
59 *Virginia Gazette and General Advertiser,* 5 Oct. 1798.
60 Ibid., 9, 16 Oct. 1798.

Clopton for sedition, even though Clopton immediately printed a denial of "Buckskin's" charge. To his credit, Marshall wrote Pickering, informed him that there was no evidence to prove that Clopton had made such a statement, and advised him not to proceed any further against his Republican opponent.[61]

After the passage of the Virginia Resolutions, supporters of the two candidates intensified their efforts. The Federalists turned from their defense of the Alien and Sedition Acts and began a counterattack against the "disloyal" activities of their Republican opponents. The Virginia Republicans, while they did not alter the substance of their criticism of federal policy, became even more sharply critical. In December 1798 Meriwether Jones, a radical Republican, began publishing the *Richmond Examiner*, one of the most irresponsible newspapers in the history of American journalism.[62]

The Federalists' offensive against Clopton and the Republican party was based largely on the debates in the legislature over the Virginia Resolves. They criticized the Republicans for usurping rights of the people and for fostering a spirit of disunion. If anyone had the right to declare a law unconstitutional, and the Federalists doubted whether anyone did, it was the people, not a state legislature. Clopton, because he approved of the actions of the Republicans in the legislature, was no less guilty than those who had voted for the Resolutions.[63]

John Thompson, a young polemicist from Fredericksburg, renewed the attack on Marshall's political principles through

[61] Timothy Pickering to Edward Carrington, Trenton, 23 Oct. 1798, Marshall to Pickering, Richmond, 30 Oct. 1798, Timothy Pickering Papers.

[62] Six months later, in May 1798, the Federalists established their own newspaper, the *Virginia Federalist*. Both newspapers reached new depths of scurrility and irresponsible journalism. The exchange between the two became so bitter that eventually, the two rival publishers, Meriwether Jones and James Rind, fought a duel. William C. Stanard, "Party Violence, 1790-1800," *Virginia Magazine of History and Biography* 29 (1921): 177. Lisle Rose, *Prologue to Democracy*, pp. 222-23, maintains that the establishment of the *Virginia Federalist* was "one of the most significant advances" in the Virginia Federalist party's history. This appears to be an overstatement. The Federalist newspaper, plagued by low subscriptions and erratic writing, survived little more than a year.

[63] Particularly effective were the arguments of "Plain Truth," *Virginia Gazette and General Advertiser*, 5, 12, 15, 26 Feb., 1 March 1799.

the pages of the *Examiner.* Writing under the pseudonym "Curtius," Thompson admitted that Marshall was respected by many good and patriotic men, but added, "if you are indeed 'an American in heart and sentiment,' you must be deeply mortified when you observe that the persons most vehement in your praise are the partizans of Great Britain and the inveterate enemies of independence."[64] This theme ran through Thompson's and, indeed, all the Republicans' attacks on Marshall. He was accused of being among those "who have long endeavoured to restore us to the abject condition of the British colonies" and of attempting to sell American independence to British merchants in order to enrich a privileged minority.[65] Great Britain had long been the symbol of corrupt, oppressive rule, and now the federal government was beginning to be viewed in the same light. As a result, it became impossible for anyone to support the Federalist administration without being labeled a partisan of the British, monarchical form of government.

Marshall refused to become embroiled in a pamphlet war with "Curtius." A few of his supporters attempted to answer in his behalf, but their efforts were short-lived, since they possessed neither the style nor the polemical skill of "Curtius."[66]

As election day approached and it became obvious that the contest would be close, the Federalists enlisted the aid of Patrick Henry. In a letter to Archibald Blair, circulated throughout the congressional district, Henry denounced the tactics of the Republicans in the legislature and threw his support to Marshall.[67] The effect of the endorsement was terrific. Henry had refused to identify himself with either party during the controversies of the past few years, and his support of Marshall had a considerable effect among the sizable group of Virginia voters who were, like Henry, as yet unaligned with either the

64 [John Thompson], *The Letters of Curtius Addressed to John Marshall* (Richmond, 1798), p. 4.

65 Ibid., p. 8.

66 Ibid., p. 37; "Hodge" and "Procopius" in the *Virginia Gazette and General Advertiser,* 11, 25 Dec. 1798.

67 Patrick Henry to Archibald Blair, Red-hill, 8 Jan. 1799, Timothy Pickering Papers; Beveridge, *Marshall,* 2: 413.

Republicans or the Federalists. In the minds of many, Patrick Henry was the man most closely associated with the struggle to preserve the liberties of Virginians from the threat of outside authority; if Marshall possessed Henry's confidence, the Republicans' accusations as to his pro-British sympathies must assuredly be false.

On election day the two candidates were seated alongside the judges at a table on the courthouse green to listen to the progress of the voting. This election was considered so important that, reportedly, not a single eligible voter was allowed to be absent. "Sick men were taken in their beds to the polls; the halt, the lame, and the blind were hunted up and every mode of conveyance was mustered into service." All the while the assembled voters were imbibing the hospitality of the two candidates, and "the majority took it straight." As each freeholder cast his vote, *viva voce,* the favored candidate would rise from his seat, bow, and publicly thank him for his suffrage. The sheriff would ask, "Mr. Blair, who do you vote for?" When he said, "John Marshall," the Federalist candidate replied, "Your vote is appreciated Mr. Blair." When the next voter voiced his preference for John Clopton, the Republican candidate avowed: "Mr. Buchanan, I shall treasure that vote in my memory. It will be regarded as a feather in my cap forever." As the afternoon wore on and the contest remained close, the partisans of each candidate became more vocal and more violent. When one citizen, Thomas Rutherford, cast his vote for Marshall, an enraged Republican snarled: "You sir, ought to have your mouth smashed." When the tumult and shouting had ended, Marshall emerged victorious by 108 votes.[68]

The conduct of Marshall and Clopton during the campaign and on election day was a curious mixture of the traditional, aristocratic style of politics and the new, highly partisan brand. The two candidates based their appeal squarely on the impor-

[68] Beveridge, *Marshall,* 2, 413 16; Sydnor, *Gentlemen Freeholders,* pp. 21-22. Both Beveridge and Sydnor take their description from George W. Munford, *The Two Parsons; Cupid's Sports; the Dream; and the Jewels of Virginia* (Richmond, 1884), pp. 208-10.

tant issues of the time. To a significant degree, the freeholders were made to feel that they had a part in shaping public policy; no longer were they simply voting for the most prestigious candidate. But certain elements of the old style remained. The treating, the personal attention, and often subtle coercion given to each voter were practices of an earlier era.[69] Virginia, in the Marshall-Clopton election, found itself at a crossroads. In one direction lay a political process where elections were decided by the people after a full and free discussion of the issues. Although there were many obstacles in this path, it was the road to democracy. In the other direction lay a method of campaigning which relied on wealth, influence, and personal prestige. Although this road had considerable appeal for traditionalists, it was a road leading back to the past, toward aristocracy. If the Federalists could continue to offer the voters popular alternatives to Republican policies and personnel, the election campaigns that followed would constitute a meaningful step toward the democratization of the political process in Virginia.

The Federalists' success was not confined to Richmond. They captured eight of Virginia's nineteen seats in Congress—a gain of four seats over the previous session. The Federalists retained strength in the Eastern Shore, in the Norfolk area, and in the northwestern district encompassing Frederick and Berkeley counties; they increased their strength in the Southern Piedmont, in the Southern Tidewater, in the two congressional districts in the Northern Neck, as well as in the city of Richmond. The shift in the Northern Neck was the most significant; there the Federalists would succeed in consolidating their gains beyond the election of 1800. The Federalist victory in the Southern Tidewater is perhaps best explained by the intensity of anti-French, and therefore by implication, anti-Republican sentiment in those areas served by the port of Norfolk. And Federalist fortunes in Richmond were enhanced both by the

[69] The new standards of campaigning were even beginning to become institutionalized. In 1798 the General Assembly prohibited the practice of treating at elections. Shepherd, *Statutes at Large*, 2: 150.

increasing disenchantment with France and by Marshall's extraordinary popularity.[70]

The Federalist gain in Virginia was but one element in a general upsurge of Federalist fortunes throughout the nation. The opposition party, now a minority in both houses of Congress, realized that it was essential to maintain control of the state government. There was little chance that they would ever lose their numerical majority in the Virginia legislature, but the Republican leaders in the Assembly needed to use that majority more effectively than they had in the past. The Republicans spared no effort to persuade their most influential spokesmen to run for the legislature. After considerable pleading by party stalwarts, both Madison and William Branch Giles agreed to serve in the legislature.[71] The triumvirate of Madison, Giles, and John Taylor promised to lend the Republican cause a wealth of prestige and organizational ability.

The Federalists had similar plans. They urged Patrick Henry to run for the legislature on the grounds that he was the only man who could halt the movement towards disunion. Henry agreed in hopes that he could "arrest the progress of the State legislature in opposition to the General Government" and like Madison and Giles was elected with no difficulty.[72] Jefferson was furious when he heard the news: "Mr. Henry will have the mortification of encountering such a mass of talents as he has never met before; for from everything I can learn, we never had an abler nor a sounder legislature. His apostacy must be unaccountable to those who do not know all the recesses of his heart."[73] Jefferson's pique overruled his judgment. Although

[70] Dauer, *The Adams Federalists*, pp. 316-21. The election of a Federalist congressman in the Southern Piedmont is more difficult to explain. The overwhelming proportion of representatives from that area to Congress and to the legislature had been, and would remain, vigorously opposed to the policies of the Federalists.

[71] Republican Members of Congress to James Madison, 7 Feb. 1799, in Hunt, ed., *Madison's Writings*, 6: 341; John Taylor to Creed Taylor, 10 April 1799, Creed Taylor Papers, University of Virginia.

[72] George Washington to Patrick Henry, Mt. Vernon, 15 Jan. 1799, in Fitzpatrick, ed., *Washington's Writings*, 37: 87-90; Spencer Roane to James Monroe, 24 March 1799, Monroe Papers, LC, quoted in Cunningham, *Jeffersonian Republicans, 1789-1801*, p. 156.

it was undeniable that the strength and quality of the Republican delegation to the legislature was superior to any other during the past decade, Henry's presence would have been an enormous aid to the Federalists.

Unfortunately for the supporters of the administration, Henry died in June 1799, before the General Assembly met. The Federalists were faced with the unpleasant fact that they would be without the services of the one man who might have been able to dampen some of the partisan spirit in the legislature. With Marshall in Congress and Henry gone from the scene, the Federalists were ill equipped to combat the combined talents of Madison, Giles, and Taylor.

The Republicans expected to accomplish three general tasks during the legislative session of 1799. First, they were intent on purging the state government of all its Federalist officials. They had failed to do so in 1798 when the Federalist Speaker of the House John Wise was reelected to his post, but they had no intention of allowing a repetition. Nor did they mean to confine themselves to the legislative branch. Governor James Wood had tried to remain neutral in the contest between the two parties, but at this crucial time the Republicans considered neutrality a danger to their cause.

Second, the Republicans wanted to pass additional resolutions clarifying the meaning of the Virginia Resolves. Jefferson, perhaps realizing that his suggestions had been too extreme the year before, mapped a more moderate course for the Republicans in the 1799 session. He believed that the Republicans in the House of Delegates should first answer the objections of those states that had condemned the Virginia legislature for passing the Resolves. He wanted the legislature to make clear, "in affectionate and conciliatory language, our warm attachment to the union with our sister states, and to the instrument by which we are united."[74] Some Republicans protested that

---

[73] Jefferson to Archibald Stuart, Monticello, 14 May 1799, in Ford, ed., *Jefferson's Writings*, 7: 378.

[74] Jefferson to Wilson Cary Nicholas, Monticello, 5 Sept. 1799, in Ford, ed., *Jefferson's Writings*, 7: 390.

this strategy was too mild and that it would not effect the desired changes in federal policy. John Taylor considered "the Republican cause as daily declining on account of its fashionable maxim of moderation in its efforts, and waiting, as it is called, for the public mind. . . . Bold truth and steady detection ought to have been all along resorted to, as the only means of counteracting their acts." He predicted that Americans would find themselves ruled by an "anglo-monarchic-aristocratic-military government" unless they immediately combined to stop Federalist policy.[75] Fortunately, moderate voices prevailed.

Third, the Republicans were determined to change Virginia's presidential electoral law. The present law permitted the residents of each of Virginia's twenty-one electoral districts to vote for only one presidential elector, thus giving the Federalist presidential candidate a chance of picking up at least a few electoral votes in those districts where the Federalist party had concentrations of strength. The Republicans, in order to assure their candidate's receiving all Virginia's electoral votes, wanted to change from a system of individual districts to the method of a single, statewide ticket. If that could be accomplished, the task of party organization for the election of 1800 would be considerably simplified.

When the Assembly convened on December 2, 1799, the Republicans systematically began to remove Federalists from every state office. The first to go was John Stuart, Federalist Clerk of the House. His association with the *Virginia Federalist* made him anathema to the Republicans, and accordingly, he was replaced by William Wirt.[76] The Republicans next nominated Larkin Smith to oppose John Wise for the speakership. The Federalists pleaded with the Republican members to consider Wise's long and distinguished service before they cast their votes. The Republicans, on the other hand, argued that

75 John Taylor to Creed Taylor, Caroline, 10 April 1799, Creed Taylor Papers. The whole tone of Taylor's letter suggests that he was prepared for more violent means of opposing the general government should the more moderate methods of Madison fail to exert any influence in government policy.

76 *House Journal*, 2 Dec. 1799; *Virginia Gazette and General Advertiser*, 6 Dec. 1799.

the Federalist administration in Philadelphia had consistently excluded Republicans from office. It was therefore imperative that they attempt to combat the effects of Federalist patronage. This time their arguments were effective; Larkin Smith defeated Wise, 83-55.[77]

The Republicans next elected Wilson Cary Nicholas to fill the United States Senate seat formerly occupied by the recently deceased Henry Tazewell. This was hardly unusual, as in the ten years that Virginia had been a member of the union, it had never had a Federalist senator. Immediately thereafter, the Republicans nominated James Monroe for governor. This move occasioned more opposition from the Federalists than any of the others. They demanded that the election be postponed until they could more fully investigate Monroe's conduct while ambassador to France. They suspected Monroe, more than any other Virginian, of being under French influence. The Federalists, however, simply did not have the votes to block Monroe's election. Monroe received 111 votes; the Federalist, James Breckinridge, 44.[78] The next day, the strongly pro-administration newspaper, the *Virginia Federalist,* mourned: "Virginia's misfortunes may be comprised in one short sentence—Monroe is elected."[79] The Republicans had succeeded in occupying every important office over which the legislature exercised control. They were not prepared to concentrate on vindicating the conduct of the last Assembly.

The *Virginia Report,* written and guided through the legislature by Madison, was the most careful and knowledgeable analysis of federal-state relations to appear up to that time.[80] Perhaps its most important feature was its exposition on the nature of the compact between the state and national

---

[77] *House Journal,* 2 Dec. 1799.

[78] Ibid., 5 Dec. 1799; *Virginia Gazette and General Advertiser,* 10 Dec. 1799.

[79] *Virginia Federalist,* 6 Dec. 1799.

[80] Historians have of course discussed the *Report,* but they have spent much more time analyzing the more brief and dramatic *Resolutions of Virginia and Kentucky.* Most Federalists and Republicans at the time viewed the *Report* as little more than a reiteration of the Virginia Resolutions. F. M. Anderson, "Contemporary Opinion of the Virginia and Kentucky Resolutions," *American Historical Review* 5 (1900): 243.

governments. While the Virginia Resolutions had used the word compact rather loosely and indeed had implied that it could be broken by the action of a single state legislature, the *Report* treated it as a solemn agreement which could be challenged only under the most serious circumstances. Although Madison maintained that the states possessed ultimate sovereignty, and therefore were vested with the power to maintain or dissolve the compact, he was careful to add: "It does not follow however, that because the states, as sovereign parties to their constitutional compact, must ultimately decide whether it has been violated, that such a decision ought to be interposed either in a hasty manner or on doubtful and inferior cases. . . . [I]n the case of an intimate and constitutional union, like that of the United States, it is evident that the interposition of the parties, in their sovereign capacity, can be called for by measures only deeply and essentially affecting the vital principles of their political system."[81] Madison stressed this again and again. Any violation of the Constitution, to warrant the interposition of the states, must be "of a nature *dangerous* to the great purposes for which the Constitution was established" and must be clearly seen as such by a majority of the people.[82]

Despite the facts that union among the states was a novelty, that precedents for judging the constitutionality of federal laws were ill defined, and that Madison used extreme caution in defining the circumstances under which a state could rule a law unconstitutional, the doctrine of nullification was nevertheless pernicious. And Madison realized this. When the General Assembly declared the Alien and Sedition Acts unconstitutional in 1798, many Republicans believed that it was

[81] J. W. Randolph, *Virginia Report* (Richmond, 1850), p. 192. The Virginia Resolutions had also used the term "states" carelessly; no one knew whether the authors of the resolutions intended the word to mean state legislatures or the people of the state as a whole. In the *Report*, Madison was careful to define the state as "the people comprising those political societies in their highest sovereign capacity." This definition was consistent with Madison's own belief that sovereignty rested with the people, not with the states. It also reflected his misgivings over the fact that the Virginia Resolutions had been passed by the state legislature, rather than a constituent assembly. Madison to Jefferson, 29 Dec. 1798, in Hunt, ed., *Madison's Writings*, 6: 328-29n.

[82] Randolph, *The Virginia Report*, pp. 192-95.

a statement of fact, not opinion, and that the practical effect of the declaration was to render the laws null and void. In the second half of the *Report,* when he was specifically discussing the constitutionality of the Alien and Sedition Acts, Madison clearly stated: "The declarations . . . are expressions of opinion, unaccompanied with any other effect than what they may produce on opinion, by exciting reflection. The expositions of the judiciary, on the other hand, are carried into immediate effect by force. The former may lead to a change of the general will; possibly to a change in the opinion of the judiciary; the latter enforces the general will, whilst that will and that opinion continue unchanged."[83]

This statement presents a striking contradiction with the first half of the *Report.* Madison had carefully laid down the conditions under which a state could resort to interposition and had stated that the circumstances surrounding the Alien and Sedition Acts had met those conditions, but in the second half of the *Report,* he was unwilling to admit that Virginia had taken the steps that would lead to interposition. Although he probably met disagreement from some of his Republican colleagues on this matter, Madison maintained that the Virginia legislature had not passed a judgment on the constitutionality of the Alien and Sedition Laws but, rather, had merely stated its opinion on the subject. This distinction, while it probably lessened the political effectiveness of the *Report,* was testimony to Madison's longstanding commitment to the union.

The Federalists were not impressed by Madison's moderation. For all its subtleties and equivocations, the *Report* still constituted a defense of the Virginia Resolutions. Accordingly, on January 7, 1800, when the *Report* came to a vote, the Federalists proposed a resolution stating "the present General Assembly, convinced of the impropriety of the Resolutions of the last assembly, deem it inexpedient to act upon the said resolutions." Their efforts failed, 57-98, and Madison's *Report* was approved, 100-60.[84]

Ten days later the Assembly acted on the Republican pro-

---

[83] Ibid., pp. 230-31.   [84] *House Journal,* 7 Jan. 1800.

posal to change the method of choosing presidential electors. The Republicans made no secret of the purpose of the general ticket law: it was intended solely to assure Jefferson all of Virginia's twenty-one electoral votes in the next election. This reform, which the Federalists claimed would "exclude one-third at least of the citizens of Virginia from a vote for the President of the United States," represented a betrayal of the political principles which Virginia's Republican leaders had espoused over the past decade and offered a striking contrast with the high-toned phrases of the *Virginia Report*.[85] For ten years, the Antifederalists had been complaining of the dangers of consolidation and domination by the Northern majority in Congress; they now sought to stamp out any influence which the minority party in their own state might possess. Indeed, the radical and unsavory Republican journalist, James Thomson Callender, in his *The Prospect before Us*, had only recently condemned the general ticket laws of the New England states as a device to facilitate consolidation.[86] The Republicans' only justification for the general ticket law was thoroughly pragmatic: the Eastern states had such laws, and "it is necessary to fight an adversary at his own weapons."[87] Many Republicans were disturbed by such an obvious departure from their own political principles, and the measure only narrowly passed, 78-73.[88]

The Federalists had lost every major battle in the legislative session of 1799. They were unable even to win approval for a resolution honoring Patrick Henry, in which it was stated, his "unrivalled eloquence and superior talents, were in times of peculiar peril and distress, so uniformly devoted to the cause of freedom and of his country." The Republicans evidently thought Henry's most recent efforts had not been devoted to the cause of freedom and defeated the resolution, 58-88. Henry could not escape the "baneful effects of faction," even in his grave.[89]

[85] Ibid., 17 Jan. 1800, *Virginia Federalist*, 19 March 1800.

[86] *House Journal*, 17 Jan. 1800.

[87] *Virginia Argus*, 21 Jan. 1800, quoted in Cunningham, *Jeffersonian Republicans, 1789-1801*, p. 175.

[88] *House Journal*, 17 Jan. 1800.

The tightening of party lines in Virginia can best be seen
in an analysis of the election and voting behavior of the members of the House of Delegates. The assembly elections of
1798 and 1799 are notable in one important respect: for the
first time in the decade, the citizens of Virginia seemed to be
interested enough in the campaigns for the Assembly to vote.
Although there are only a few counties where election records
are sufficiently complete to allow a comparison of the rate of
voter participation throughout the decade, the evidence that
exists suggests that the citizens of Virginia were experiencing
a change of attitude toward the electoral process. In Essex
County it was customary for 250 voters, or 25 percent of the
free adult white male population, to cast ballots for members
of the General Assembly; in both 1798 and 1799 nearly 350
citizens, or 35 percent voted in the Assembly election. In Brunswick County the increase was even more striking. In 1798 and
1799 nearly 800 citizens, or 45 percent of those eligible voted
in the Assembly election. The usual turnout had been about
half that figure. Thus, the voters of these two Virginia counties,
long apathetic, were finally beginning to respond to the increased competition between Republicans and Federalists for
public support.[90]

As could be expected, partisan divisions were even more
pronounced among the politically conscious gentry who served
in the General Assembly than among the electorate as a whole.
An analysis of the voting behavior of the fifty-four delegates
serving all three terms in the legislature during the years
1797-1800 indicates that each of the delegates, without excep-

---

[89] Ibid., 13 Dec. 1799. George Washington, who died on December 14, escaped
this display of partisanship. The Virginia General Assembly unanimously agreed
to wear black armbands throughout the session in honor of Washington. The
only hint of ill feeling in the Republican ranks was the rumor that James Monroe
had initially refused to attend the funeral of the former chief executive.
Columbian Mirror, 11 March 1800.

[90] Essex County, House of Delegates' Election Poll Lists, 21 April 1788, 14 April
1790, 18 April 1791, 16 April 1792, 15 April 1793, 18 April 1796, April 1797, April
1798, 24 April 1799, Essex County Deed Books, nos. 33 and 34, VSL; Brunswick
County, House of Delegates' Election Poll Lists, April 1789, April 1790, 25 April
1791, 27 April 1795, 24 April 1797, 23 April 1798, 24 April 1799, Election Returns,
Brunswick County Records, VSL.

tion, was aligned with one of the two parties. Despite the Federalists' increased efforts to win popular support, they continued to be hopelessly outnumbered in the lower house. Forty of the fifty-four delegates were Republicans, fourteen were Federalists.[91] As in previous years, there were no marked differences in the occupational or economic interests of the members of the two voting blocs.[92]

It is possible, however, to detect some patterns of regional voting within the state. Using the 1788 vote on ratification of the federal Constitution, the December 21, 1790, vote condemning assumption as unconstitutional, the November 20, 1795, vote on the Jay Treaty and the December 21, 1798, roll call on the Virginia Resolutions as guides to party voting over time, at least one area of strong and consistent Federalist support in the extreme west becomes apparent.[93] The Federalist success there probably resulted from a number of factors. First, the promise of federal protection against hostile Indians had always proved particularly attractive to the citizens of the west. It was generally conceded that the western delegates to the ratifying Convention were ultimately persuaded to support the Constitution because of the inability of the Confederation government to provide defense for them. And federal Indian policy, after a shaky beginning, actually began to yield tangible benefits to the western residents by the mid 1790s. Second, the Jay Treaty had proved advantageous to the citizens of the extreme west. The British, to the surprise of nearly everyone, had lived up to their promise in the Jay Treaty and had promptly relinquished their posts on the western frontier.

91 The Federalist-Republican ratio among the sample group is probably more lopsided than it was in the Assembly as a whole. If the votes on the Virginia Resolutions and the *Virginia Report* are any indication, the Republicans outnumbered their opponents by slightly less than two to one.

92 The divisions listed in the third part of Appendix 2 are based on a computer analysis of the voting behavior, on national issues, of the fifty-four men who served in the House of Delegates every year between 1797 and 1800. A rate of 75 percent agreement was set as the minimum requirement for inclusion within either voting bloc.

93 Accomac and Northampton counties on Virginia's Eastern Shore also tended to be solidly Federalist during the 1790s, but they were not numerically strong enough in the legislature to constitute a meaningful voting bloc.

Finally, the western counties had a number of compelling reasons for disliking the Republican-dominated state government in Richmond. They were particularly dissatisfied with the state constitution, believing that its provisions concerning apportionment of the legislature had consistently denied them adequate representation. Moreover, the national government in Philadelphia, no matter how distant it was in actual fact, seemed no more inaccessible than the capital in Richmond. In the absence of strong ties with either government, the western residents probably felt that the federal government could help them more than the state. The one rationale for their support of the Federalists that was conspicuously lacking was a belief in the nationalist precepts of Hamiltonian ideology. As was so often the case in Virginia, their allegiance to Federalism was based on particular, local interests and not on broad principles of public policy.

Federalist strength was less impressive elsewhere. Although the Federalists had picked up two congressional seats in the Northern Neck in the election of 1798, they actually lost ground in that area in the state legislature at the same time. In fact, Federalist strength in the Northern Neck throughout the entire decade seemed to fluctuate markedly; the Northern Neck representatives strongly supported ratification, mildly opposed assumption, narrowly favored the Jay Treaty, and disapproved of the Alien and Sedition Acts.

Republican domination in all other areas of the state by 1798 was even more pronounced than it was in the Northern Neck. In the Piedmont, which had been a strong source of Antifederalist support in 1788 and a nearly united source of opposition to both assumption and the Jay Treaty, the delegates overwhelmingly supported the Virginia Resolutions. And in the Tidewater, which provided the key to Republican fortunes, Republican-dominated counties outnumbered Federalist counties by more than four to one by 1798. This was an important development, since the Tidewater had been moderately Federalist in 1788 and rather evenly divided in 1790 and 1795 (see maps on pages 244, 245, 247, and 248).

Thus the Republicans, looking forward to the presidential election of 1800, had considerable cause for optimism in most parts of the state. And the small pockets of Federalist strength that did exist would be of no consequence in the election unless the supporters of the Federalist administration could somehow work a miracle throughout the rest of the state. With the general ticket law in effect, the party with a bare majority would gain all Virginia's twenty-one electoral votes. After the Assembly adjourned in January 1800, both Republicans and Federalists immediately began preparations for the campaign.

CHAPTER EIGHT

Triumph of Agrarian Republicanism

THE REPUBLICANS were the first to take advantage of the new presidential elector law. On January 21, 1800, the very day after the general ticket proposal had become law, ninety-three members of the legislature and a number of other persons met to lay plans for an efficient party organization for the election. It had long since been decided that Jefferson and Aaron Burr would be Republican candidates for president and vice president, so the first task was to nominate a slate of electors pledged to these two candidates. They succeeded in enlisting the aid of nearly every prominent Republican in the state. Among those chosen to run on the Republican ticket were George Wythe, Edmund Pendleton, James Madison, William Branch Giles, Archibald Stuart, and William Cabell.[1] With the general ticket law in operation, the prestige of these men would undoubtedly enhance Republican prospects in those districts where the party's strength might otherwise not have been so great.

On January 23, after the General Assembly had adjourned, the Republicans met a second time. They first appointed a General Standing Committee, headed by Philip Norborne Nicholas, which constituted the central body of the Republican organization and which was to oversee the campaign throughout the state. All the members of the committee lived in or near Richmond and could easily communicate with each other.

Moreover, Richmond, as the hub of political activity in the state, was the distribution point for most of the important news on the progress of the campaign throughout the nation and was thus the logical choice for the home base for Republican organization. The Republicans next appointed five-man committees in every county except three, Princess Anne in the east and Kanawha and Randolph in the west. In these counties, the Republicans were enough in doubt about the political loyalties of the leading residents that they did not appoint county committees. The task of the committees was to distribute any communications received from the General Committee throughout their respective counties and to send back to the central organization in Richmond any information that would promote the Republican ticket.[2] Republican leaders, particularly Jefferson, had been so plagued by the snooping of Federalist postal employees that the General Committee instructed the county committeemen to write Philip Norborne Nicholas, *"without annexing the word chairman;* this is enjoined to avoid interruption in their correspondence."[3]

Before the Republican strategy meeting adjourned, each member agreed to contribute a dollar to defray the expense of printing and distributing the list of Republican electoral college candidates. This was particularly important, since the new electoral law had eliminated *viva voce* voting and it was now the responsibility of each voter to write the names of all twenty-one candidates for elector, together with his own name, on a piece of paper which was to be used in place of a printed ballot. Since it would be difficult for the voters to remember the names of all twenty-one candidates, the Republicans printed sample ballots, sent them to each county committee, and suggested that the committeemen distribute them to the freeholders to be used as ballots on election day.[4]

---

[1] *Calendar of Virginia State Papers,* 9: 74-75.   [2] Ibid. 9: 75-87.

[3] Letter from Philip Norborne Nicholas, Chairman of the General Committee of Correspondence, Richmond, 1 Feb 1800, in *Virginia Argus,* 25 March 1800, quoted in Cunningham, *Jeffersonian Republicans, 1789-1801,* p. 153.

[4] Ibid., pp. 194, 196; *Calendar of Virginia State Papers,* 9: 76; Shepherd, *Statutes at Large,* 2: 197-200.

The Federalists met in February to plan their campaign.[5] In May they printed a list of their own candidates for presidential elector along with an address to the voters. The Federalist ticket was woefully inferior to that of the Republicans. Not one of Virginia's revolutionary heroes was on the list; even John Marshall, who was in the nation's capital serving a brief term as secretary of state, was unavailable as a candidate. Only John Wise, James Breckinridge, and George K. Taylor had any kind of statewide reputation and even they possessed none of the prestige of Wythe, Pendleton, or Madison. The Virginia Federalists were aware of their disadvantage. To avoid the stigma of being associated with such Northern Federalists as Hamilton, Wolcott, and Pickering, they styled themselves "The American Republican Ticket." Nowhere in their address to the voters did they attempt to praise President Adams. Instead, they carped at the unfairness of the general ticket law and pleaded with the voters to uphold the honor of the late President Washington.[6]

The embattled Federalists, because of the lackluster quality of their own ticket, were even driven to berating the Republicans for the "imposing names" used in behalf of Jefferson. The Federalists claimed that their candidates, because they had not enjoyed positions with the state government, would not "regard the rival authorities of the union with a jealousy, too apt to degenerate into hatred."[7] This last observation, although tinged with malice, contained some truth. So accustomed to directing the affairs of the largest and most populous state in the union, the Republicans had been unhappy about yielding any of their power to the new federal government; conversely, the Federalists, shut out of important statewide offices by 1800, looked to the federal government for a source of patronage and political power.

[5] Broadside, from William Austin, Secretary of "The Committee Entrusted with the Ticket of the Minority," 11 Feb. 1800, John Cropper Papers.

[6] William Austin, "An Address to the Voters for Electors of President and Vice President of the United States, in the State of Virginia," 26 May 1800, John Cropper Papers.

[7] Ibid.

After their long denunciation of Republican electioneering tactics, the Federalists gave a brief defense of the policies of the federal government, giving particular emphasis to the accomplishments of Washington.[8] The Republicans, whose efforts had been hindered by the legend of Washington when he was still alive, were determined not to allow the Federalists to resurrect him for their own partisan gain. They asked the voters "to consummate your reverence for the memory of Washington, not by employing it as an engine of election, but by declaring that even his name shall not prevent the free use of your own understandings."[9]

All this activity—the nomination of candidates for elector, the printing of sample ballots, and the publication of campaign platforms—had been completed by May, less than five months after the two parties had begun organizing in earnest. Although the party machinery of both the Republicans and Federalists was not complex, the changes that did occur represented a revolution in the political practices of Virginia. Prior to the changes, the candidates in most counties had relied solely on their own influence and prestige and that of close friends to be elected to office. After the change, the campaign was managed from headquarters in Richmond and the candidates and issues were selected by a small committee. For the first time, the politics of the Old Dominion were taken out of the hands of amateurs.

It proved impossible for the two central committees to maintain a tight hold on the course of the campaign. The trial of James Thomson Callender for seditious libel, held in Richmond in May and June of 1800, injected new life and considerable confusion into the presidential race. The case was important both because it was the most celebrated test of the Sedition Act and because Callender had close association with many of the most prominent Virginia Republicans. The brief, and in the end unhappy, romance between Callender and the Republican party of Virginia had begun in the autumn of 1798, when Callender, fearing arrest under the Sedition Act,

8 Ibid.   9 *Virginia Argus,* 11 July 1800.

fled from Philadelphia to Virginia. Senator Stevens Thomson Mason agreed to feed and lodge him at his home in Loudon County and Thomas Jefferson sent the pamphleteer and rumor-monger fifty dollars to help him renew his journalistic efforts. It was at Mason's home that Callender began his *The Prospect before Us,* the work which was eventually to land him in jail. Callender asked Jefferson for more financial aid to carry the project forward, and Jefferson, believing that it "cannot fail to produce the best effect," sent Callender another fifty dollars.[10] Callender was hoping that his tracts would make enough money to allow him to "come up the James River . . . and try to find 50 acres of clear land, and a hearty Virginia female, that knows how to fatten pigs and boil hominy, and hold her tongue."[11] Although he did not know it at the time, Callender was headed not for the James River but for the Richmond jail.

When the trial opened on May 23, the courtroom "was thronged with spectators from every quarter."[12] The two principal combatants, Federalist Judge Samuel Chase and Callender, personified the extreme wings of each party. Before he reached Richmond, Judge Chase had been given a copy of *The Prospect before Us* with the inflammatory passages underlined. He had determined to secure a conviction against Callender before the trial had even started. Chase's only fear was that "we shall not be able to get the damned rascal in this Court." He managed to get an indictment against Callender, which described the Republican propagandist as "a person of wicked, depraved, evil disposed, disquiet and turbulent mind and disposition,"

---

10 All the relevant correspondence between Jefferson and Callender is printed in *Thomas Jefferson and James Thomson Callender,* ed. Worthington C. Ford (Brooklyn, N.Y., 1897), pp. 10-20 (hereafter referred to as Ford, ed., *Jefferson and Callender*). Actually, Jefferson's financial dealings with Callender began before the journalist fled Philadelphia for Virginia. In 1797 and 1798 Jefferson made several small contributions to Callender, totaling slightly more than fifty dollars. A sympathetic, but on the whole balanced account of Jefferson's relationship with Callender is given by Malone, *Jefferson and the Ordeal of Liberty,* pp. 332-33, 466-72.

11 Callender to Jefferson, Richmond, 26 Sept. 1799, in Ford, ed., *Jefferson and Callender,* p. 17.

12 Ford, ed., *Jefferson and Callender,* p. 23. My account of Callender's trial is largely derived from the excellent description in James Morton Smith, *Freedom's Fetters,* pp. 334-58.

and then set the rules for the trial. The federal government would not have to prove Callender's allegations against the Adams administration as false; rather it was the defendant's task to prove that they were true.[13] In short, Callender was presumed guilty until proved innocent.

Virginia's state officials, because they had publicly opposed the Sedition Act as a violation of the Constitution, decided that they had a responsibility to defend Callender. Jefferson advised Governor Monroe that "Callender should be substantially defended, whether in the first stage by public interference, or private contributions."[14] Callender's supporters used both methods. John Taylor raised a defense fund exceeding one hundred dollars and Monroe enlisted Attorney General Philip Norborne Nicholas and the clerk of the House of Delegates, William Wirt, to provide legal counsel for the penniless defendant.[15] The participation of Nicholas, who was also chairman of the Republican General Committee, was a clear indication that the Republicans had decided to make an issue of the trial.

It is doubtful whether any defense attorney in the nation could have saved Callender. Chase had laid plans so well against the defendant that it was well-nigh impossible to prove Callender's innocence. The defense attorneys were barely allowed to rise from their seats without being overruled, the testimony of Callender's key witnesses was disallowed, and the jury was heavily packed with Federalists.[16] Perhaps even more unfavorable to Callender's case were his own writings. The Sedition Act was certainly unjust, and it may have been unconstitutional, but it was nevertheless the law of the land and Callender's guilt or innocence was determined by the standards it laid down. *The Prospect before Us* was not a timid piece of prose. It charged: "The reign of Mr. Adams has been one continued tempest of malignant passions. As President, he has *never* opened his lips, or lifted his pen without threatening

13 Smith, *Freedom's Fetters*, pp. 343-45, 348-54.
14 Jefferson to Monroe, 26 May 1800, in Ford, ed., *Jefferson's Writings*, 7: 448.
15 Beveridge, *Marshall*, 3: 38-39; Smith, *Freedom's Fetters*, p. 346.
16 Smith, *Freedom's Fetters*, pp. 346-56.

and scolding; The grand object of his administration has been to exasperate the rage of contending parties to calumniate and destroy every man who differs from his opinions. . . . The object of Mr. Adams was to recommend a French war, professedly for the sake of supporting American commerce, but in reality for the sake of yoking us into an alliance with the British monarch." Callender proceeded to call Adams a "hoary-headed incendiary" and a "professed aristocrat." He gave his readers a choice "between Adams, war and beggary, and Jefferson, peace and competency."[17]

Judge Chase, in his instructions to the jury, gave an election speech of his own. He noted that Adams had been "one of the principal characters of the revolution" and praised him for his work during the peace negotiations that followed. Chase reviewed Adams's illustrious service during his two terms as vice president and his one term as president and asked the jury "if it was possible for any rational man to believe such a man guilty of the atrocious crimes laid to his charge by the traverser?"[18] The jury evidently thought not, for they rendered a verdict of guilty and sentenced Callender to nine months in prison and assessed him a two hundred dollar fine.[19]

The Federalists may have derived some initial propaganda benefits from the trial, but the Republicans got what they needed most—a martyr who would rally opposition against the Sedition Act and President Adams. Callender's imprisonment only made his writings more vituperative. He issued the second volume of *The Prospect* in installments, each bearing the postmark of "The Richmond Jail." He termed Adams a "repulsive pedant, a gross hypocrite, and an unprincipled oppressor" who was entitled "not only to the laughter, but likewise the curses of mankind."[20]

While Callender was cranking out more abuse against the

---

17 Francis Wharton, *State Trials of the United States during the Administrations of Washington and Adams.* . . . (Philadelphia, 1849), pp. 688-90 (hereafter referred to as Wharton, *State Trials*).

18 Judge Chase's charge to the jury is printed in Ford, ed., *Jefferson and Callender*, pp. 23-24.

19 Wharton, *State Trials*, p. 718.

20 Smith, *Freedom's Fetters*, p. 358.

president, another group of Richmond residents was organizing a protest of a more serious nature. On August 30, 1800, rumors of a massive slave insurrection panicked the city of Richmond. Gabriel's Rebellion—one of the largest slave conspiracies in American history—temporarily quieted the contest between the two political parties; Republicans and Federalists united in the face of a crisis that threatened to undermine one of the cornerstones of their society.[21]

Surprisingly, once the threat posed by the rebellion had ended, neither party attempted to make political capital of it. Although some of the testimony taken during the aftermath of the conspiracy suggested, wrongly, that two white Frenchmen were the first instigators of the insurrection, the Virginia Federalists were not inclined to resort to their usual tactic of linking the Republicans to French intrigue.[22] That the Republicans escaped such charges was no doubt due in part to Republican Governor James Monroe's vigorous action in initiating an inquiry into the causes of the rebellion and his relentless prosecution of all the conspirators. Monroe was himself so horrified by the abortive rebellion that no one could properly accuse him of being soft on the question of maintaining the security of the slave system. Moreover, the Federalists feared the possible consequences of the rebellion too much even to consider making a partisan issue of it.[23] They differed with the Republicans on many important questions, but the two parties were united on the necessity of preserving the social and economic fabric of society.

21 The first concrete proof that an insurrection was to take place was given by Mosby Shepherd in a communication to the Governor, Richmond, 30 Aug. 1800, in *Calendar of Virginia State Papers*, 9: 134. For a detailed discussion of the events and aftermath of the rebellion see Richard R. Beeman, "The Old Dominion and the New Nation, 1788-1801" (Ph.D. diss., University of Chicago, 1968), pp. 369-77.

22 The pro-Federalist *Gazette of the United States* of Philadelphia claimed that "the insurrection of the negroes in the Southern states, which *appears to be organized on the true French plan*, must be decisive with every reflecting man in those states of the election of Mr. Adams and Gen. Pinckney," quoted in Herbert Aptheker, *American Negro Slave Revolts* (New York, 1943), p. 150. I have not found any similar statements in the newspapers of Virginia.

23 Beeman, "The Old Dominion and the New Nation, 1788-1801," pp. 369-77.

The only way in which Gabriel's Rebellion affected the campaign was through the residue of bitterness left against the black man. Recognizing that the white citizens of Virginia were determined to adopt a much more harsh policy toward the slave population, the Federalists dragged out evidence from Jefferson's *Notes on Virginia* to prove that the Republican presidential candidate desired a program of general emancipation. This was a plan that was, needless to say, particularly unpopular at the present, unsettled time.[24]

For the most part, however, the Federalists concentrated on the same themes used during the election of 1796. Jefferson's religious beliefs were again an easy target. Blurring the distinction between deism and atheism, the Federalists asked the voters: "Is that man fit to preside over a Christian nation who does not believe in the Christian Religion? Can that man be a believer in Christianity who thinks it does him no injury whether his neighbor believes in twenty Gods or in no God, and who attempts to prove from the principles of natural philosophy that the Mosaic account of the deluge cannot be true?"[25] The Federalists thought not. They predicted that if Jefferson were elected, "religion itself & a belief in the immortality of the soul . . . may possibly be discarded as anile fictions. Churches are little more than heaps of bricks & stones, but sufficient for him who was born in a manger, & virtue itself may soon perhaps be declared to be nothing more than a name."[26]

Nor could Jefferson escape the charges of cowardice. The Federalists no longer directly accused him of cowardice during the Revolution, but made oblique references to "want of firmness" and the necessity of electing a president who was "not

---

[24] Malone, *Jefferson and the Ordeal of Liberty,* p. 480.

[25] *Columbian Mirror,* 21 Oct. 1800.

[26] Thomas Evans to Levin Powell, Accomack, 30 Oct. 1800, in *John P. Branch Historical Papers of Randolph-Macon College,* 1 (1901): 54-56. One of the stories circulating about Jefferson's religious beliefs was that, on seeing a church in a state of disrepair, Jefferson had remarked to his friend Philip Mazzei: "It is good enough for him who was born in a manger." *Serious Considerations on the Election of a President; Addressed to the Citizens of the United States* (New York, 1800), pp. 16-17.

one who shrinks from danger." This time the Republicans were armed with answers. Philip Norborne Nicholas, acting for the Republican General Committee, issued a seven-page circular letter defending Jefferson's wartime conduct. The circular reprinted all the correspondence relevant to the British invasion of the capital in 1781, including a copy of the resolution passed by the General Assembly in 1782 absolving Jefferson of cowardice.[27]

Finally, the Federalists sounded the alarm over the disastrous results of such a radical change in administration. They warned the voters: "The political sentiments of him and his party are diametrically opposed to those of the present officers of our government. . . . and remember that . . . to make the desperate change, that you will do it at the risk of everything dear to mankind; that you may find war, poverty and misery substituted for the peace, plenty and happiness which we at present enjoy; and that the ploughshare may be again wrested from the rustic swain and reconverted into the exterminating sword!!"[28]

The Federalists, genuinely fearful of the results of a Republican victory, would have accused any Republican opponent of attempting to sow the seeds of anarchy and disunion, but Jefferson was particularly vulnerable to charges of political radicalism. In a letter to his Italian friend, Philip Mazzei, written in 1796 and published without permission in 1797, Jefferson made some highly intemperate remarks. Referring to the Washington administration, he had complained of those "who were Samsons in the field, Solomons in the Council, but who have had their heads shorn by the harlot of England." He described the supporters of the administration as "timid men who prefer the calm of despotism to the boisterous sea of liberty, British merchants & Americans trading on British capitals, speculators & holders in banks & public funds, a contrivance invented for the purposes of corruption & for assimilating us in to the rotten as well as the sound parts of the British model."[29] Jefferson's nearly

27 Cunningham, *The Jeffersonian Republicans, 1789-1801*, p. 154.
28 *Columbian Mirror*, 21 Oct. 1800.

direct censure of Washington gave the Federalists another opportunity to invoke the memory of the former chief executive. To the Federalists, the Mazzei letter was concrete proof of the radical and irresponsible nature of Jefferson's political principles.

The themes of anarchy and disunion raised by the Federalists were expressions of some deep concerns. Political styles, at least on the level of national politics, were in a state of flux and the members of the Federalist administration were having great difficulty adjusting to the new mode of political discourse. Jefferson, as the head of the Republican ticket, symbolized the evils the Federalists so feared.

If the Federalists appeared eager to defame Jefferson, the Republicans were hardly models of objectivity when discussing the merits of Adams.[30] They accused the members of his administration of every crime from financial corruption to adultery.[31] Adams bore the brunt of the abuse. He was never able to escape the charge that he was a partisan of monarchy. As was the case in the election of 1796, Republican publicists combed his writings, extracting passages, many out of context, to prove Adams was sympathetic to the "monocratic" government of Great Britain.[32]

---

29 Jefferson to Philip Mazzei, Monticello, 24 April 1796, in Ford, ed., *Jefferson's Writings*, 7: 72-78.

30 Charles O. Lerche, "Jefferson and the Election of 1800: A Case Study in the Political Smear," *William and Mary Quarterly*, 3d ser., 5 (1948): 471, has concluded that the Federalist attacks on Jefferson were so malicious that they "were executed with something of the same imagination and finesse as were those of the late Herr Goebbels." This judgment appears to be a bit harsh on the Federalists. Although the attacks on Jefferson in New England exceeded those of Virginia in their intensity, they did not differ significantly from the mudslinging that has taken place in many hotly contested elections in America.

31 These charges were directed in particular at Alexander Hamilton, and dated back to 1793, when William Branch Giles introduced a resolution in the House of Representatives claiming that the secretary of the treasury was "guilty of maladministration in the duties of his office." After a thorough investigation, Hamilton was completely exonerated. He was, however, caught in his indiscretions with Mrs. James Reynolds, and James Thomson Callender, in his *History of the United States for 1796* (Philadelphia, 1797), exploited fully Hamilton's amorous adventures. The blame for Hamilton's indiscretions should not have been laid at the door of the Adams administration, however, for Hamilton was never an official member of that administration.

32 *The Examiner*, 14, 17, 21, 24, 28, 31 Oct. 1800.

On at least one occasion the Virginia Federalists tried to turn the popular aversion to "monocratic" rule to their own advantage. "An American Republican," writing in Alexandria's *Columbian Mirror,* included a letter from the Republican candidate for elector, Edmund Pendleton, to Carter Braxton written in 1776. Pendleton, hazarding some observations on the nature of government, had ventured: "Of all the others, I own I prefer the true English constitution, which consists of a proper combination of the principles of honor, virtue and fear." It followed, the Federalist writer claimed, that Pendleton favored "an hereditary king, and a hereditary House of Lords." If this was the type of man who supported Jefferson, the citizens of Virginia would do well to think twice before casting their votes for such a partisan of monarchy.[33]

This was precisely the tactic which the Republicans had been using against Adams. By borrowing from Pendleton's speculative writings on the nature of the English constitution, a form of government which was revered by most American Whigs in 1776, the Federalists were able to make it seem as if Pendleton, twenty-five years later, preferred the present English system of government to that of the United States. Unfortunately for the Federalists, the writings of Adams contained more passages praising the British system of government than the writings of all the nation's Republicans combined. As a consequence, this device was never fully exploited.

It is unlikely that any tactic the Federalists could have devised would have saved them from defeat in Virginia. The election, held on November 3, 1800, was a triumph for the Republican ticket. The final tally in the state stood: Jefferson-Burr, 21,002; Adams-Pinckney, 6,175.[34] The Federalist ticket received a majority in only seven of Virginia's ninety-four counties and townships. In only four of these areas—Accomac, Northampton, Bath, and Greenbrier—did it gain substantial majorities.[35] Furthermore, Adams and Pinckney owed their success in those

---

[33] *Columbian Mirror,* 23 Oct. 1800.
[34] Election Records, no. 259, "Presidential Election of 1800," VSL.
[35] Ibid.

counties not to their own popularity but to the personal prestige of the electors campaigning for them in the particular districts. In Accomac and Northampton, the Federalist candidate for elector was John Wise, the former Speaker of the House of Delegates; the Republican candidate was William Nevison, a man of no fame in the district. In spite of the combined prestige of the candidates for elector on the Republican ticket, the individual influence of John Wise was enough to carry the lackluster Federalist ticket to victory. Similarly, Greenbrier and Bath counties probably supported Adams and Pinckney because of the popularity of James Breckinridge, the Federalist candidate for elector in that district.

In most of the state, Adams's unpopularity, in combination with more traditional patterns of deferential voting, worked directly to the advantage of the Republicans. In Amelia County, where William Branch Giles was the Republican candidate, the Jeffersonian ticket won, 243-0. In Buckingham. Archibald Stuart carried the Republicans to a 501-0 victory. Madison's presence on the Republican ticket was undoubtedly the main reason for Jefferson's and Burr's 337-7 victory over the Federalists in Orange County. In Caroline County, Edmund Pendleton was largely responsible for the Republicans' 369-6 victory.[36]

Although the margin of the Republican victory was not everywhere so dramatic, this pattern of deferential voting held generally true throughout the state. The citizens of Virginia, despite attempts by the organizations of the respective parties to gear their campaigns toward questions of national policy and despite some recent indications that party affiliation was becoming as important as personality in local elections, persisted in following the recommendations of the well-born and socially prominent when casting their ballots. Virginians, with their agrarian values and localist traditions, were not yet prepared to abandon their narrow view of the national interest.

Only in towns such as Richmond, Norfolk, and Alexandria, where party machinery was well established and where the

36 Ibid.

partisan newspapers gained wide circulation, did the voters
show any inclination to act independently. The Jeffersonian
ticket only narrowly triumphed in Richmond despite the fact
that George Wythe was the Republican candidate for elector
representing that district. The presence of two pro-Federalist
newspapers, the *Virginia Gazette* and the *Virginia Federalist,*
helped Adams. In Norfolk, although the Federalist candidate
for elector, John Nevison, was nowhere near as popular as the
Republican candidate, Mayor Thomas Newton, the Adams
ticket nevertheless narrowly defeated the Jeffersonian organization. The continuing hostility of the Norfolk residents toward
the French, together with Jefferson's well-publicized attachment
to France, more than offset any advantage the Republicans
gained by having Newton on the ticket.[37]

The Federalists derived little solace from these isolated
victories and near-victories in the politically sophisticated towns
of Virginia, for the inescapable fact presented by the election
returns was that the supporters of government had proved
unable to gain a majority in any region in the state. The mag-
nitude of Jefferson's and Burr's success would virtually extin-
guish Federalism as a political force in the Old Dominion.

The presidential electors were to meet in the state capitals
on December 3, 1800, to cast their ballots; due to poor communications, however, it was several weeks later when Virginia's
residents heard the final results: Jefferson and Burr—seventy-
three electoral votes each; Adams—sixty-five; Pinckney—sixty-
four; and John Jay—one. With Jefferson and Burr tied, the
election was thrown into the House of Representatives.[38] Most
Virginians had not expected party discipline to be so strict that
Jefferson and Burr would get the same number of votes from

---

37 Ibid. Historians have generally assumed that the more commercialized towns
of Virginia were naturally more sympathetic to Federalism than was the country-
side. This does not seem to be the case, since the citizens of both Richmond and
Norfolk had supported Republican candidates more often than Federalists during
the 1790s.

38 There are a number of sources that give a detailed treatment of the election
throughout the nation: Cunningham, *Jeffersonian Republicans, 1789-1801,* pp.
175-248; Malone, *Jefferson and the Ordeal of Liberty,* pp. 484-506; and John C.
Miller, *The Federalist Era, 1789-1801* (New York, 1960), pp. 251-77.

each state. They had expected that Jefferson, as the Republican presidential candidate, would get more votes than Burr, the candidate for vice president. The Republican General Committee had made certain that Burr, as well as Jefferson, received all Virginia's electoral votes, but they had done so only because they had been promised that the Republicans in either South Carolina or Georgia would withhold at least one vote from Burr.[39] They never imagined that any Republican other than Jefferson would be considered for the presidency. Now that the election was to be determined by the House of Representatives, Virginians realized for the first time the incompatibility between the present electoral laws and the new party system.

The congressional delegation of each state had only one vote in balloting for president. Since the Republicans constituted a majority of Virginia's delegation, there was never any danger that the Federalists would wrest Virginia's vote from Jefferson. But no one knew what the Federalists from the Northern states might do to thwart the will of the people.

The most important maneuverings in the nation's capital centered around attempts of the dissident elements in the Federalist party to throw their support to Burr. The citizens of Virginia, located far from the scene of action, heard many wild rumors, from one report that Adams would remain in office until another election could be held to the rumor that the Federalists in the House of Representatives were planning, by legislative fiat, to elevate John Marshall to the presidency.[40]

[39] Cunningham, *The Jeffersonian Republicans, 1789-1801*, p. 240. Some Virginians had been alert to the danger of being too staunch in support of Burr. James Madison recalled: "It was with much difficulty that a unanimous vote could be obtained in the Virginia College of Electors for both lest an equality might throw the choice into the House of Reps, or otherwise endanger the known object of the people. J. Madison had received assurances from a confidential friend of Burr that in a certain quarter votes would be thrown from B. with a view to secure a majority for Jefferson. This authority alone with the persuasive language of the other electors overcame the anxiety of Mr. Wythe, whose devoted regard for Mr. Jefferson made him nearly inflexible." Douglass Adair, ed., "James Madison's Autobiography," *William and Mary Quarterly*, 3d ser., 2 (1945): 206.

[40] St. George Tucker to John Page, Williamsburg, 7 Feb. 1801, Tucker-Coleman Papers; Monroe to Jefferson, Richmond, 6 Jan. 1801, in Hamilton, ed., *Monroe's Writings*, 2: 253-55.

The Virginia Republicans were certain of one thing: if the Congress of the United States attempted to thwart the will of the people, either by electing Burr instead of Jefferson or by arranging for a Federalist to retain the presidency, they were prepared to secede from the union. These sentiments were not confined to a few radical Republicans. Party leaders in positions of political power—men like Monroe, St. George Tucker, and Philip Norborne Nicholas—had stated their determination to see the union dissolved if Jefferson were not elected.[41]

Fortunately for Virginians, and the union, the House of Representatives, on February 17, 1801, elected Jefferson on the thirty-sixth ballot. Federalist James Bayard, the lone representative from the state of Delaware, made the election possible by changing his vote from Burr to Jefferson at the last minute. Whether Jefferson, or the Republican floor leader in the House of Representatives, Samuel Smith, made concessions to Bayard on subjects concerning future appointments and policy in order to persuade him to change his vote has long been a source of contention among historians. Circumstantial evidence indicates that one of the two Republican leaders did make promises to the Delaware representative, but there is no written evidence to corroborate any story of a bargain between Jefferson and Bayard.[42] In any case, the citizens of Virginia were jubilant at Jefferson's election. The Republican victory represented for them the salvation of the union.

[41] Ibid.; St. George Tucker to John Page, Williamsburg, 7 Feb. 1801, Tucker-Coleman Papers; Philip Norborne Nicholas to A. Stuart, Richmond, 17 Feb. 1801, Archibald Stuart Papers.

[42] Malone, *Jefferson and the Ordeal of Liberty*, p. 505, offers what is probably the best explanation. While Jefferson himself did not make any specific promises to Bayard, Samuel Smith of Maryland undoubtedly made some vague promises that Jefferson would not take any drastic steps to undo the work of previous administrations.

CHAPTER NINE

Virginia and the Revolution
of 1800

JEFFERSON AND REPUBLICANISM had triumphed. Joseph C. Cabell commented: "It is the triumph of principles & not the triumph of men which now causes the heart to vibrate with joy & the eye to swim in tears of delight. . . . The men who would make this country a scene of tyranny and ruin are now giving place to those who wish to keep us in peace to share our treasure & to administer our government upon the purest principles of republican liberty."[1] But what did this triumph mean for Virginians and how was it to affect their state's internal polity and its relations with the federal government?

Jefferson's election signified a return to the nonpartisan, gentlemanly style of Virginia politics. Yet the importance of this should not be overemphasized, for Virginia, even during the years when opposition to the Federalist administration was greatest, never fully abandoned her traditional patterns of political behavior. Even in the election of 1800, most counties continued to pay deference to the gentlemen-politicians who had so long ruled their affairs. Virginia, during the 1790s, had experienced some changes. The use of county meetings to make direct appeals to the people, the growing political awareness of the citizens living in urban areas such as Richmond, Norfolk, and Alexandria, and the beginnings of centralized party organizations in the election of 1800—these seemed to signal the arrival of a new era in Virginia politics.[2] But Jefferson's victory sounded the knell for the two-party system in Virginia. The Federalist General Committee, organized in 1800 to promote John Adams's candidacy, was disbanded immediately after the election, never to be revived. Never again would the Federalist party in Virginia attempt to stake out an official position on the important issues of the time. While Federalists in other states continued to denounce the Republicans as anarchists and atheists, the Federalists in Virginia quietly returned to their nonpolitical duties. These Federalists continued to be elected to statewide offices, and in some cases to Congress, but this occurred only when the prestige of such a candidate was powerful enough to surmount the handicap imposed by his party affiliation or when the particular regional interests of the district he represented happened to be at odds with the policies of the Republican administration.[3]

When Federalism declined as a political force in Virginia, so too did the slow trend toward democratization of the political system. Twenty-five percent of Virginia's free adult white males voted in the election of 1800. Although this figure may seem low in light of the fact that 85 to 90 percent could have voted had they desired to do so, it was nevertheless a considerably higher percentage than in any previous congressional or presidential election in the state.[4] If the Federalist organization had not folded, that percentage might have continued to rise. In-

[1] Joseph C. Cabell to his father, Williamsburg, 5 March 1801, Cabell Family Papers.

[2] Ironically, the Republican gentry in the counties, whose primary aim had been to resist innovation in the political structure of their state, unintentionally initiated changes that they had not foreseen. In their opposition to the general government, they were forced to formulate strategies and policies which would have drastically changed the nature of local politics. Their support of the General Ticket Law, for example, was in direct contradiction to their long fight against consolidation.

[3] David Hackett Fischer, *The Revolution of American Conservatism: The Federalist Party in the Era of Jeffersonian Democracy* (New York, 1965), argues that the Federalist party throughout the nation as a whole was much more active in the decades following Jefferson's election than most historians have previously believed. It seems safe to assume, judging from the dearth of evidence in Fischer's book attesting to the vitality of Virginia Federalism, that the "supporters of government" in Virginia were a major exception.

[4] Brown and Brown, *Virginia: Democracy or Aristocracy?* pp. 125-46; J. R. Pole, "Representation and Authority in Virginia," p. 49.

stead, Virginia's citizens entrusted their political power to the Republican gentrymen who had traditionally guided their affairs, and voter participation in subsequent elections dropped sharply. In 1804 only 11 percent of those eligible voted in the presidential election. This figure rose to 17 and 18 percent in the elections of 1808 and 1812, primarily because of the competition from within the Republican party by the *tertium quids*. It was only a momentary increase, and by 1820 voter participation among free adult white males had dropped to a mere 3 percent.[5]

A New Englander, traveling through Virginia in 1804, noted the striking contradiction between the rhetoric and reality of Jeffersonian democracy:

> Though we hear so much about *democracy* from this quarter, the State approaches nearer a pure aristocracy than any other state in the union. The great landholders are Lords; and their tenants, as decidedly as their negroes, are slaves. They are amused, indeed, with *incantations of republicanism liberty and equality*, whereas in truth, their *public affairs* are in an absolute monopoly by the rich. The poor have, unquestionably, the liberty to quarrel about the support of a patron at an election, but as to *equality*, it no more exists here than it does in the French, English, or Turkish Dominions.[6]

Nor did political practice seem to change much in the half-century that followed. John S. Wise, reminiscing about the manners and customs of Virginia during antebellum days, described a congressional election held in 1855 that could well have taken place in the eighteenth century:

> voting was done openly, or *viva voce*, as it was called, and not by ballot. The election judges, who were magistrates, sat upon a bench with their clerks before them. When practicable it was customary for the candidate to be present in person, and to occupy a seat at the side of the judges. As the voter appeared,

5 Pole, "Representation and Authority in Virginia," p. 49.

6 William Eaton to Col. Alexander Sessions, Hampton, 24 June 1804, in Louis B. Wright, ed., "William Eaton Takes a Dismal View of Virginia," *William and Mary Quarterly*, 3d ser., 5 (1948): 106.

his name was called out in a loud voice. The judges inquired, "John Jones (or Bill Smith), for whom, do you vote?" . . . He replied by proclaiming the name of his favorite. The clerks enrolled the vote, and the judges announced it as enrolled. The representative of the candidate for whom he voted arose, bowed, and thanked him aloud; and his partisans often applauded.[7]

This scene took place fifty-five years after the triumph of Jeffersonian democracy. It is no wonder that V. O. Key, in his study of *Southern Politics,* described Virginia as "a political museum piece."[8]

The return to the old style of politics did not of course signify an end to political disagreement in the Old Dominion. Issues that had always caused divisions within the ruling elite—constitutional reform, establishment of new counties, and legislation affecting the slave population—continued to divide individuals and regions in Virginia in much the same way as they had before 1801. And some regions, such as the extreme west, could still be counted on to give their support to Federalist proposals in Congress.[9] But the lessening of competition between the two parties would make it easier for members of the ruling elite to settle their differences among themselves, without the necessity of appealing to the people for support. And the decisions in those disputes would most often go to those who thought it "safer to remain as we are rather than risk a reform which may be more defective."

Not until 1829 did a majority of the ruling oligarchy agree to call a convention to consider amending the state constitution, and even then their commitment to constitutional revision was minimal at best. Many of the members of the Virginia Constitutional Convention of 1829 had been in the fore of the Republican movement in 1800, and not surprisingly they

[7] John S. Wise, *The End of an Era* (Boston, 1900), pp. 55-56.

[8] V. O. Key, *Southern Politics in State and Nation* (New York, 1949), p. 19.

[9] For the persistence of local political divisions in Virginia see Hall, "A Quantitative Approach to . . . Virginia." Risjord, "The Virginia Federalists," pp. 486-517, is the best account of the continuation of Federalist-Republican divisions after 1801.

showed the same disinclination to alter Virginia's internal political structure as they had in the 1790s. The 1829 Convention liberalized, but did not eliminate, the freehold qualification for voters. It refused to consider changing the basis for apportioning representation in the lower house, despite protests from the western delegates that the present system was inequitable.[10] In general, the proceedings of the Convention illustrated the unwillingness of Virginia's ruling oligarchy to do anything which might diminish their political power.

The county government, the backbone of Virginia's political system, remained alert to thwart any attempt at innovation. Nowhere is the essential conservatism of Virginia political life more clearly displayed than in the attitude of the county governments toward free, public education. In 1796, the General Assembly passed a long overdue act to establish a public school system. It placed responsibility for laying out the school districts and for expenses of the schools with the individual counties. Thirteen years later, in 1809, Governor John Tyler complained to the legislature that not one single county had put the public school law into operation. He lamented that "an enlightened stranger, if he were making a tour thro' the states, [would] readily conclude that in the general passion for war which pervades the civilized world, we had, for want of an enemy at our gates, declared an exterminating war against the arts and sciences."[11] It was not until 1845 that the state government established a system of public education; in the meantime the rich and the well-born were educated at private academies, while the remainder of the population taught themselves or remained illiterate.[12] It is not surprising that Virginians protested against federal taxes for the maintenance of defense or payment of the public debt when they would not even tax themselves for the education of their children.

[10] See David L. Pulliam, *The Constitutional Conventions of Virginia from the Foundation of the Commonwealth to the Present Time* (Richmond, 1901), pp. 63-70.

[11] Shepherd, *Statutes at Large*, 2: 3-5; Governor Tyler to the Speaker of the House of Delegates, 4 Dec. 1809, Cabell Family Papers.

[12] Porter, *County Government in Virginia*, p. 222.

Many Virginia Republicans hoped that Jefferson's election, in addition to restoring calm to their internal political affairs, would work revolutionary changes in the conduct and structure of the federal government. They would be disappointed. To be sure, Jefferson would rely less on Great Britain and would continue the policy, begun by Adams during his last year in office, of seeking a rapprochement with France. He would also use his power of patronage to replace Federalist cabinet members with Republicans who would take a more sympathetic view of the interests of the agrarian South. This would not satisfy the Antifederalists, who composed a majority of the Republican party in Virginia. They desired not only a change in personnel but also a radical alteration of the structure of the federal government. John Taylor was the most vocal and articulate champion of the Antifederalist position. He was convinced that the United States Constitution, as it stood, did not allow for a true division of sovereignty. As a consequence, the American form of government was drifting toward that "produced by the English original—namely—concert and union among the three branches of government—influences—corruption—and force, so as to leave the people a nominal, but not a real influence over the measures of government."[13] A mere change of men could not effect the desired reforms. "It . . . might operate temporary public benefits, but they would certainly be transient, and constitutional error will still ultimately prevail. It would be only like the lucid intervals of a madman."[14]

Most Republicans in positions of political power did not give in to the Antifederalist demands for drastic changes in the structure of the general government. Wilson Cary Nicholas, who, with James Madison, was responsible for guiding the new president along a course of moderation, cautioned: "It depends very much upon the temper of the administration and the people of America for the next four years whether the present

[13] John Taylor to Harry Innes, Caroline County, 25 April 1799, Innes Papers, LC.
[14] John Taylor to James Monroe, Caroline County, 25 March 1798, in *John P. Branch Historical Papers of Randolph-Macon College*, 2 (1907): 269.

parties in this country shall be entirely extinguished, or whether they shall be perpetuated until they produce all the mischiefs that have flown from the like excess in other countries, and either make us prey to some other country, engender a despotism in our own, or cause a separation of the states.[15] Nicholas suggested that through cautious use of executive patronage and by constant assurances that federal policy would not be radically changed, Jefferson could mitigate many of the animosities that had been engendered over the past decade. This was precisely the course that the new president followed, even though it meant risking harmony within the Republican party.

The position of the moderate Republicans was precarious. They had joined the Republican party not because they quarreled with the principles upon which the federal government was founded, but because they opposed the particular policies of Alexander Hamilton. They had worked with the Antifederalists, and had even used the rhetoric of Antifederalism, in order to wage an effective fight against a common enemy. But this was an alliance of expediency. When the moderate Republicans gained control of the federal government in 1800, they found themselves flanked by extremists. Because the moderates had borrowed the language of Antifederalism in their assault on Hamiltonian policy, the Federalists viewed them as wild-eyed radicals bent on destroying the central government. The Antifederalist wing of the party, believing they had converted the moderates to their point of view, expected them to take precisely those drastic steps the Federalists so feared.

Jefferson's term in office would help allay, but not eliminate, the fears of the Federalists. It would partially satisfy, but not fulfill, the hopes of the old Antifederalists. Jefferson would change the style of the federal government, but not its substance. Virginians would feel more comfortable with Jefferson in the executive mansion, but their battle against consolidation and domination by the general government had not ended.

15 W. C. Nicholas to James Madison, 1801, Carter-Smith Papers, University of Virginia.

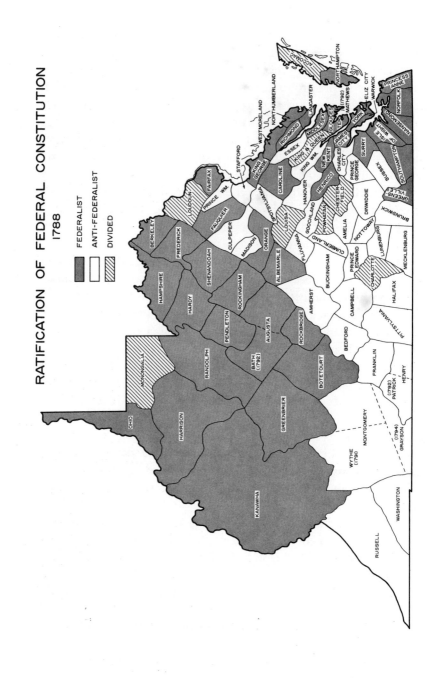

RATIFICATION OF FEDERAL CONSTITUTION
1788

FEDERALIST
ANTI-FEDERALIST
DIVIDED

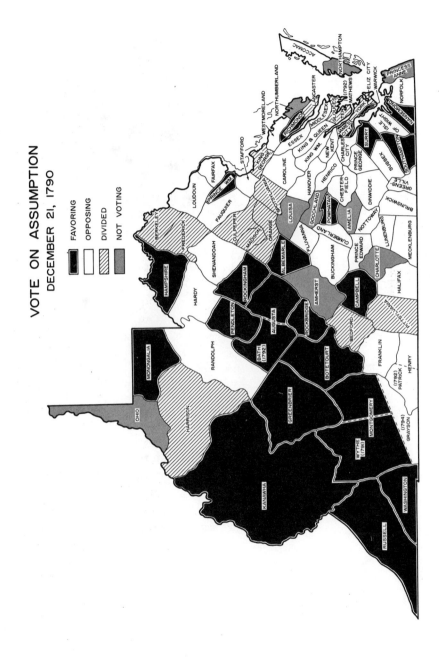

VOTE ON ASSUMPTION
DECEMBER 21, 1790

FAVORING
OPPOSING
DIVIDED
NOT VOTING

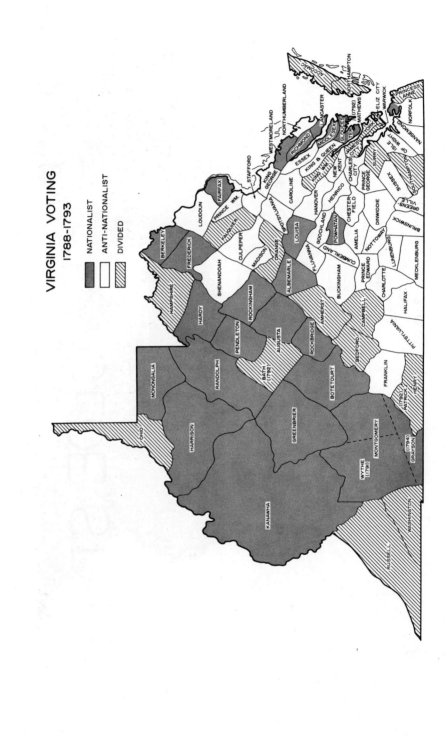

VIRGINIA VOTING
1788-1793

NATIONALIST
ANTI-NATIONALIST
DIVIDED

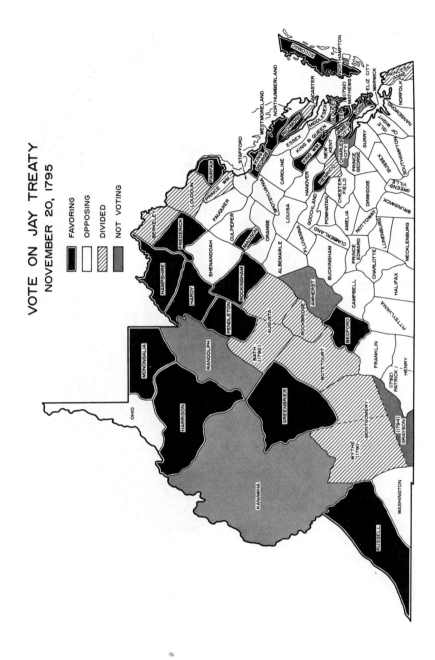

VOTE ON JAY TREATY
NOVEMBER 20, 1795

FAVORING
OPPOSING
DIVIDED
NOT VOTING

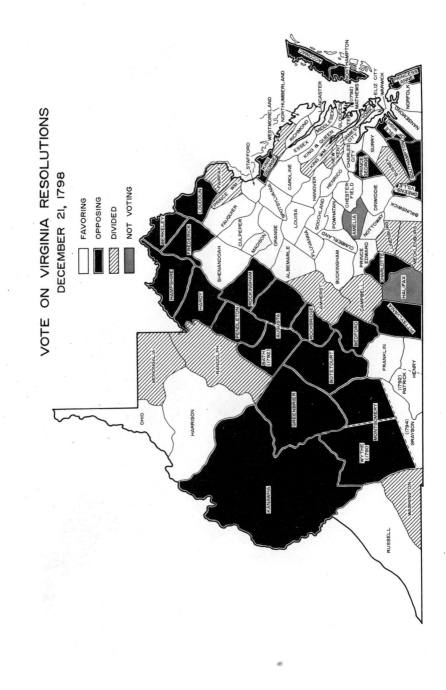

VOTE ON VIRGINIA RESOLUTIONS
DECEMBER 21, 1798

FAVORING
OPPOSING
DIVIDED
NOT VOTING

Leadership of the House of Delegates, 1788-1800

Name and County	Occupation	Property
Robert Andrews (Williamsburg)	Minister	1 house in town 2 lots in town 8 Negroes 2 horses
Carter Braxton* (King William)	Planter	8,508 acres 91 Negroes 75 horses
Samuel Jordan Cabell (Amherst)	Planter	1,444 acres 38 Negroes 24 horses
William Cabell* (Amherst)	Planter	15,237 acres 93 Negroes 20 horses
William O. Callis (Louisa)	Planter	5,330 acres 16 Negroes 12 horses

* The individuals listed here were selected on the basis of an analysis of their service on the important standing and special committees of the House of Delegates. The real and personal property holdings of those men with the asterisk following their names were taken from Jackson T. Main, "The One Hundred," *William and Mary Quarterly,* 3d ser., 10 (1954): 368-83. The real and personal property holdings of all others were found in the Real and Personal Property Tax Lists, 1795, VSL.

Name and County	Occupation	Property
Wilson Miles Cary* (Elizabeth City)	Planter	11,426 acres 286 Negroes 72 horses
Francis Corbin (Middlesex)	Planter	4,194 acres 119 Negroes 9 horses
Joseph Eggleston (Amelia)	Planter	1,895 acres 56 Negroes 26 horses
Thomas Evans (Accomac)	Lawyer	556 acres 7 Negroes 6 horses
William Foushee (Henrico)	Physician	1,344 acres 2 lots in town 6 Negroes 3 horses
William Branch Giles (Amelia)	Lawyer	400 acres 23 Negroes 10 horses
John Guerrant (Goochland)	Planter	491 acres 12 Negroes 7 horses
Benjamin Harrison* (Charles City)	Planter	21,266 acres 2½ lots, 1 house 304 Negroes 109 horses
Collier Harrison (Charles City)	Planter	3,512 acres 67 Negroes 21 horses
Patrick Henry* (Prince Edward)	Planter	22,100½ acres 66 Negroes 38 horses

Name and County	Occupation	Property
Zachariah Johnston (Augusta)	Planter	607 acres 11 Negroes 24 horses
Miles King (Elizabeth City)	Physician	1,303 acres 40 Negroes 19 horses
Henry Lee* (Westmoreland)	Planter	4,626 acres 97 Negroes 13 horses
Richard Lee (Westmoreland)	Planter	6,103 acres 138 Negroes 17 horses
Richard Bland Lee (Westmoreland)	Planter	4,098 acres 16 Negroes 2 horses
Thomas Madison (Botetourt)	Planter	3,326 acres 50 Negroes 20 horses
John Marshall (Henrico)	Lawyer	(land books destroyed— owned at least 4,000 acres) 9 Negroes 4 horses
Thomas Mathews (Norfolk)	Merchant	1 lot in town 3 Negroes 1 horse
Wilson Cary Nicholas* (Albemarle)	Planter	7,100 acres 62 Negroes 22 horses
John Page* (Gloucester)	Planter	6,015 acres 234 Negroes 47 horses

Name and County	Occupation	Property
Edmund Randolph* (Williamsburg)	Lawyer	7,463 acres 101 Negroes 19 horses
Larkin Smith (King and Queen)	Planter	1,087 acres 7 Negroes 4 horses
French Strother (Culpeper)	Planter	1,310 acres 22 Negroes 12 horses
William Tate (Washington)	Planter	346 acres 2 Negroes 7 horses
George K. Taylor (Prince George)	Lawyer	130 acres 2 horses
John Taylor* (Caroline)	Planter	12,907 acres 47 Negroes 9 horses
Nathaniel Wilkinson (Henrico)	Planter	1,685 acres 8 Negroes 3 horses
John Wise (Accomac)	Lawyer	1 lot in town 1 Negro 1 horse

Party Divisions in the House of Delegates[*]

1788-1790

Antifederalist Bloc

Name and County	Occupation	Property
John Trigg (Bedford)	Planter	363 acres 15 Negroes 2 horses
Notley Conn (Bourbon)	No record	
Binns Jones (Brunswick)	Planter	732 acres 13 Negroes 6 horses
Anthony New (Caroline)	Lawyer	566 acres 11 Negroes 5 horses

[*] The real and personal property holdings of those men with the asterisk following their names were taken from Jackson T. Main, "The One Hundred," pp. 368-83. The holdings of those with the double asterisk were taken from Forrest McDonald, *We the People: The Economic Origins of the Constitution* (Chicago, 1958), pp. 269-81. The holdings of all others were found in the Real and Personal Property Tax Lists, 1795, VSL. It is likely that the holdings of many of the men listed here were actually much larger; the figures given here account only for their holdings within the county in which they resided.

Name and County	Occupation	Property
Benjamin Harrison (Charles City)	Planter	7,225 acres 64 Negroes 25 horses
Matthew Cheatham (Chesterfield)	Planter	400 acres 12 Negroes 5 horses
George Markham (Chesterfield)	No record	
French Strother (Culpeper)	Planter	1,100 acres 22 Negroes 12 horses
John Woodson (Cumberland)	Planter	388 acres 14 Negroes 10 horses
Robert Bolling (Dinwiddie)	Merchant	2,860 acres 13 Negroes 10 horses
George Booker (Elizabeth City)	Planter	400 acres 30 Negroes 11 horses
James Upshaw, Jr. (Essex)	Planter	599¼ acres 16 Negroes 7 horses
Joshua Rentfro (Franklin)	Planter	400 acres 12 Negroes 8 horses
John Guerrant (Goochland)	Planter	491 acres 12 Negroes 7 horses
Batte Peterson (Greensville)	Planter	2,457 acres

Name and County	Occupation	Property
Miles Selden (Henrico)	Planter	721 acres 31 Negroes 16 horses
Thomas Cooper** (Henry)	Planter	1,163 acres 7 Negroes 11 horses
Benjamin Eley (Isle of Wight)	Planter	330 acres 12 Negroes 3 horses
Francis Boykin (Isle of Wight)	Planter	440 acres 13 Negroes 3 horses
John Roane (King William)	Planter	1,000 acres 19 Negroes 8 horses
Richard Kennon (Mecklenburg)	Planter	1,094 acres 46 Negroes 29 horses
Willis Riddick (Nansemond)	Planter	4,500 acres
Henry Guy (Northampton)	Planter	493 acres 10 Negroes 5 horses
Benjamin Lankford (Pittsylvania)	Planter	400 acres 8 Negroes 3 horses
Tarlton Woodson (Prince Edward)	Planter	1,248 acres 11 Negroes 10 horses
Patrick Henry* (Prince Edward)	Lawyer	22,190½ acres 66 Negroes 38 horses

Name and County	Occupation	Property
Andrew Buchanan (Stafford)	Planter	423 acres 9 Negroes 4 horses
Thomas Edmunds (Sussex)	Planter	3,979 acres 32 Negroes 10 horses
Samuel Edmiston (Washington)	Planter	400 acres 5 Negroes 5 horses
Robert Sheild (York)	Planter	570 acres 17 Negroes 6 horses
William Nelson (York)	Lawyer	8 Negroes

Federalist Bloc

Name and County	Occupation	Property
Zachariah Johnston (Augusta)	Planter	607 acres 11 Negroes 24 horses
Francis Walker (Albemarle)	Planter & Merchant	6,300 acres 45 Negroes 10 horses
Joseph Swearingen (Berkeley)	No record	
James Ball (Lancaster)	Planter	1,077 acres 26 Negroes 6 horses
Ralph Wormley* (Middlesex)	Planter	15,707 acres 325 Negroes 74 horses
John Stringer (Northampton)	Planter	408 acres 1 horse

Name and County	Occupation	Property
Walker Tomlin** (Richmond)	Planter	274 acres 60 Negroes 7 horses
George Baxter (Rockingham)	Lawyer	1,196 acres 3 Negroes 8 horses
Francis Kirtley (Rockingham)	Planter	394 acres 21 Negroes 12 horses
John Allen (Surry)	Planter	2,200 acres 49 Negroes 19 horses

1794-1796

Repubican Bloc

Wilson Cary Nicholas* (Albemarle)	Planter	7,100 acres 62 Negroes 22 horses
Joseph Eggleston (Amelia)	Planter	1,000 acres 56 Negroes 26 horses
Joshua Chaffin (Amelia)	Planter	353 acres 16 Negroes 8 horses
John White (Bath)	Planter	106 acres 2 horses
Thomas Madison (Botetourt)	Planter	3,326 acres 50 Negroes 20 horses
Thomas Washington (Brunswick)	Planter	704 acres 18 Negroes 9 horses

Name and County	Occupation	Property
Collier Harrison (Charles City)	Planter	3,512 acres 67 Negroes 21 horses
Matthew Cheatham (Chesterfield)	Planter	400 acres 12 Negroes 5 horses
Philip Thompson (Culpeper)	Planter	1,149 acres 15 Negroes 11 horses
John Hatcher (Cumberland)	Planter	126 acres 6 Negroes 3 horses
Anderson Cocke (Cumberland)	Planter	400 acres 9 Negroes 7 horses
Alexander McRae (Dinwiddie)	Lawyer	
Augustine Jennings (Fauquier)	Planter	200 acres 6 Negroes 4 horses
Joseph Hadden (Fluvanna)	Planter	1,099 acres 8 Negroes 3 horses
Thomas Miller (Goochland)	Planter	828 acres 28 Negroes 18 horses
John Guerrant (Goochland)	Planter	491 acres 12 Negroes 7 horses
Joseph Wilkins (Greensville)	Planter	1,100 acres 11 Negroes 11 horses

Name and County	Occupation	Property
John Goodwyn (Greensville)	Planter	890 acres 12 Negroes 5 horses
Joseph Martin (Henry)	Merchant & Planter	810 acres 14 Negroes 15 horses
Martin Shearman (Lancaster)	Planter	332 acres 8 Negroes 4 horses
Peter Garland (Lunenburg)	Planter	446 acres 6 Negroes 2 horses
Holder Hudgins (Mathews)	Planter	1,075 acres 27 Negroes 7 horses
Thomas Smith (Mathews)	Planter	252 acres 40 Negroes 11 horses
Willis Riddick (Nansemond)	Planter	4,500 acres
William Chamberlayne (New Kent)	Merchant	414 acres 20 Negroes 8 horses
John Quarles (Norfolk)	Merchant	½ lot 3 Negroes
Charles Wells (Ohio)	Planter	1,690 acres
Isaac Davis (Orange)	Planter	527 acres 12 Negroes 14 horses
William Mosely (Powhatan)	Lawyer	925 acres 14 Negroes 9 horses

Name and County	Occupation	Property
George K. Taylor (Prince George)	Lawyer	130 acres 2 horses
William Dulaney (Shenandoah)	Planter	266 acres 1 Negro 1 horse
James Wilkinson (Southampton)	Planter	366 acres 18 Negroes 12 horses
John Willis (Spotsylvania)	Merchant	50 acres 18 Negroes 7 horses
Nathaniel Fox (Stafford)	Planter	200 acres 9 Negroes 6 horses
William Boyce (Surry)	Planter	305½ acres 5 Negroes 5 horses
Nicholas Faulcon (Surry)	Planter	604 acres 1 lot 14 Negroes 8 horses
William Massenburg (Sussex)	Planter	535 acres 17 Negroes 7 horses

Federalist Bloc

Name and County	Occupation	Property
Thomas Evans (Accomac)	Lawyer	556 acres 7 Negroes 6 horses
Joseph Burrus (Amherst)	Planter	818 acres 15 Negroes 8 horses

Name and County	Occupation	Property
Samuel Hancock (Bedford)	Planter	677 acres 8 Negroes 5 horses
Miles King (Elizabeth City)	Physician	1,303 acres 40 Negroes 19 horses
William Cavendish (Greenbrier)	Planter	
John Hutcheson (Greenbrier)	No record	6 horses
Isaac Parsons (Hampshire)	No record	
Thomas Tinsley (Hanover)	Planter & Merchant	57 acres 1 lot 15 Negroes 6 horses
James Machir (Hardy)	Lawyer	3 Negroes 1 horse
John Pierce (James City)	Planter	731 acres 13 Negroes 3 horses
Charles Stuart (King George)	Planter	732 acres 25 Negroes 8 horses
William Claiborne (King William)	Planter	939½ acres 28 Negroes 18 horses
Peter Hull (Pendleton)	No record	
William Bentley (Powhatan)	Planter	600 acres 12 Negroes 9 horses

Name and County	Occupation	Property
William Nimmo (Princess Anne)	Merchant	476 acres 3 lots 5 Negroes 3 horses
John Bowyer (Rockbridge)	Planter	1,733 acres 19 Negroes 23 horses
Robert Andrews (Williamsburg)	Minister	1 house 2 lots 8 Negroes 2 horses

1797-1800

Republican Bloc

Francis Walker (Albemarle)	Planter & Merchant	6,300 acres 45 Negroes 10 horses
Wilson Cary Nicholas* (Albemarle)	Planter	7,100 acres 62 Negroes 22 horses
Joshua Chaffin (Amelia)	Planter	353 acres 16 Negroes 8 horses
James Fletcher (Brunswick)	Planter	344 acres 7 Negroes 5 horses
William Ruffin (Brunswick)	Planter	1,887 acres 17 Negroes
George Buckner (Caroline)	Planter	718 acres 10 Negroes

Name and County	Occupation	Property
John Taylor* (Caroline)	Planter	12,907 acres 47 Negroes 9 horses
Samuel Tyler (Charles City)	Lawyer	75 acres 17 Negroes 15 horses
Thomas A. Taylor (Chesterfield)	Planter	557 acres 6 Negroes 4 horses
Matthew Cheatham (Chesterfield)	Planter	400 acres 12 Negroes 5 horses
John Roberts (Culpeper)	Planter	523 acres 5 Negroes 10 horses
Peterson Goodwyn (Dinwiddie)	Lawyer	1,837 acres 45 Negroes 25 horses
John Pegram (Dinwiddie)	Planter	600 acres 15 Negroes 4 horses
George Booker (Elizabeth City)	Planter	400 acres 30 Negroes 11 horses
Joseph Hadden (Fluvanna)	Planter	1,099 acres 8 Negroes 3 horses
James Payne (Fluvanna)	No record	3 Negroes 2 horses
William Hall (Gloucester)	Planter	460 acres 14 Negroes 4 horses

Name and County	Occupation	Property
James Pleasants (Goochland)	Lawyer	100 acres 4 Negroes 3 horses
Greenberry McKenzie (Grayson)	Planter	405 acres 2 horses
Thomas Starke (Hanover)	No record	235 acres 7 Negroes 4 horses
William Price (Henrico)	Planter	3,172 acres 16 Negroes 6 horses
Miles Selden (Henrico)	Planter	721 acres 31 Negroes 16 horses
Joseph Martin (Henry)	Planter	810 acres 14 Negroes 15 horses
John Redd (Henry)	Planter	1,103 acres 10 Negroes 14 horses
William O. Callis (Louisa)	Planter	5,330 acres 16 Negroes 12 horses
Francis Eppes (Lunenburg)	Planter & Lawyer	100 acres 14 Negroes 11 horses
Henry Hill (Madison)	Planter	1,064 acres 22 Negroes 11 horses
Josiah Riddick (Nansemond)	Planter	575 acres

Name and County	Occupation	Property
William Claughton (Northumberland)	Planter	422½ acres 11 Negroes 6 horses
William Mosely (Powhatan)	Lawyer	925 acres 14 Negroes 9 horses
Richard Barnes (Richmond)	Planter	1,016 acres 20 Negroes 6 horses
William Dulaney (Shenandoah)	Merchant	267 acres 1 Negro 1 horse
John Gatewood (Shenandoah)	No record	
John Mercer (Spotsylvania)	No record	
Nathaniel Fox (Stafford)	Merchant	200 acres 9 Negroes 6 horses
Samuel Meek (Washington)	Planter	460 acres 3 Negroes 6 horses
Samuel Shields (York)	Minister	1,106 acres 33 Negroes 6 horses
William Foushee (Richmond)	Physician	1,344 acres 1 lot in town 6 Negroes 3 horses
James Johnson (Isle of Wight)	Lawyer	300 acres 3 Negroes 3 horses

Federalist Bloc

Name and County	Occupation	Property
Andrew Anderson (Augusta)	Planter	540 acres 6 Negroes 9 horses
James Breckinridge (Botetourt)	Lawyer	520 acres 8 Negroes 2 horses
John Miller (Botetourt)	Planter	1,343 acres 6 Negroes 3 horses
Archibald Magill (Frederick)	Lawyer	239 acres 4 Negroes 5 horses
William Cavendish (Greenbrier)	No record	12 horses
Jacob Fisher (Hardy)	No record	2 Negroes 8 horses
Christian Simons (Hardy)	No record	5 horses
William Morris (Kanawha)	Planter	400 acres 1 horse
Robert Pollard (King William)	Merchant	772 acres 20 Negroes 5 horses
John Evans (Monongalia)	Planter	4 Negroes 4 horses
John Upshur (Northampton)	Planter	1,213 acres 16 Negroes 5 horses

Name and County	Occupation	Property
James Cureton (Prince George)	Planter	1,279 acres 18 Negroes 8 horses
George K. Taylor (Prince George)	Lawyer	130 acres 2 horses
Thomas Griffin (York)	Physician	100 acres 11 Negroes

Local Interest Groups in the House of Delegates, 1788-1790*

Group A		
Name and County	Region	Political Affiliation
Binns Jones (Brunswick)	East	Antifederalist
Anthony New (Caroline)	West	Antifederalist
Henry Southall (Charles City)	East	Antifederalist
Robert Bolling (Dinwiddie)	East	Antifederalist
George Booker (Elizabeth City)	East	Antifederalist
James Upshaw (Essex)	East	Antifederalist
Batte Peterson (Greensville)	East	Antifederalist
Miles Selden (Henrico)	East	Antifederalist
Francis Boykin (Isle of Wight)	East	Antifederalist
Ralph Wormley (Middlesex)	East	Federalist
Tarlton Woodson (Prince Edward)	West	Antifederalist

* This appendix is based on an analysis of the voting behavior, on local issues, of the fifty-four delegates serving all three terms in the lower house during the years 1788-1790. All roll call votes, except those pertaining to national issues and those of a strictly procedural nature, were examined. Although the two groups listed below suggest a pronounced east-west division within the state, the small number of men aligned with each group indicates that this factor should not be overemphasized.

Name and County	Region	Political Affiliation
John Allen (Surry)	East	Federalist
Thomas Edmunds (Sussex)	East	Antifederalist
William Nelson (York)	East	Antifederalist

Group B

Name and County	Region	Political Affiliation
John Trigg (Bedford)	West	Antifederalist
Notley Conn (Bourbon)	West	Antifederalist
John Clarke (Campbell)	West	Unaligned
Matthew Cheatham (Chesterfield)	East	Antifederalist
George Markham (Chesterfield)	East	Antifederalist
French Strother (Culpeper)	West	Antifederalist
John Guerrant (Goochland)	West	Antifederalist
Thomas Cooper (Henry)	West	Antifederalist
Richard Kennon (Mecklenburg)	West	Antifederalist
Willis Riddick (Nansemond)	East	Antifederalist
Hardin Burnley (Orange)	West	Unaligned
Benjamin Lankford (Pittsylvania)	West	Antifederalist
William McKee (Rockbridge)	West	Unaligned
Thomas Carter (Russell)	West	Unaligned
Samuel Edmiston (Washington)	West	Antifederalist

Bibliographical Note

IT IS SURPRISING, when one considers the important role that Virginia, and Virginians, played in the political struggles of the late eighteenth century, that there is so little secondary literature devoted exclusively to Virginia politics during the revolutionary and post-revolutionary years. H. J. Eckenrode, *The Revolution in Virginia* (Boston, 1916), and Freeman H. Hart, *The Valley of Virginia in the American Revolution, 1763-1789* (Chapel Hill, N.C., 1942) are the only two detailed accounts of the Revolution in Virginia and neither is entirely satisfactory. For the Confederation period one must rely on two doctoral dissertations, Augustus Low, "Virginia in the Critical Period, 1783-1789" (University of Iowa, 1949), and Myra L. Rich, "The Experimental Years: Virginia, 1781-1789 (Yale University, 1966), and one important article, Jackson T. Main, "Sections and Politics in Virginia, 1781-1787," *William and Mary Quarterly,* 3d ser., 12 (1955): 96-112. Although all three make important contributions to our understanding of certain facets of Virginia politics during the Confederation, none provides an adequate synthesis of the period. Harry Ammon, "The Republican Party in Virginia, 1789-1824" (Ph.D. diss., University of Virginia, 1948), "The Formation of the Republican Party in Virginia, 1789-1796," *Journal of Southern History* 19 (1953): 283-310, "The Jeffersonian Republicans in Virginia," *Virginia Magazine of History and Biography* 71 (1963): 153-67, and "Agricola vs. Aristedes: James Monroe, John Marshall and the Genêt Affair in Virginia," *Virginia Magazine of History and Biography* 74 (1966): 312-20 are all important contributions to our knowledge of Virginia during the years 1788-1801. Ammon has directed his attention at Virginians in Congress and has uncovered important material relating to the mechanics of party organization at the national level. He does, however, tend to overlook the essentially chaotic state of party organization on the local level. Norman Risjord, "The Virginia Federalists," *Journal of Southern History* 33 (1967): 486-517, has made a useful contribution to our understanding of party development by showing the intimate connection between the factional divisions of the 1780s and the party divisions of the 1790s.

More general studies of party development, particularly Noble Cunningham, *The Jeffersonian Republicans: The Formation of Party Organization, 1789-1801* (Chapel Hill, N.C., 1957), and Lisle A. Rose, *Prologue to Democracy: The Federalists in the South, 1789-1801* (Lexington, Ky., 1968), seem to suffer from their tendency to assume that the mechanisms of national party organization actually worked the way they were supposed to when transferred to the state and county level. This focus on the formal mechanisms rather than the actual operation of the political system often obscures rather than illuminates our understanding of late eighteenth-century Virginia. Eugene P. Link, *Democratic-Republican Societies, 1790-1800* (New York, 1942), avoids the pitfalls of an approach based solely on national politics, but he too tends to overestimate the cohesiveness of party organization on the local level.

Van Beck Hall, "A Quantitative Approach to the Social, Economic and Political Structure of Virginia, 1790-1810" (unpublished paper presented at the annual meeting of the Southern Historical Association, 1969), is the only systematic approach to local politics in Virginia. Charles H. Ambler, *Sectionalism in Virginia from 1776 to 1861* (Chicago, 1915), is less helpful.

Biographies of prominent Virginians, particularly Albert J. Beveridge, *The Life of John Marshall*, 4 vols. (New York, 1916-1919), Irving Brant, *James Madison*, 5 vols. (New York, 1941-1961), Dumas Malone, *Jefferson and the Ordeal of Liberty* (Boston, 1962), and David John Mays, *Edmund Pendleton, 1721-1803: A Biography*, 2 vols. (Cambridge, Mass., 1962), provide some of the best commentary on Virginia during the first decade of government under the federal Constitution. Of lesser value are Dice Robins Anderson, *William Branch Giles: A Study in the Politics of Virginia and the Nation from 1790 to 1830* (Menasha, Wis., 1914), Thomas Boyd, *Light Horse Harry Lee* (New York, 1931), Robert Douthat Meade, *Patrick Henry*, 2 vols. (Philadelphia, 1957-1969), Eugene Mudge, *The Social Philosophy of John Taylor of Caroline: A Study of Jeffersonian Democracy* (New York, 1939), and Kate Mason Rowland, *The Life of George Mason* (New York, 1892).

Charles Sydnor, *Gentlemen Freeholders: Political Practices in Washington's Virginia* (Chapel Hill, N.C., 1952), stands in a class by itself. Sydnor has perhaps overlooked too many of the negative features of the "county oligarchies," but his book remains the most intelligent analysis of Virginia political life written to date.

The primary source material on eighteenth century Virginia, although voluminous, has some unfortunate gaps. The *Journal of the House of Delegates* (Richmond, 1776-   ) and the *Journal of the Senate* (Richmond, 1776-   ) together comprise the single most important source for reconstructing the basic framework of political activity in Virginia, but, unhappily, we have no records of debate in either the House of Delegates or the state senate. The Virginia Ratifying Convention and the important 1798 session of the House of Delegates are recorded in more detail. Debate on ratification of the Constitution can be found in Jonathon Elliot, *The Debates in the Several State Conventions on the Adoption of the Federal Constitution,* 4 vols. (Washington, D.C., 1836), and a full record of the discussion in the House of Delegates on the Virginia Resolutions is printed in *Resolutions of Virginia and Kentucky . . . and Debates in the House of Delegates of Virginia* (Richmond, 1832). Other published official records are W. W. Hening, *The Statutes at Large: Being a Collection of the Laws of Virginia from the First Session of the Legislature in the Year 1619,* 12 vols. (Richmond, 1823), Samuel Shepherd, *Statutes at Large of Virginia, 1792-1806: Being a Continuation of Hening Statutes at Large,* 3 vols. (Richmond, 1835-1836), and William P. Palmer, ed., *Calendar of Virginia State Papers and Other Manuscripts Preserved in the Capitol at Richmond,* 11 vols. (Richmond, 1875). The Executive Communications to the General Assembly, Executive Correspondence, Executive Letterbooks, Legislative Petitions, and Rough Bills of the House of Delegates, all in manuscript in the Virginia State Library, further fill in our picture of the operation of the state government.

The published papers of the people involved in Virginia political life are of course an invaluable source for a study of this kind. Those that I found most helpful are Julian Boyd, ed., *The Papers of Thomas Jefferson,* 17 vols. (Princeton, N.J., 1950-   ), Paul Leicester Ford, ed., *The Writings of Thomas Jefferson,* 12 vols. (New York, 1904-1905), John C. Fitzpatrick, ed., *The Writings of George Washington from the Original Manuscript Sources, 1745-1799,* 39 vols. (Washington, D.C., 1931-1944), Worthington C. Ford, ed., *The Writings of George Washington,* 14 vols. (New York, 1889-1893), William Wirt Henry, *Patrick Henry: Life, Correspondence, and Speeches,* 3 vols. (New York, 1891), Gaillard Hunt, ed., *The Writings of James Madison,* 9 vols. (New York, 1900-1910). Stanislaus M. Hamilton, ed., *The Writings of James Monroe,* 7 vols. (New York, 1898-1903), Henry Cabot Lodge, *The Works of Alexander Hamilton,* 12 vols. (New York, 1912), James C. Ballagh, ed., *The Letters of Richard Henry Lee,* 2 vols. (New York, 1911-1914), and U. S., Department of State, *Documentary History of the Constitution of the United States of America,* 5 vols. (Washington, D.C., 1894-1905).

The following manuscript collections were of particular importance: Breckinridge Family Papers, Harry Innes Papers, the Papers of Thomas Jefferson, Richard Bland Lee Papers, the Papers of James Madison, James McHenry Papers, Garret Minor Papers, Wilson Cary Nicholas Papers, and Henry Tazewell Papers (all in the Library of Congress); David Campbell Papers, John Clopton Papers, Joseph Jones Papers, and William and John Preston Papers (all at Duke University); Cabell Family Papers, Edgehill-Randolph Papers, Lee Family Papers, Wilson Cary Nicholas Papers, and Creed Taylor Papers (all at the University of Virginia); Real and Personal Property Tax Lists, Zachariah Johnston Papers, and Tazewell Family Papers (all in the Virginia State Library); John Cropper Papers, Ludwell-Lee Papers, Preston Family Papers, Archibald Stuart Papers, and Stuart Family Papers (all at the Virginia Historical Society); Tucker-Coleman Papers (College of William and Mary).

Newspapers are probably the most valuable source available to the historian of eighteenth-century Virginia. Although they still reflect the biases of the literate portion of the population, they at least are free of the legalistic tone set by the official records and their content is more representative than the writings of such highly atypical members of the Virginia elite as Jefferson, Madison, and Washington. I have relied most heavily on the [Alexandria] Columbian Mirror and Alexandria Advertiser, the [Richmond] *Virginia Gazette and General Advertiser,* the [Richmond] *Examiner,* and the [Richmond] *Virginia Federalist.* Other newspapers of importance are [Alexandria] *Virginia Journal and Alexandria Advertiser,* the [Dumfries, Va.] *Republican Journal, Fredericksburg Herald and General Advertiser, Norfolk and Portsmouth Chronicle,* [Richmond] *Virginia Gazette and Manchester Advertise,* and [Richmond] *Virginia Gazette and Richmond Chronicle.*

Index

Accomac County, 3

Adams, John: proposes system of titles, 59; and anti-British legislation, 138; and presidential election of 1796, 161-68; cooperates with Jefferson, 168; strengthens American defenses, 169; defended, 196-97; and presidential election of 1800, 223, 231-35; attacked by Callender, 226-27; mentioned, 170-81 passim

Address from the Minority: of 1798, 196-97

Address of the General Assembly . . .: regarding assumption, 79-82, 90

Address to Congress from the General Assembly: of 1798, 195-96

Adet, Pierre, 181-82

Albemarle County, Va.: complaint of citizens of, 32; meeting in 1798, 177-78; Jefferson in disfavor in, 179

Alexandria, Va., 149, 178

Alien and Sedition Acts: passage of, 184-85; reaction in Virginia to, 185-98; and Virginia Resolves, 190-94; defended by Federalists, 196-97, 204; and congressional elections, 206; and Virginia Report, 214-15; mentioned, 200, 218, 219

Amelia County: opposes Proclamation of Neutrality, 131; opposes Jay Treaty, 141

amendments, U.S. Constitution. *See* Constitution, U.S.

American Revolution: and state debts, 68; Jefferson's conduct during, 162-63; mentioned, x, 7, 17, 28

Ames, Fisher, 160

Andrews, Robert, 46, 144

Antifederalists in Virginia: in Ratifying Convention, 1-13; favor second convention, 12-15; unseat Carrington, 16; seek amendments in legislature, 17-22; campaign against Madison, 18-19, 24-27; disappointed with congressional amendments, 58-59, 65-66; and site of capital, 59-60; move to Republican party, 111; mentioned, passim

Articles of Confederation, 2, 5, 200

assumption of state debts: proposed by Hamilton, 68; Virginia's reaction to, 69-73, 75-77; and Virginia's interests, 73-75; compromise on, 74-75; reaction of House of Delegates to, 78-82; and executive domination, 181

Bank of the United States, 115-18, 181

Banks, Henry, 148n

Baptists: political organization of, 26; and federal Constitution, 65-66; and glebe lands, 93-95, 198-99; philosophy of government, 115-16

Bayard, Ferdinand, 38

Bayard, James, 236

Beckley, John, 14, 155

Bill of Rights. *See* Constitution, U.S.

Blair, Archibald, 207

Bland, Theodorick, 57n, 72

Boutetourt County, Va.: supports Adams, 178

Braxton, Carter, 46, 232

Breckinridge, James: defeated for governorship, 213; candidate for elector, 223, 233

Breckinridge, John: of Kentucky, 188

Brent, Daniel: defends Jefferson, 162-63; chosen elector, 165; denounces Adams, 175; mentioned, 176

British debts: evasion of, by Virginians, 123-25

Brooke, Robert, 136

Brown, B. Katherine, 40-41

Brown, Robert E., 40-41